E TO

Arizona's
Wilderness Areas

TEXT BY
TOM DOLLAR

PHOTOGRAPHY BY
JERRY SIEVE

WESTCLIFFE PUBLISHERS

www.westcliffepublishers.com

Table of Contents

Acknowledgments 7

Arizona Wilderness Areas Map 8

Preface 11

Arizona's Extraordinary Diversity 13

What Is Wilderness? 18

Along the Trail 25

How to Use This Guide 34

Northern Arizona: Grand Canyon and Colorado Plateau 36

1   Beaver Dam Mountains Wilderness 38

2   Grand Canyon National Park 41

3   Grand Wash Cliffs Wilderness 56

4   Kachina Peaks Wilderness 58

5   Kanab Creek Wilderness 63

6   Kendrick Mountain Wilderness 68

7   Mount Trumbull Wilderness 71

8   Paiute Wilderness 74

9   Paria Canyon–Vermilion Cliffs Wilderness 77

10   Petrified Forest Wilderness 81

11   Saddle Mountain Wilderness 85

12   Strawberry Crater Wilderness 89

Rim Country: Mogollon Rim to the Salt River 92

13   Bear Wallow Wilderness 94

14   Blue Range Primitive Area 97

15   Castle Creek Wilderness 106

16   Escudilla Wilderness 109

17   Fossil Springs Wilderness 111

18   Granite Mountain Wilderness 114

19   Hellsgate Wilderness 117

20   Juniper Mesa Wilderness 121

Light filters through Paria Canyon

21   Mazatzal Wilderness.. 124

22   Mount Baldy Wilderness... 132

23   Munds Mountain Wilderness... 135

24   Red Rock–Secret Mountain Wilderness 138

25   Salome Wilderness 144

26   Salt River Canyon Wilderness 147

27   Sierra Ancha Wilderness.. 150

28   Sycamore Canyon Wilderness 155

29   West Clear Creek Wilderness 159

30   Wet Beaver Wilderness.. 162

31   Woodchute Wilderness 166

Southeastern Arizona: Basin and Range Sky Islands................................. 168

32   Aravaipa Canyon Wilderness.. 170

33   Chiricahua Wilderness 173

34   Dos Cabezas Mountains Wilderness.. 179

35   Four Peaks Wilderness... 182

36   Galiuro Wilderness... 186

37   Miller Peak Wilderness.. 192

38   Mount Graham Wilderness Study Area 196

39   Mount Wrightson Wilderness 204

40   Pajarita Wilderness... 209

41   Peloncillo Mountains Wilderness 212

42   Pusch Ridge Wilderness 216

43   Redfield Canyon Wilderness 222

44   Saguaro Wilderness East.. 224

45   Saguaro Wilderness West... 230

46   Superstition Wilderness... 234

47   White Canyon Wilderness 239

Western Arizona: Sonoran and Mohave Deserts 242

48   Big Horn Mountains Wilderness 244

49   Cabeza Prieta Refuge Wilderness 246

50   Eagletail Mountains Wilderness 250

51   Harquahala Mountains Wilderness 253

52   Hassayampa River Canyon Wilderness 256

53   Hells Canyon Wilderness 259

54   Hummingbird Springs Wilderness 262

55   Imperial Refuge Wilderness 265

56   Kofa Refuge Wilderness 268

57   Mount Tipton Wilderness 272

58   Mount Wilson Wilderness 274

59   North Maricopa Mountains Wilderness 276

60   Organ Pipe Wilderness 279

61   Sierra Estrella Wilderness 283

62   South Maricopa Mountains Wilderness 285

63   Tres Alamos Wilderness 287

64   Trigo Mountains Wilderness 289

Appendix 1: Wilderness Areas 292

Appendix 2: Addresses for Further Information 293

Appendix 3: Map Sources 295

Appendix 4: Selected Bibliography 295

Index 297

ISBN: 1-56579-280-7

TEXT COPYRIGHT: Tom Dollar, 1998. All rights reserved.

PHOTOGRAPHY COPYRIGHT: Jerry Sieve, 1998. All rights reserved.

EDITOR: Kristen Iversen

PRODUCTION MANAGER: Harlene Finn

DESIGN AND PRODUCTION: Rebecca Finkel, F + P Graphic Design; Boulder, CO

PUBLISHED BY: Westcliffe Publishers, Inc.
P.O. Box 1261
Englewood, Colorado 80150
www.westcliffepublishers.com

PRINTED IN: Hong Kong
PRINTED BY: H & Y Printing, Ltd.

LIBRARY OF CONGRESS CATALOGING-IN-PUBLICATION DATA

Dollar, Tom.
    Guide to Arizona's wilderness areas / by Tom Dollar ; photography by Jerry Sieve.
        p. cm.
    Includes bibliographical references and index.
    ISBN: 1-56579-280-7
    1. Wilderness areas—Arizona—Guidebooks.
    2. Hiking—Arizona—Guidebooks. 3. Arizona—Guidebooks. I. Title.
    QH76.5.A6 D65 1998   98-24594
    333.78'2'09791—DC21   CIP

For more information about other fine books and calendars from Westcliffe Publishers, please contact your local bookstore, call us at 1-800-523-3692, write for our free color catalog, or visit us on the Web at www.westcliffepublishers.com.

COVER CAPTION:
Brittle Bush plant in bloom below Superstition Mountains, Superstition Wilderness

PLEASE NOTE:
Risk is always a factor in backcountry and high-mountain travel. Many of the activities described in this book can be dangerous, especially when weather is adverse or unpredictable, and when unforeseen events or conditions create a hazardous situation. The author has done his best to provide the reader with accurate information about backcountry travel, as well as to point out some of its potential hazards. It is the responsibility of the users of this guide to learn the necessary skills for safe backcountry travel, and to exercise caution in potentially hazardous areas, especially on avalanche-prone terrain. The author and publisher disclaim any liability for injury or other damage caused by backcountry traveling, mountain biking, or performing any other activity described in this book.

Acknowledgments

THANKS, FIRST, to family and friends who accompanied me on my backcountry jaunts. To Jack Dykinga, Charlie Dee, Patrick and Laura McCarthy, Lynne Dollar, Bill Bendt, Marty and Annette Cordano, Richard Lyons, Peter Noebels, Smokey Knowlton, Randy Epperson, thanks all; and thanks especially to my one true mate, Kate McCarthy, for her loving support and encouragement.

Without the kind assistance of people at various state and federal managing agencies, this book would not have been possible. Thanks to all the nameless people who staffed information desks and answered my telephone queries. And thanks in particular to Ken Mahoney, Arizona Bureau of Land Management Wilderness Coordinator; Pete Weinel, Tonto National Forest; Eric Smith, Arizona State Parks Trails Coordinator; Larry Gearhart, Bureau of Land Management, Arizona Strip; and Carrie Templin, Coronado National Forest.

Thanks to Ron Holubiak and Charles Smith of Tucson Map and Flag for their invaluable assistance. Thanks to Libby O'Shea and the river guides at Far Flung Adventures.

And thanks, finally, to the editorial and production group at Westcliffe Publishers for their forbearance. Linda Doyle, Kiki Sayre, Dean Galiano, Kristen Iversen, and Harlene Finn—thank you all.

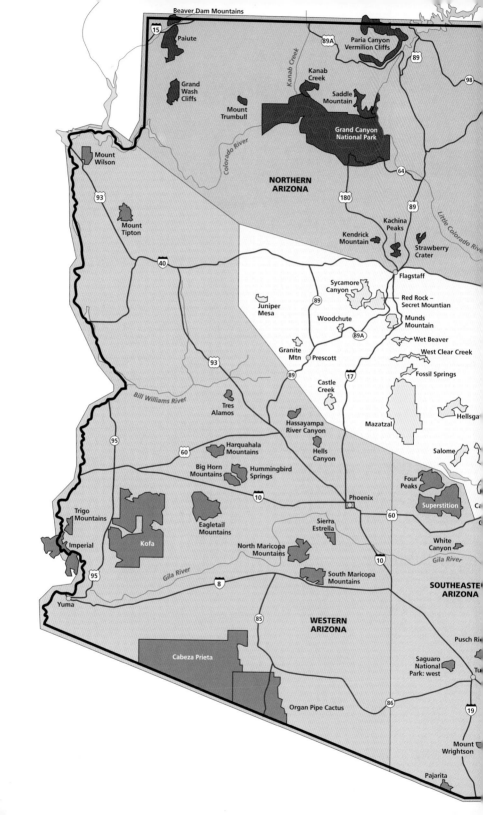

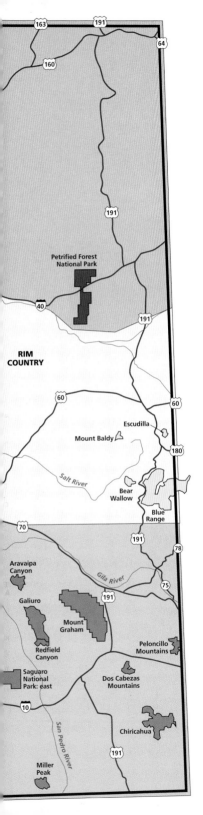

Arizona Wilderness Areas

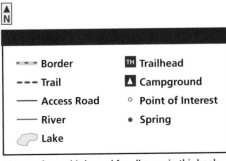

N

▪▪▪ Border	**TH** Trailhead
--- Trail	▲ Campground
— Access Road	○ Point of Interest
— River	• Spring
◯ Lake	

Please refer to this legend for all maps in this book.

Preface

WHEN I ARRIVED IN ARIZONA more than sixteen years ago, the state contained fifteen wilderness areas, counting Grand Canyon National Park and the Blue Range Primitive Area. Today, there are ninety-two designated wilderness areas (again, including the Grand Canyon and Blue Range, both still awaiting long-overdue wilderness designation). Wilderness dedications came in two great waves. The first occurred with passage of the Arizona Wilderness Act of 1984, setting aside forty-two new wilderness areas for protection, most of them on National Forest lands. The second wave came in 1990 with enactment of the Arizona Desert Wilderness Act, assigning wilderness status to more than two million acres of Bureau of Land Management (BLM) and National Wildlife Refuge terrain. Arizona now has nearly five million acres under wilderness protection.

To prepare for this book I visited most, but not all, of Arizona's wilderness areas. Entry to some is blocked by private land, to others by Indian Reservation lands. Access to a handful is too difficult and recreational opportunities too few to include them in a guide of this sort.

For the most part, what remains of my backcountry excursions are memories of solitude, adventure, and the impressive physical and environmental diversity of Arizona's wild places. I remember especially a cold, winter backpack amid the slumped bentonite cones and fractured trees-turned-to-stone of the Petrified Forest Wilderness; a hike among cool conifers along Ash Creek in the Mount Graham Wilderness Study Area; an eleven-mile mid-summer trek through the Aravaipa Canyon Wilderness where cooling creek waters saved me from serious dehydration when air temperatures exceeded 100 degrees Fahrenheit; a four-day rafting adventure through the Salt River Canyon Wilderness; a two-day cross-country hike in the Organ Pipe Wilderness carrying a ton of water; and a lonesome, mid-winter kayak float through the Imperial Refuge Wilderness on the lower Colorado River where in four days I saw only one other boat.

Although this guidebook can convey but slight impressions of my top wilderness experiences, it does, I hope, provide sufficient factual and descriptive detail to help you find your way into the wilderness areas described here and to enhance your appreciation of Arizona's wonderful backcountry.

Happy trails!
—TOM DOLLAR

A serene moment for Tristan Sieve, age 14, in the Woodchute Wilderness

Arizona's Extraordinary Diversity

ARIZONA'S WILDERNESS SYSTEM consists of 92 units, totaling 4,864,673 acres managed by four different federal agencies: the Fish and Wildlife Service (1,343,544 acres); the National Park Service (443,700 acres); the Forest Service (1,518,732 acres); and the Bureau of Land Management (1,558,697 acres). In size Arizona's designated wild lands range from the tiny 2,065-acre Baboquivari Peak Wilderness to the expansive 803,418-acre Cabeza Prieta National Wildlife Refuge Wilderness. In natural setting they represent every ecological and topographical feature Arizona offers: sheer-walled canyons, mountain meadows, boreal forests, alpine tundra, riparian oases, badlands, grasslands, and deserts. And what's extraordinary is that by auto and on foot you can take in the full range of Arizona's wild diversity in a single day.

On an early morning in mid-June, for example, I can leave my home near the Saguaro National Park Wilderness in the Arizona uplands just outside Tucson, elevation 3,000 feet, and drive north to the Kachina Peaks Wilderness near Flagstaff, where late that afternoon I can traverse alpine tundra while hiking to the summit of Humphreys Peak, elevation 12,643 feet.

This journey, spanning some 300 miles, is environmentally akin to traveling from Mexico to Alaska in roughly eight hours. From the desert uplands, where giant Saguaro cacti are just beginning to set circlets of succulent ruby fruits, my route descends into the broiling agricultural fields south of Phoenix before rising gradually north onto grassland benches and into piñon-juniper woodlands. Dropping into the Verde Valley, it crosses the Verde River to climb atop the Mogollon Rim and into ponderosa pine forests surrounding Flagstaff. Fifteen miles north of Flagstaff, I park my pickup at a trailhead near the Snow Bowl Ski Area, don hiking boots, and hoist my daypack. The trail to Humphreys Peak in the Kachina Peaks Wilderness leads through groves of aspen only recently come into full leaf, meadows sprinkled with Rocky Mountain iris, and spruce-fir forests where in deep shade snow still lies in ragged patches. Passing a few gnarled bristlecone pines, it then moves onto seemingly barren tundra above treeline as it approaches the summit of Humphreys Peak.

Motoring and hiking from dawn until dusk, I will have passed through every life zone in Arizona, from lower Sonoran desert scrub to treeless arctic-alpine tundra. At Humphreys Peak the temperature flirts with 50 degrees Fahrenheit, and if a scudding cloud obscures the descending sun and the breeze freshens a bit, I scurry to dig another layer from my daypack. Meanwhile, back in Tucson, as the sun just now dips below a nearby peak, the ribbon of mercury on the thermometer beneath my backyard ramada is nailed to 106 degrees Fahrenheit, the day's high.

The fifth largest of the lower 48 states, Arizona divides into two large and distinctive chunks of ground—the Colorado Plateau and the Basin and Range regions—separated by a transitional strip of highlands called the Mogollon Rim. The Colorado Plateau sprawls across the northern half of the state, extending beyond Arizona's borders into Colorado, Utah, and New Mexico. The Basin and Range portion takes up the state's southern half, but on Arizona's western edge, it extends north along the lower Colorado River to the Nevada border.

Wildflower-covered ridgeline in late summer,
Chiricahua Wilderness

The Mogollon Rim, girdling Arizona's midsection, splits the Colorado Plateau and the Basin and Range land areas. A fantastically rugged and heavily forested plateau, the rim extends southeast to northwest from the White Mountains near the New Mexico line, up through Flagstaff, and beyond to the Grand Canyon. Fifty to 100 miles wide, the Mogollon Rim defines the southern edge of the Colorado Plateau as it drops steeply to the Salt River to form some of the most striking but forbiddingly rough terrain in the state.

The most arresting feature of the Colorado Plateau—a vast expanse creased by deep gorges, punctuated by high peaks, mesas, and plateaus—is, of course, the 277-mile-long Grand Canyon, the widest and deepest chasm of them all. North of the Grand Canyon lies the Arizona Strip. Edging the Utah border, the Strip consists of a chain of high, sparsely populated plateaus: the Shivwits, Kanab, Kaibab, and Paria.

The 9,000-foot Kaibab Plateau is the site of the North Rim headquarters of Grand Canyon National Park. Its name derives from a Southern Paiute Indian word meaning "mountain lying down." Early Mormon settlers in the area called it Buckskin Mountain for the plentiful deer hides they acquired from tribal hunters. Rising abruptly from adjacent plateau country, the Kaibab is heavily forested with Boreal spruce, fir, and aspen. The weather, too, is northern, with the entire plateau often lying under a deep blanket of snow from October through May. On one of my hiking excursions to the North Rim shortly after the National Park opened for the season in mid-May, heavy snow still lay across many trails and roads, rendering them impassable.

East of the Kaibab, defining the south rampart of the Paria Plateau, are the stunning, polychromatic Vermilion Cliffs, the site of a California condor reintroduction in 1997. On the eastern edge of the Paria Plateau, the Paria River cuts a deep, 38-mile, north-south slash through spectacular sandstone formations of the Paria Canyon-Vermilion Cliffs Wilderness Area, all the way from the Utah border down to the Colorado River near Lees Ferry.

Navajo National Monument, the Painted Desert, Glen Canyon National Recreation Area, Petrified Forest National Park and Wilderness, and Canyon de Chelly National Monument are among the notable features of the northeast quadrant of the Colorado Plateau—harsh, barren, windswept steppes, fiercely hot in summer and piercingly cold in winter.

In the vicinity of Flagstaff, roughly dead center on the Colorado Plateau, the volcanic peaks of the San Francisco Mountains' Kachina Peaks Wilderness rise to nearly 13,000 feet. Sacred to Zuni, Hopi, Havasupai, Navajo and other Indian groups, the "Peaks" show evidence of volcanic eruptions, lava flows, erosion, glaciation, and frost action. Although bereft of perennially flowing water, the Peaks are a popular destination for backpackers, cross-country skiers, snow-shoers, and climbers.

Southeast of Flagstaff, the rough country below the Mogollon Rim, known as the Tonto Basin, was once the stronghold of the redoubtable Tonto Apaches. Some of the toughest-to-reach wild areas in Arizona, including West Clear Creek, Hellsgate, Wet Beaver, Fossil Springs, and the Salt River Canyon Wilderness, are located along and below the Mogollon Rim.

Arizona's Basin and Range region divides into three quite distinct units. In the southeast corner of Arizona, east of a line that slices north to south through Phoenix and Tucson, is the Arizona Uplands portion of the Basin and Range, an area of broad desert valleys interspersed with mountain ranges trending along a northwest-to-southeast line. Perennial creeks and springs and forests of pine, spruce, fir, and aspen are commonplace in these "sky island" mountains where many peaks rise above 8,000 feet. Close to the Mexican border to the south and to the Continental Divide just east of the Arizona–New Mexico line, the mountains of Southeastern Arizona are unique in their biological diversity. In these mountains, Sierra Madrean, Rocky Mountain, eastern, and western species of plants, animals, and birds freely intermingle. Nearly all of the designated wild lands in this portion of the Basin and Range region are in the upper mountain elevations.

West of the Mexican Highlands, extending to the Colorado River and north to the Colorado's confluence with the Bill Williams River, lies the Sonoran Desert region of the Basin and Range Province. North of the Bill Williams River, the Mohave section of the Basin and Range Province follows a narrow corridor all the way up to Lake Mead and beyond.

Arizona's reputation for bone-dry aridity is legitimately earned by its low-elevation southwestern region where in some years less than three inches of annual precipitation is recorded. Except for a few die-hard, desert-outback survivalists, no one risks summertime backcountry travel in Organ Pipe, Cabeza Prieta Refuge, Kofa Refuge, and other wilderness areas in the Sonoran Desert and Mohave sections along Arizona's western edge. Because permanent water is either scarce or non-existent in these arid-lands regions, even fall, winter, and spring outings may be dangerous for inexperienced hikers.

Arizona's commitment to wilderness preservation started early. The Galiuro Wilderness in the Coronado National Forest was Arizona's first; established in 1932 when 52,717 acres were set aside, it was later enlarged to 76,317 acres under the 1984 Arizona Wilderness Act. In 1933, the Chiricahua Wilderness, the Sierra Ancha Primitive Area, and Blue Range Primitive Area were created. The Sierra Ancha eventually became a wilderness area, but efforts to change the status of the 173,762-acre Blue Range Primitive Area—where Mexican gray wolves were reintroduced in March 1998—continue to be blocked by a powerful lobbying force of stockmen and mining companies. Three additional wilderness areas were protected in the 1930s and 1940s— Sycamore Canyon Wilderness in 1935, Superstition Wilderness in 1939, and the Mazatzal Wilderness in 1940.

Thirty years later, on October 23, 1970, 50,260 acres of Petrified Forest National Park were designated as the Petrified Forest National Wilderness. It was the first wilderness area established in the National Park System under the provisions of the Federal Wilderness Protection Act of 1964, and it was also the first wilderness area created in Arizona since passage of the 1964 act. Three National Park wilderness preservations followed—a small portion of the Chiricahua National Monument in 1976; Saguaro National Monument (now a national park) in 1976; and Organ Pipe Cactus National Monument in 1978.

In 1976 Congress passed the Federal Land Policy Management Act, a law that made it possible to consider for wilderness preservation areas managed by the Bureau of Land Management. Then, in 1984, responding to a bill introduced by Arizona Congressman Morris K. Udall, Congress passed the Arizona Wilderness Act, creating an additional one million acres of wilderness in the state and raising the total number of wilderness acres protected to two million, still less than three percent of the state's land area. Most of the forty-two new areas established in 1984 are in National Forests, but a handful, including Paria Canyon and Aravaipa Canyon, are on Bureau of Land Management (BLM) lands.

A milestone for the creation of wilderness areas in Arizona was the Arizona Desert Wilderness Act of 1990, the first major piece of wilderness legislation to set aside more than one million acres of BLM land. The law also designated 1.3 million acres in Havasu, Imperial, Kofa, and Cabeza Prieta National Wildlife Refuges for wilderness protection. These game refuges are all within Arizona's arid western region; two of them, Imperial and Havasu, lie along the lower Colorado River, Arizona's "west coast." More than half of the total wilderness acreage created by the Arizona Desert Wilderness Act is in the Kofa and Cabeza Prieta Wilderness Areas. The 1990 act also added 12,710 acres to the Aravaipa Canyon Wilderness and established the 20,900-acre Gila Box Riparian National Conservation Area. Arizona now has 4.8 million wilderness acres in 92 distinct units.

Stately Bell Rock against a blue sky,
Munds Mountain Wilderness

What is a Wilderness?

THE WORD WILDERNESS, rooted in the Old English *wildeor*, meaning "wild beast," has long been associated with dark, frightful regions, inhospitable to humans and haunted by fierce, wild creatures. From the beginning, Americans in the New World seem to have had two minds about wilderness. On the practical, pioneering side, wilderness stood for vast, untracked, bewildering places where one could easily become swallowed up, forever lost. On the romantic side, wilderness stood for virgin terrain, a new Eden where one could seek physical and spiritual renewal. Seen from the first perspective, wilderness was to be mastered, brought under control, converted into resources. According to the second, wilderness was best accepted on its own terms, not only for its beauty and opportunity for new beginnings but also for adventure, physical isolation, and risk.

Today, more than four-and-a-half centuries after the first Europeans entered the American Southwest, both attitudes still prevail. Adherents to the first point of view seem bent on logging off the remaining old-growth forests, overgrazing arid grasslands, and poisoning rivers and streams in pursuit of mineral resources. Adherents to the second point of view are just as determined to stop dam-building and logging, prevent species extinctions, preserve what's left of our wild places, and restore damaged ground to some dream of former purity.

But what, in fact, is wilderness? The answer may depend on recreational, aesthetic, political, or philosophical inclinations. A component of many definitions is size. Indeed, the wording of the 1964 Wilderness Act establishes a rather imprecise size guideline by describing wilderness as a tract of Federal land that contains "at least five thousand acres…or is of sufficient size as to make practical its preservation and use in an unimpaired condition." The notion of "sufficient size" is interesting. In Arizona, as we will see, there are wilderness areas that barely nudge past the 5,000-acre mark, and a few others that fall significantly short of that standard. As parcels of ground go, 5,000 acres is not much by any measure. Imagine a tract of land consisting of eight 640-acre sections squared, and you've got roughly 5,000 acres. A fit hiker, traveling at a brisk pace on level terrain, could walk across it in about an hour—a nice size for a small working cattle ranch, perhaps, but not what most of us visualize when we think of wilderness. On the other hand, few wilderness areas in the lower 48 states, and none in Arizona, fit Aldo Leopold's criterion: "a continuous stretch of country preserved in its natural state…big enough to absorb a two weeks' pack trip."

In its catch-all phrasing, the 1964 Wilderness Act also provides for setting aside lands that offer "ecological, geological, or other features of scientific, educational, scenic, or historical value." In Arizona, the tiny, 2,065-acre Baboquivari Peak Wilderness southwest of Tucson fits nearly all those criteria. Baboquivari Peak's massive granite dome is unique in being the only major peak in Arizona that requires technical climbing skills to summit. For the Tohono O'odham Indians, on whose reservation it is situated, the peak is a sacred place, the home of their creator, I'itoi. And Baboquivari's canyons, noted for wildlife diversity, preserve a remnant population of the endangered Kearney's blue star. Any of those features is reason enough to protect Baboquivari Peak.

Whether wilderness status is the proper designation, or whether Baboquivari is large enough "to make practicable its preservation and use in an unimpaired condition" is debatable.

While heavy recreation in some wilderness areas has required managing agencies to limit recreational use, for a great many wilderness advocates, outdoor recreation is the touchstone of any definition. For hikers and backpackers, bird watchers and botanists, kayakers and rafters, hunters and anglers, rock climbers and others, a backcountry experience is enhanced by activity. And, although wilderness recreational pursuits for their own sake require no justification, it may be argued that they often lead not only to a deeper appreciation for wild country but also to conscientious efforts to protect and preserve it, awakening in many what Aldo Leopold labeled the "land ethic." Among my backcountry companions are a good number of strong preservationists who, like Leopold himself, shouldered a rifle on their first outdoor excursions. The authors of the 1964 Wilderness Act may have envisioned such a result in urging that wild terrain should offer "outstanding opportunities for solitude or a primitive and unconfined type of recreation"—an intriguing pairing, implying, perhaps, that one engenders the other.

The 1964 Act further defines wilderness as "an area where the earth and its community of life are untrammeled by man, where man himself is a visitor who does not remain," and the act elsewhere characterizes true wilderness as pristine, "unscathed by human intervention." Untrammeled, pristine, unscathed—illusory words, all. Even the word human is tricky, its usual referent in this context being European.

In Arizona, arguably, you would have to go back more than 10,000 years to find anything approaching pristine. Indigenous people were present almost that far back in Arizona's wild country, and, long before Europeans arrived, Indians were at home in what we now call wilderness. They forged trails across it; they conducted commerce in it; they "managed" it. They dug canals and diverted water for irrigation; they introduced new species of domesticated plants; they slaughtered game animals by stampeding them; and they used fire as a tool in both hunting and agriculture. They also left their mark on the land. Ruined pit houses, cliff dwellings, pictographs and petroglyphs, pots, baskets, spear points and tools, granaries, ball courts, and kitchen middens are mute evidence of their former prosperity in our so-called wilderness.

Today, cattle still graze in some wilderness areas, while other areas have been mined, logged, or otherwise "trammeled." And in two wilderness areas, the Kofa—a sanctuary for desert bighorn sheep—and the Cabeza Prieta—a last retreat for the only U.S. population of endangered Sonoran pronghorn—military aircraft routinely roar through at full throttle, only one hundred feet above the ground. Moreover, virtually all designated wilderness areas are in some ways managed: visitors are counted, activities restricted, fires suppressed, animal populations monitored, predators controlled. Untrammeled? Some purists would maintain that once it's mapped, wild land is no longer virgin territory.

"Wilderness without wildlife," writer Lois Crisler has said, "is just scenery." Others go further. Expanding on Leopold's idea of the "natural state," they assert that wilderness is defined by the presence of arch predators—wolves, grizzlies, jaguars—creatures that kill and eat people. Without them, the argument goes, there is no "wild" in wilderness.

Of the large predators that once roamed Arizona, only the mountain lion and the black bear remain, and recurring backcountry confrontations between black bears and campers may diminish the black bear's odds for survival in some of Arizona's more popular wilderness areas. Mountain lions still thrive throughout Arizona and recently a rare Mexican jaguar, thought to be extirpated here, was observed and photographed by a rancher along the Arizona-Mexico border. In July 1997, the U.S. Fish and Wildlife Service, acting on a federal court order, listed the Mexican jaguar as endangered in Arizona, New Mexico, and Texas.

The grizzly bear, which once roamed the mountains, grasslands, and riparian corridors from the Kaibab Plateau north of the Grand Canyon all the way down to the Arizona-Mexico border in southeastern Arizona, was wiped out in Arizona 60 years ago, the last killed in 1939 in what is now the Mount Baldy Wilderness.

Mexican gray wolves were systematically exterminated in Arizona by federal Animal Damage Control agents. The Fort Apache Indian Reservation in east-central Arizona was the site of the last wolf killed by federal agents in March 1960. In the mid-1970s, a lone wolf was reported moving north from the Mexican border along a historical runway through the Mule, Dragoon, and Galiuro Mountains. After local ranchers put a $500 price on its head, a bounty hunter pursued and killed the wolf in what is now the Aravaipa Canyon Wilderness. In March 1998, one of our lost predators was restored to Arizona's wild country. Eleven wolves, in three groups, were released into the Blue Primitive Range on the Arizona-New Mexico border.

Echoing Henry David Thoreau's "in Wildness is the preservation of the world," other ideas of wilderness underscore the ethical, spiritual, and mythic significance of wild places, which may be what conservationists and politicians who framed the 1964 Act had in mind when they wrote in the requirement that wilderness provide "opportunities for solitude."

John Muir, perhaps the first advocate for wilderness, said, "In God's wildness lies the hope of the world—the great fresh, unblighted, unredeemed wilderness."

In 1960 Wallace Stegner wrote, "Something will have gone out of us as a people if we ever let the remaining wilderness be destroyed. We simply need wild country available to us, even if we do no more than drive to its edge and look in. For it can be a means of reassuring ourselves of our sanity as creatures, a part of our geography of hope."

Other voices endorsed the idea. Nature writer and literary critic Joseph Wood Krutch, writing about the Grand Canyon, said, "The wilderness and the idea of wilderness is one of the permanent homes of the human spirit." And still others echoed these sentiments. Edward Abbey noted, "Wild country has the power to remind civilized people that out there is a different world, older and greater and deeper by far than ours, a world which surrounds and sustains the little world of man." Gary Snyder emphasized that "Wildness is not just the 'preservation of the world', it is the world."

Autumn morning view from Centella Point,
Chiricahua Wilderness

A common thread running through these declarations is the conviction that we are sustained by wild places, that without wilderness our lives would be unimaginably impoverished. Implicit in them is an understanding that, however civilized we may have become in our towns and cities, we ourselves are wild, and our essentially wild selves seek equivalency, renewal, and sustenance in Muir's "great fresh, unblighted, unredeemed wilderness." That, more than anything, is the meaning of wild ground.

So where do we find wilderness? In Arizona, at least, we have presently preserved a potpourri of wilderness lands. They range in size from the tiny Baboquivari Peak Wilderness to the vast, bigger-than-Rhode-Island Cabeza Prieta National Wildlife Refuge, which sprawls across 1,300 square miles of southwestern Arizona's Sonoran Desert. Nearly urban in their proximity to towns and cities, some wilderness areas offer no chance for solitude; even to refer to them as wilderness seems absurd. And wilderness areas containing live streams and rivers, rare in the arid Southwest, are so popular among recreational users that visitor numbers must be curtailed by permit-dispensing agencies. On the other hand, some Arizona wild lands are so remote that to reach them requires hard travel through rough terrain; these remain virtually inaccessible outbacks.

A few of Arizona's wild places seem to have been tossed into the wilderness hopper after extractive industries got through with them. But among those, wonderfully, are a number that have self-restored to at least a semblance of untrammeled lands. Other wilderness areas where daytime thermometer readings routinely peg 115 degrees Fahrenheit in summer seem good-for-nothing piles of rocks in waterless deserts, hostile to life in any form. Yet these regions have always been home to lizards, snakes, scorpions, toads, and drought-adapted plants and mammals. And then there are the peaks and canyons of Northern Arizona, the forests, lakes, and streams of Rim Country, and the perennially flowing streams and unmatched biological diversity of southeastern Arizona's splendid "sky islands."

We could wish for more in Arizona. The Blue Range Primitive Area, the Gila Box National Riparian Conservation Area, the Mount Graham Wilderness Study Area in the Pinaleño Mountains (the site of the controversial Mt. Graham astrophysical observatory) should all be afforded wilderness protection. And long overdue for wilderness status is the Grand Canyon, where, according to a biologist friend, "some of the biggest chunks of nowhere left in Arizona" lie along the North Rim.

Beyond striving to bring those areas into the wilderness fold, however, we must be vigilant to protect what we already have. In southern Arizona a large mining company wants to resume operations within a few miles of the Mount Wrightson Wilderness, thus cutting off an important wildlife corridor between the Santa Rita Mountains and nearby ranges. And in the Cabeza Prieta Refuge Wilderness, the last great autonomous slice of Sonoran Desert north of Mexico, all-terrain vehicle operators and hunting groups are putting pressure on the U.S. Fish and Wildlife Service for greater access.

We are saving much more than a place for introspection or recreation when we set aside a wilderness tract, but the language of preservation doesn't always reflect that. Our discussions are oddly anthropocentric in their emphasis on wilderness

Cholla blossom in the Pusch Ridge Wilderness,
Catalina Mountains

"resources" for humans, solitude or recreation for people, and scenery that appeals to human aesthetic sensibilities. And, invariably, it's the human spirit to which we refer when we talk about the uplifting effect of wild places. Such ways of speaking deflect our attention from the underlying value of wilderness.

More than any particular region of wild and stunning beauty, more than miles of hiking or snowshoeing trails, more than opportunities for isolation and contemplation, what we should hope to save, and what we do save when we set aside wilderness areas, are entire ecosystems and their watersheds, migratory routes and corridors that guarantee freedom of movement and safety for animals, biological and genetic diversity, clean air and pure water, and—ultimately—an opportunity for the land to self-regulate and renew itself. To fully understand these things is to understand David Brower's epigrammatic warning, "Wild places are where we began; when they end, so do we."

Along the Trail

FOR WILDERNESS TRAVELERS, two things are essential. The first is personal safety, which you can reasonably assure by equipping yourself properly and avoiding risk. The second is to leave the wilderness as unspoiled as you found it, which can be accomplished by practicing common-sense wilderness etiquette and minimum impact camping:

- Leave no trace.
- If you pack it in, pack it out.
- Tread lightly.

These have long been the bywords of wilderness etiquette. To leave the wilderness as we found it, or wish to have found it, is an admirable precept, but seasoned backcountry travelers know that in actual practice it requires adherence to a few guidelines about equipment, group size, length of stay, campsites and campfires, and other minimum-impact basics.

EQUIPMENT

True, Arizona is synonymous with sunshine. Don't be fooled. At higher elevations weather conditions often change quickly and overnight temperatures in the mountains may drop sharply even in summer. Violent thunderstorms arrive in late June and continue into September, and winter weather systems moving overland from the Pacific may last for several days, bringing heavy snow to mountain regions. Year-round heat and aridity at lower elevations can put the unwary and unprepared at great risk. Prepare for anything.

GROUP SIZE

In some Arizona wilderness areas, managing agencies set limits on visitor numbers; in a few, reservations and permits are required. Where no limits are imposed, sound conservation practice suggests that group size be limited to between eight and ten. To lessen impact when hiking off-trail, even smaller groups are a good idea. Pack animals, if used, should never exceed the number of people.

CROSS-COUNTRY HIKING

Cross-country jaunts through wilderness areas enhance your outdoor experience by taking you to places that are otherwise inaccessible. But off-trail hiking can do lasting damage, particularly in desert terrain where, once disturbed, fragile soils take years to heal. Here are some guidelines for hiking in wilderness areas where no developed trail systems exist.

- Avoid fragile areas, particularly unstable slopes, areas covered by dwarf shrubs or ferns, and areas of desert vegetation. If you must hike across such terrain, avoid treading on plants.
- Where possible, hike on bare rock, sand, gravel, the deep duff of the forest floor, or in areas regularly scoured by water, such as the beds of desert arroyos.
- Keep group size small. On fragile surfaces, spread out to avoid wearing a path. But on extremely fragile surfaces, such as tundra, walk single-file in order to cut only one path.
- Avoid descending steep, loose slopes. If possible choose another route.

Fall color along Ramsey Creek, Miller Peak Wilderness

CAMPSITES

A rule of thumb: If a campsite already exists, use it, even if you have to tidy it a bit. It takes only a few days of camping to trample and compact the vegetation in a pristine area, thus creating a new campsite where none existed. If you come upon a campsite in the backcountry that is just becoming noticeable, pick a new location, allowing the hardly used site to restore itself over a season. Do not camp in desert arroyos; sudden storms may produce killer flash floods. Finally, avoid causing water or visual pollution by camping more than 200 feet from any water source, trail, or scenic location.

FIRES AND STOVES

For people who care about backcountry preservation, campfires are out, camp stoves are in. Romantic though they may be, fires and fire rings leave ugly, long-lasting scars on the landscape. A basic tenet of wilderness etiquette is to build a fire only if your stove malfunctions or if you need a fire in an emergency. If you require a fire, use an existing fire ring and select smaller wood sticks. Large logs seldom burn through, leaving campsites littered with their charred, ugly remains. When no previously used fire ring is available, build a fire on a rock covered with a thin layer of soil, if possible, or in a dug pit. Save both topsoil and sod to cover the fire site after the ashes have cooled. These practices help prevent superheating which sterilizes topsoil.

WASTES

Waste is the biggest problem in wilderness travel, and the pack-it-in-pack-it-out rule of wilderness etiquette applies especially to waste disposal. Wrappers of any kind, tins, empty propane or butane cartridges, cigarette butts—if you carried it in, carry it out. And while you're at it, carry out a piece or two of junk discarded by sloppy campers.

Human waste disposal should not be a problem in the backcountry, but all of us have been disgusted by toilet paper, sometimes even human feces, scattered near a trail or campsite. Fouling the wilderness in this way is easily avoided. Use a light-weight trowel to dig a "cat hole" no deeper than 6 to 8 inches. This will deposit feces in the most biologically active layer of soil, hastening decomposition. Save any sod you have removed and replace it, tamping it down after filling the hole with soil. You can do one of two things with toilet paper—burn it and mix the ashes with the soil returned to the cat hole, or place it in a resealable plastic bag and pack it out. A word of caution about burning, however. If fire danger is high, you should not risk burning toilet paper. In fact, during periods of drought in Arizona, managing agencies often ban backcountry fires of any kind (sometimes including camp stoves), leaving you no choice but to carry out all burnables.

Do not bury tampons or sanitary napkins; they do not decompose and animals will dig them up. Instead, bag them along with other refuse and carry them out.

PACK ANIMALS

Just as disgusting as a campsite marred by human litter is one that pack stock have trampled and fouled. To lessen the wilderness impact of horses and mules, hobble them, erect temporary electric-wire corrals, or tether them far apart on lines strung between trees. These practices will prevent pack stock from trampling and denuding a plot of ground.

A winter afternoon in Petrified Forest National Park

Packers can further limit the impact of stock animals by using lightweight camping equipment, thus reducing load weights and the number of animals required to haul gear. To prevent streambank erosion, water stock animals on graveled shorelines, not on soft streambanks. And feeding pellets to pack animals will prevent the introduction of destructive exotic plants harbored in hay bales.

In Arizona some trekkers have abandoned horses and mules in favor of llamas or even goats, which do less damage to the natural environment.

NOISE

Except for the wind in the trees, the sound of cascading water, the singing of birds, the call of a loon, or the bugling of a bull elk, the pleasures of a wilderness experience are heightened by the absence of noise. Loudness is an intrusion; respect the rights of others to solitude and quiet in the vast silences of wilderness. Don't disturb the peace by partying late into the night. Don't shout. And if you've brought a guitar, harmonica, or other musical instrument, ask nearby campers if they mind your playing.

WATER

Giardiasis is wicked. Ask anyone who has had a run-in with it. You become nauseated, can't eat, feel feverish, lose weight—all the symptoms you associate with a severe case of flu. It goes on and on and on, and, worse, it comes back on you just when you think you're cured. It's caused by *Giardia lamblia,* a parasite deposited in water by animal feces. Assume that all water anywhere is contaminated.

Treat water obtained at wilderness sources by boiling, filtering, or adding chemicals. Experts disagree about boiling times needed to purify water. If you prefer to boil, for safety's sake bring water to a rolling boil for at least 3 minutes. Commercial water-purification filters will remove giardia cysts, but if you do not follow manufacturers' instructions carefully, you may actually contaminate the filter attachments. Iodine tablets, which to some taste bad, kill giardia cysts. You can mask the taste of iodine by adding powdered lemonade, or other fruit flavors.

HYPERTHERMIA AND HYPOTHERMIA

Hyperthermia means too hot, hypothermia too cold. Both are life threatening. The most effective way to prevent dangerous swings in your body's core temperature is to protect yourself against the elements with proper clothing, adequate nourishment, and great care to maintain hydration.

Because much of our state becomes extremely hot and dry during summer, hyperthermia is the more common condition in Arizona. "It's a dry heat," you will hear people say, by way of suggesting that temperatures above 100 degrees Fahrenheit are somehow tolerable. But aridity is in many ways as dangerous as heat. In a place where capacity for evaporation is many times greater than actual precipitation, everything, including the human body, rapidly desiccates. Thus, great care must be taken to avoid overheating and water loss leading to heat exhaustion or, worse, heat stroke.

The symptoms of heat exhaustion, a dangerous condition that should be treated immediately, include weakness; disorientation or panic; clammy, pale skin; and chills. The symptoms of heat stroke or hyperthermia, a life-threatening condition requiring a physician's attention, are a flushed complexion, dry, hot skin, and complete collapse or unconsciousness.

The first line of protection against heat and aridity is sunglasses, sunscreen, and clothing. Use sunscreen with an SPF of at least 15, put it on thirty minutes to an hour before exposing your skin to the sun, and renew it after four to six hours, depending on the season and the sun's intensity. Long-sleeved shirts, long trousers, and wide-brimmed hats—a bit old fashioned, perhaps, but effective—offer not only excellent solar protection but help prevent overheating. Remember to wear sunglasses with UV protection.

Even when you think you are drinking plenty of water, maintaining proper hydration in a desert climate is tough, particularly under heavy exertion such as backpacking or hiking. Before you set out, "camel up" by drinking lots of water and drink frequently along the way. Drink even when you do not feel thirsty. Do not try to ration water. Monitor the color of your urine. If it becomes deep yellow, you are already dehydrated.

Watch for any of the following symptoms in your hiking companions: difficulty maintaining pace or loss of muscular control; slowness or slurring of speech; faintness or dizziness; paleness; nausea; and extreme fatigue. Any of these may indicate the onset of serious dehydration, and require immediate first aid:

- Get the victim out of the sun and into the shade. Shade is scarce in the desert, but if you are hiking near a dry wash you may find mesquite or palo verde trees large enough to provide shade.
- Calm the victim. As mentioned, panic is often a symptom of heat exhaustion.
- Encourage the victim to drink in small sips.
- Wipe the victim's face and neck with a bandanna or cloth soaked in cool water.
- Wait until sunset to continue hiking, even if the victim's condition is improved.

Hypothermia, the opposite of heat stroke (hyperthermia), is not unheard of in Arizona. A number of years ago, a man hiking in a party of three died while on a winter backpack in the Galiuro Wilderness. He was strong and athletic, so his companions did not worry when he fell behind while hiking in wet, sloppy snow. By the time they doubled back to find him, it was too late. The group was wrong to think that the victim's falling behind was insignificant. The victim himself was terribly wrong in his choice of clothing—a cotton denim jacket and jeans that had become saturated, chilling him to the bone. "Cotton kills," you will hear experienced backcountry travelers say. Wear wool or synthetic fleece instead. Both provide thermal protection even when wet.

Ironically, victims of hypothermia, also called exposure, show some of the same symptoms as victims of heat stroke—a stumbling gait, slurred speech, and disorientation. In addition, victims of cold often begin to shiver uncontrollably, particularly in cold, damp, windy weather; alert hikers should watch for any of the above symptoms in their companions. If they occur, give immediate first aid:

- Remove the victim's wet clothing and quickly dress him or her in layers of warm, dry clothing.
- Bundle the victim in a sleeping bag with another hiker; two, if possible.
- Give the victim plenty of warm fluids to drink.

Of course, prevention is the best remedy for either of these life-threatening conditions. Before undertaking an arduous backcountry expedition, be certain that your physical condition is equal to it. Carefully check your equipment before leaving to be sure you have the essentials for survival. Make sure that you pack adequate clothing, especially protection against wind, rain, and other extreme weather conditions. While on the trail, consume high-energy foods and know your own energy needs. Some hikers—and I am one—need to "refuel" more frequently than others. Drink plenty of water. Here, again, individual requirements vary. Although I drink "tons" of water while on trail and carefully monitor the color of my urine, I always feel a bit dried out after a long outing.

Finally, common sense prevails always. Know your limits and don't exceed them. Do not act impulsively. Remember, always, to carry extra food and water and to leave a well-stocked vehicle at the trailhead.

ALTITUDE

Adjusting to mountain altitudes is important, particularly for hikers from low-elevation locations. If you live at sea level and begin hiking at elevations approaching 7,000 feet without going through a period of adaptation, you are likely to be hit by altitude sickness. The symptoms—headache, faintness or dizziness, shortness of breath, nausea, and diarrhea—will vary depending on individual tolerances. A more serious form of altitude sickness, pulmonary edema, is rare in Arizona where no peaks rise above 13,000 feet. Along with the symptoms listed above, pulmonary edema causes extreme fatigue, painful coughing, rasping or bubbling noises in the chest, and bloody sputum. Since it is life threatening, anyone suffering from it should be quickly removed to lower elevations. To avoid altitude sickness, acclimate yourself by spending one or two days of normal activity at elevation. Other tips: Don't smoke. Avoid alcohol. Get plenty of sleep. Be in peak physical condition.

Be mindful that difficulty breathing is not the only problem in the rarefied air at high elevations. The thin atmosphere also increases the sun's power, making exposed skin far more vulnerable to solar radiation. Protect yourself against painful sunburn at high elevation by wearing sunglasses, garments that leave little skin exposed, and a wide-brimmed hat. And don't forget to slather on lots of high-SPF sunblock and lip protection.

LIGHTNING

About 300 people are killed by lightning strikes in the United States annually. During the summer monsoon, which unofficially lasts from July 4th through Labor Day, Tucson and surrounding Pima County in southern Arizona become the virtual capital of lightning strikes. Scientists regularly gather here to study the phenomenon.

The average square mile of ground throughout the United States will be hit by ten lightning bolts each year. In the vicinity of Tucson, that number rises to fifteen bolts per square mile, and the chance that lightning will hit the ground within 100 yards of where you stand is once every two years. More than fifty people have been killed by lightning throughout Arizona over the past thirty-five years, with most of the fatalities occurring during July, August, and early September.

Just about every Arizona outdoors person I know has a lightning story to tell. Take precautions. Summer thunderstorms tend to hit during the afternoon hours, so try to leave the high country early or seek shelter before the storm arrives. If you are caught out in the open, however, there are things you can do to prevent getting zapped.

Green-gold aspens in Coronado National Forest, Chiricahua Wilderness

- Crouch down and curl into a ball, taking up as little space as possible. Do not, however, lie on the ground; a lightning charge disperses when it enters the earth.
- Do not seek shelter under lone trees; avoid wire fences and metal pipes.
- Avoid all high, exposed places.
- If you are near your vehicle, get in it and close the windows.
- If a hiking companion is struck by lightning, you may save his life by performing immediate CPR.

FLOODING

Over the past 50 years, more than 100 people have been killed in Arizona by flash flooding. During periods of heavy rain, dry washes become raging rivers capable of tumbling Volkswagen-Bug-sized boulders and uprooting tall trees. The unwary, miscalculating the depth and hydraulic ferocity of moving water, are often caught trying to cross a running wash. Twenty-three people were killed statewide during the heavy rains of September 1970. In July 1981, eight people were drowned by a flash flood at Tanque Verde Falls, a favorite recreational area in the Rincon Mountains near Tucson.

Heed all warning signs about the dangers of entering a flooded wash; never try to drive your vehicle through a wash at flood stage. A mere two feet of rushing water will carry away most vehicles. Backcountry hikers should use extreme caution fording swollen streams and washes. It is easy to lose your footing in a strong current while carrying a fully loaded backpack. Only six inches of fast-moving water can knock you off your feet. One mistake could be fatal. Flood waters usually subside quickly; a short wait may save your life.

TEN ESSENTIALS

Nearly everyone has seen a list or two of the ten essentials necessary to backcountry survival. Wilderness survival schools teach from these lists, Forest Service pamphlets publish them, and kids learn them at summer camp. Below is my list of ten:

- Matches or lighter and fire starter.
- Flashlight with extra batteries and bulb.
- Emergency shelter: space blanket, poncho, or ground cloth.
- First aid kit.
- Map of area and compass.
- Knife.
- Emergency food.
- Signaling device: stainless-steel mirror or whistle.
- Extra clothing: windbreaker, polypro cap, and gloves.
- Sun protection: sunglasses, sunscreen, lip balm, and hat.

Except for the map, these are stock items in my daypack, many of them packaged together in heavy, resealable plastic bags. Over time I have added or subtracted from the list. Periodically, I check to see what needs replacing.

Reflections along the west fork of Oak Creek Canyon show mounds of columbine and monkeyflower on the rock walls of Secret Mountain Wilderness

MAPS

Maps in this guidebook detail salient features of the areas they describe and are not intended to be used for orientation in the field. For route finding you will need to obtain one or more of the 7.5-minute topo maps listed at the beginning of each entry. Map sources are listed in Appendix 3.

- ▪▪▪▪ Border
- --- Trail
- —— Access Road
- —— River
- ⌒ Lake
- TH Trailhead
- ▲ Campground
- ○ Point of Interest
- ● Spring

Please refer to this legend for all maps in this book.

How to Use This Guide

THE ARIZONA WILDERNESS GUIDE groups the state's wilderness areas by geographic region. The chapter on Northern Arizona describes wilderness areas on the Colorado Plateau, including those lying north of the Grand Canyon. The Rim Country chapter describes those that are positioned along and below the Mogollon Rim down to the Salt River. Wilderness areas in southeastern Arizona's Basin and Range terrain are treated in the Southeast Arizona chapter. The chapter titled Western Arizona describes wilderness areas located in both the Sonoran Desert Region of southwestern Arizona and the Mohave Desert Region in northwestern Arizona.

Each of the four parts of this guide begins with an overview of the region and current status of its wilderness areas. The descriptions of individual wilderness areas in each section begin with a short table of pertinent information about each site, such as size, location, elevation range, habitats, miles of trails, and pertinent 7.5-minute U.S.G.S topographic maps.

Each wilderness area is described according to its notable land features, vegetation, wildlife, and pertinent historical data. Finally, hikes of varying lengths and degree of difficulty are detailed for each wilderness section, along with other recreational opportunities, such as skiing, snowshoeing, river rafting, and canoe or float trips. Hikes are classified as follows:

DAY HIKES. Trails and destinations that fit an approximate eight-hour period.

DESTINATION HIKES. Waterfalls, peaks, or historic sites that may require an overnight stay.

LOOP HIKES. Routes that circle through the wilderness to return the hiker to the trailhead via a different route. These include both day trips and overnighters.

SHUTTLE HIKES. Hikes that require shuttling vehicles between the start and finish points of a one-way route—typically a multi-day trek through a long canyon or across a mountain pass.

Distance in miles and elevations are recorded for all hikes, and each is graded, subjectively, by degree of difficulty. Easy hikes, for example, are low-mileage day trips on well-maintained trails with easy grades and little elevation gain. Moderate hikes, also on developed trails, require longer distances, steeper grades, and greater elevation gain. Strenuous hikes mean long distances, substantial elevation gain, and may require bushwhacking or following faint trails over rough terrain. Other factors, such as weather and availability of water, may influence the ratings. Along the way, hike descriptions point out natural features such as plant life, wildlife viewing opportunities, and aesthetic values.

A blanket of wildflowers in Chiricahua Wilderness High Country

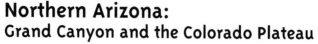

Northern Arizona:
Grand Canyon and the Colorado Plateau

Except for Arizona's extreme northwest corner, the Colorado Plateau stretches across the entire northern portion of the state, extending into New Mexico, Colorado, and Utah. The terrain is cut by deep canyons, such as the Grand Canyon, Canyon de Chelly, Paria Canyon, and the Little Colorado Canyon. The eastern portion of the plateau, sometimes identified as the Navajo Section, is Great Basin desert scrub, dry country, where even during Arizona's summer monsoon season very little rain actually falls to the ground—sometimes only an inch or two annually. Driving across the broad steppes of Arizona's eastern Colorado Plateau, a place of endless sky punctuated by vast tablelands, elongated mesas, and knobby buttes, you often see dark rain tendrils angling toward the earth from the lobes of cumulus clouds. But in the crackling dry atmosphere, they evaporate before they can pelt the parched earth. *Virgas,* these tendrils are called, Latin for twigs or whisks. The Navajo call it "ghost rain," or the "hair of the rain." Most precipitation arrives as snow, often heavy, during brutally cold winters.

The land wears a thin skin on these plains, rubbed raw by slashing rain, scorching sun, and winds that sometimes approach hurricane velocity. Sagebrush, salt bush, winterfat, bunch grasses, and a few other plants grow at roadside. Hardy in winter, adapted to prolonged drought in summer, they thrive here. In the wetter uplands, atop mesas, there are mixed pines, oaks, piñon-juniper, mountain mahogany, and cliff rose. And growing in the cooler, still wetter, microclimates of some of the deeper canyons are Douglas fir and quaking aspen.

This Navajo Section of the Colorado Plateau contains the barren, eroded hills, slumped cliffs and cones, and rain-severed gullies of the Painted Desert; the lava-capped Hopi Mesas; the wind-sculpted pinnacles, spires, and buttes of Monument Valley; the enchanted Petrified Forest; and the pine-clad, domed summit of 10,384-foot Navajo Mountain.

The Grand Canyon and the Arizona Strip, which extend north of the great gorge to the Utah border, comprise the western portion of Arizona's Colorado Plateau. Consisting of five parallel plateaus of varying heights, interspersed with Great Basin Desert valleys, the Arizona Strip is remote and sparsely populated. At greater than 9,000 feet, the Kaibab Plateau, a region of alpine meadows and mixed conifer and aspen forests, is the highest of these plateaus. Ponderosa pine forests dominate the upper reaches of some of the other plateaus, with piñon-juniper coming in at

Paria Canyon–Vermilion Cliffs Wilderness Area

mid-level elevations. Vegetation at the lowest elevations consists of drought-adapted desert shrubs, blackbrush, and Great Basin sagebrush. Toward the northwestern margins of the Colorado Plateau, Joshua Trees and other Mohave Desert trees and shrubs mingle with Great Basin species.

South of the Grand Canyon lies the Flagstaff Section of the Colorado Plateau, level terrain dominated by the San Francisco Peaks, which rise to nearly 13,000 feet. Heavily forested by ponderosa pine, the landscape is punctuated by numerous volcanic cinder cones.

Beaver Dam Mountains Wilderness

Steve Bruno

A Joshua tree in bloom at sunset

LOCATION:
16 miles southwest
of St. George, Utah

SIZE: 19,600 acres

ELEVATION RANGE:
2,000 to 4,629 feet

MILES OF TRAILS:
No marked or
maintained trails

HABITATS: Mohave
and Great Basin Desert
mountains and canyons

ADMINISTRATION:
BLM, Arizona Strip Field
Office

TOPOGRAPHIC MAPS:
Littlefield, Mountain
Sheep Spring, Castle
Cliff, Jarvis Peak

IN THE NORTHWEST CORNER OF ARIZONA, in
a narrow band north of the Grand Canyon known as the
Arizona Strip, the Virgin River slices through layers of limestone and sandstone to form steep walls rising hundreds of
feet above the river bottom. For roughly fifteen miles, from
a few miles south of the Arizona-Utah border downstream to
where the river flows into the Virgin Valley near Littlefield,
Arizona, the spectacular Virgin River Gorge parallels
Interstate 15.

South of the river, lying entirely within Arizona,
is the Paiute Wilderness; north of the river, straddling the
Arizona-Utah border, is the Beaver Dam Mountains
Wilderness.

The Beaver Dam Mountains Wilderness sits astride
a biological edge between two great North American deserts:
the Mohave, synonymous with Joshua trees, and the Great

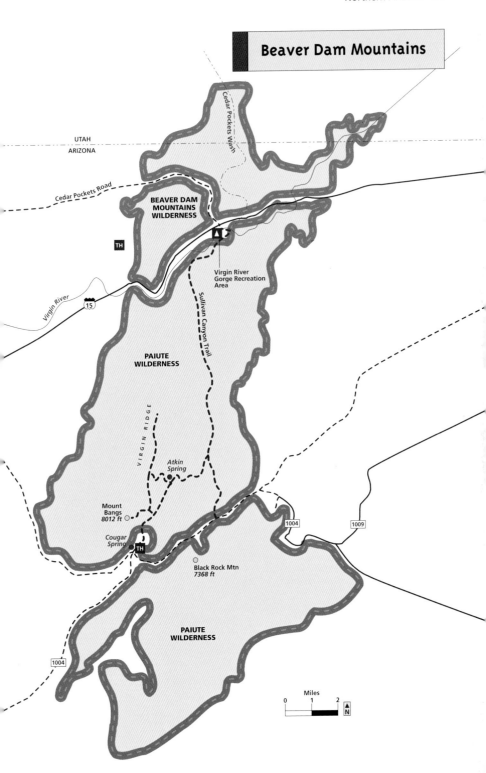

Beaver Dam Mountains

Cedar Pockets Wash

UTAH

ARIZONA

Cedar Pockets Road

BEAVER DAM MOUNTAINS WILDERNESS

TH

Virgin River Gorge Recreation Area

Sullivan Canyon Trail

Virgin River

15

PAIUTE WILDERNESS

VIRGIN RIDGE

Atkin Spring

Mount Bangs
8012 ft

Cougar Spring

TH

1004   1009

Black Rock Mtn
7368 ft

PAIUTE WILDERNESS

1004

Miles
0   1   2

N

Basin, where several types of sagebrush thrive. Joshua trees, smaller here than in their native habitat, grow mostly on the warmer, south-facing slopes. Sagebrush, preferring the cooler climes of the Great Basin, proliferate on the north-facing slopes.

Desert bighorn sheep, pronghorn, peregrine falcon, and desert tortoise are at home in the Beaver Dam Mountains Wilderness, as are black-tailed jack rabbit, bobcat, and coyote. In spring, wildflowers are often abundant. Most striking are the showy pink blossoms of beavertail prickly pear and the startling purple-blue indigo bush. The rare dwarf bearclaw poppy is sometimes seen in the uplands and the endangered woodfin minnow inhabits the Virgin River.

For many outdoor recreationists, the Virgin River Gorge itself is the preferred destination. In spring when snowmelt swells the river's volume, whitewater kayakers and rafters challenge the rapids, a short portion of which lie within the wilderness. In winter and spring, rock climbers flock from all over the world to test their skills at Blasphemy, Sun, Planet Earth, and other climbing routes on either side of the gorge.

For hikers and backpackers, bird watchers, geology buffs, and amateur botanists, the gorge is also a destination. Except during summer when temperatures can exceed 100 degrees Fahrenheit or in spring when the river occasionally becomes a raging torrent, backpackers hike the gorge along the river bottom.

HIKING THE WILDERNESS

No trails exist within the Beaver Dam Mountains Wilderness, but the terrain is open enough to allow for easy cross-country hiking. The backcountry is best entered from the Cedar Pockets Road, which divides the wilderness. The Cedar Pockets Road may be accessed from the Virgin River Gorge Recreation Area, 16 miles southwest of St. George, Utah on Interstate 15. The road, which runs up the bed of the Cedar Pockets Wash for the first mile or so, heads north into the wilderness from the recreation area before turning west to climb into the uplands. A high-clearance two-wheel-drive vehicle should be adequate except when the roadway has been rutted by heavy rains. Hiking options include bushwhacking up Cedar Pockets Wash or heading cross-country across upland slopes.

Grand Canyon National Park

Sunset, South Rim, Grand Canyon

LOCATION: 81 miles north of Flagstaff

SIZE: 1,218,376 acres

ELEVATION RANGE: 1,600 to 9,089 feet

MILES OF TRAILS: More than 300 miles

HABITATS: Sonoran Desert, piñon-juniper, ponderosa pine, boreal forest

ADMINISTRATION: National Park Service

TOPOGRAPHIC MAPS: Bright Angel, Grand Canyon, Phantom Ranch, Cape Royal, Grandview Point, Bright Angel Point, Vulcans Throne, Vulcans Throne SE, Whitmore Rapids, Mount Trumbull SE, Mount Trumbull NE, Mount Logan, Hancock Knolls, Little Park Lake, Columbine Falls, Bat Cave, Tincanebitts Point, Mount Dellenbaugh, Whitmore Point SE, Whitmore Point SW, Snap Canyon East, Snap Canyon West, Snap Draw, Whitmore Point, Yellow John Mountain, Devils Slide Rapids, Travertine Rapids, Separation Canyon, Spencer Canyon, Granite Park Price Point, Amos Point, Quartermaster Canyon, Quaking Aspen, Tapeats Amphitheater, Fishtail, Kanab Point, Hitson Tank, Hancock Knolls, Fern Glen Canyon, S B Point, Havasu Falls, Fossil Bay, Powell Plateau, King Arthur Castle, Kanabownits Spring, Little Park Lake, Gateway Rapids, Yunosi Point, Topocoba Hilltop, Explorers, Havasupai Point, Shiva Temple, Paiute Point, Navajo Bridge, Bitter Springs, Emmett Wash, North Canyon Point, Buffalo Tanks, Buffalo Ranch, Tatahatso Point, Nankoweap Mesa, Point Imperial, Cape Solitude, Walhalla Plateau, Cape Royal, Desert View, Tusayan East

MULTILINGUAL EXCLAMATIONS OF SURPRISE AND WONDER spring from the lips of millions of visitors who annually arrive from all over the world to stand awestruck at the Grand Canyon's rim. A mile deep, and more than eight miles at its widest, the Grand Canyon reveals some two billion years of geologic time in the exposed limestone, shale, and sandstone walls that extend from Lees Ferry below the Glen Canyon Dam to Pearce Ferry on upper Lake Mead. Beheld from one of its rim viewpoints, the Grand Canyon is indeed stupendous, fantastic, and awe-inspiring. Even if there were enough adjectives in English to drop one for each of the 277 miles of Colorado River plunging through the canyon's gorge, such a string of superlatives could not capture the majesty of what it's like to gaze into the Grand Canyon for the first time.

Yet, below the rim, accessible by miles of hiking trails, there's another canyon that very few of the five million annual visitors to Grand Canyon National Park ever see. It's a place of high-elevation Boreal forests and low-elevation desertscapes, a landscape of rushing streams and abundant wildlife. A hike from the North Rim of the canyon all the way to Phantom Ranch on the Colorado River, dropping 5,850 feet and covering 14.2 miles, takes you from the Canadian Life Zone of aspen, spruce, and fir down to the Lower Sonoran life zone of cacti, ocotillo, barrel cactus, and cholla. Along the way, you will have passed through the transition zone of ponderosa pine and Gambel oak and the Upper Sonoran Zone of piñon-juniper, sagebrush, mountain mahogany, and cliff rose to arrive at the Colorado River's desert riparian zone of willow, ash, tamarisk, hackberry, redbud, cottonwood, cattails and bullrushes.

The Grand Canyon and its many natural environments supports a staggering array of birds, mammals, reptiles, amphibians, and fishes. Birds common along the Colorado River include great blue heron, blue-winged teal, white-throated swift, yellow-bellied sapsucker, black phoebe, indigo bunting, violet-green swallow, Western tanager, dark-eyed junco, common merganser, red-tailed hawk, and canyon wren. The golden eagle is occasionally sighted, and the bald eagle is quite numerous in the vicinity of Nankoweap Creek where it feasts on introduced rainbow trout.

Mammals along the river include ringtail, Western spotted skunk, rock squirrel, mule deer, desert bighorn sheep, white-throated woodrat, and various bats. The Rocky Mountain toad, red-spotted toad, chuckwalla, yellow-backed spiny lizard, side-blotched lizard, Grand Canyon rattlesnake, and California kingsnake are among the amphibians and reptiles common or abundant along the river corridor. Among native fishes, only the speckled dace, flannelmouth sucker, and bluehead sucker are numerous in the Colorado River through the Grand Canyon. Introduced trout, particularly rainbow, thrive in the river's cold water.

As you climb away from the river, wildlife profiles change. Mountain lion, bobcat, elk, beaver, gray fox, black bear, porcupine, raccoon, badger, wood rat, American kestrel, blue grouse, turkey, peregrine falcon, band-tailed pigeon, cedar waxwing, Steller's jay, raven, rufous-sided towhee, common poorwill, meadowlark, American robin, Western and mountain bluebird, and pygmy nuthatch are commonly found in Grand Canyon National Park. Two small mammals, very much alike in appearance, reveal how markedly the great chasm separates species. The Abert squirrel lives only on the 7,300-foot South Rim; the Kaibab squirrel only on the 9,000-foot North Rim.

Years ago, someone told me, "If you want to study geology, go to Arizona where there's lots of it." True, which explains why almost every spring in Arizona I encounter groups of students from Midwestern universities on field trips to study Arizona's geology. And no place in Arizona is more popular among geology buffs than the Grand Canyon. It is a geology text laid open. In simple terms, the Grand Canyon was formed by the simultaneous uplifting of the Colorado Plateau and downcutting of the Colorado River. Over a period of about sixty-five million years, these processes carved away layer upon layer of rock to expose cross sections of limestone, sandstone, shale, and harder bedrock. Each of these layers, like the pages of a book, reveals a complex geologic history spreading over eons. Summed up, the pages comprise a history in rock that goes back nearly two billion years.

In the 1930s, a group of river runners entered a recess in the canyon wall at about mile 30. Known as Stanton's Cave, it was where members of a failed 1890 expedition led by Robert Brewster Stanton stashed their gear before climbing out of the canyon. But what the river runners discovered was far more important than a stash of moldy gear; they found tiny split-twig animal figurines, formed in the shapes of sheep, deer, elk, antelope, and birds. These figurines were made by Archaic Pinto Basin peoples, hunter-gatherers who roamed the river gorge and its tributaries more than 4,000 years ago. Other unearthed debris included the bones of birds and animals now extinct. Also found in the cave were plant fragments that revealed significant climate changes—showing a trend from wet to dry—over the past 10,000 years.

The Anasazi people, whose cliff dwellings may be seen in the eastern portions of the gorge, moved into the Grand Canyon around A.D. 500 as did the Cohonina, who occupied the western regions. In the 14th century, ancestors of present-day canyon dwellers, the Havasupai ("People of the Place that is Green") and Hualapai ("People of the Pine Trees") occupied the Grand Canyon. In more recent times, Navajo and Southern Paiute Indians have lived in or near the canyon. Many regional names are evidence of the strong Paiute influence in the area.

In 1540, the first Europeans, Spanish soldiers led by Captain Garcia Lopez de Cardenas, explored the Grand Canyon region. Operating on orders from Francisco Vasquez de Coronado, their mission was to find a route through the canyon to the fabled Seven Cities of Cibola. They failed, and no Europeans returned until 1776 when Spanish padres Francisco Atanasio Dominguez and Silvestre Velez de Escalante explored Glen and Marble Canyons and the North Rim in search of a path across the Grand Canyon.

American trappers came next in 1826, among them James Ohio Pattie, who led several parties of mountain men and trappers. In the 1850s, Jacob Hamblin, a Mormon missionary sent into the field by Brigham Young, discovered crossing sites at both Lees Ferry and Pierce Ferry. In 1857, Lieutenant Joseph Ives, on orders from the War Department, sailed upriver from the Gulf of California in the Explorer, a sternwheel steamboat on a mission to determine whether or not upstream navigation were possible. When the boat was grounded in Black Canyon, some 350 miles upriver from the gulf, the mission was aborted, but Ives and his men continued on foot to the confluence of the Colorado and Little Colorado rivers, a first.

Major John Wesley Powell, geologist, paleontologist, ethnologist, and a one-armed veteran of the Civil War, led the first full-length exploration of the Grand Canyon in 1869. Despite losing most of their supplies when a boat flipped, suffering heavy damage to their pine and oak boats, having their food turn bad, and being abandoned by three members of the party who climbed to the North Rim where they were presumably killed by hostile Paiutes, the expeditioners made it through. A second expedition, begun by Powell in 1871, had to be abandoned at Kanab Creek a year later. Powell is credited with naming the Grand Canyon and for most of the place names in the canyon.

In 1893 the Grand Canyon was set aside as a National Forest Reserve by President Benjamin Harrison. When President Theodore Roosevelt first saw the Grand Canyon in 1903, he said "Leave it as it is. You cannot improve it. The ages have been at work on it, and only man can mar it." Three years later, Roosevelt declared the Grand Canyon a National Game Reserve, a status upgraded to National Monument in 1908.

In 1919 President Woodrow Wilson proclaimed the Grand Canyon a National Park. By executive order, Herbert Hoover made the western Grand Canyon a National Monument in 1932 and in 1969 President Lyndon Johnson signed an order to make Marble Canyon a National Monument. Finally, in 1975, President Gerald Ford combined all these units and the North Kaibab National Forest into one—the 1,900-square-mile Grand Canyon National Park, administered by the National Park Service.

Although the Grand Canyon has not yet been so designated, a draft management plan released in June 1998 by the National Park Service would treat ninety-four percent of the 1.3 million-acre park as virtual wilderness. The plan would stop development of roads and buildings and ban motorized vehicles in those portions of the park to be managed as wilderness. Once instituted, the plan would require that more than 120 miles of old roads be converted to trails or restored to their natural condition. The Park Service hoped to begin implementing the plan by the end of 1998.

Since 1980, when the Grand Canyon was first proposed as wilderness, the Park Service has systematically purchased grazing, mining, and other private development rights. And subsequent land-use studies increased the acreage originally proposed for wilderness by nearly ten percent.

The new draft Wilderness Management Plan calls for the current 1,109,257-acre Wilderness Study Area—nearly all of the Canyon's inner gorges, the South Rim west of Hermit's Rest, and most of the North Rim—to be set aside as wilderness as soon as Congress can act.

CROSS-COUNTRY SKIING

Although the North Rim of the Grand Canyon is closed by heavy snow from about mid-November to mid-May each year, cross-country skiers with backcountry permits from the Park Service and the ability to undertake a 45-mile trek from Jacob Lake can enjoy the absolute solitude of the North Rim in winter.

RIVER RUNNING

Commercial raft trips on the Colorado River through the Grand Canyon usually put in at Lees Ferry and take out at Diamond Creek, some 225 miles downstream. In all, the river drops 1,800 feet in that distance over approximately 160 rapids. Private trips, for which obtaining a permit may take years, can be arranged through the River Permits Office (see Appendix 2).

HIKING

Summer temperatures on the North Rim are mild, making hiking there quite pleasant throughout the summer. South Rim temperatures can be quite warm in summer and cold in winter. As you drop from the rim into the canyon the temperature rises at a rate of approximately 4 to 6 degrees Fahrenheit for every thousand feet lost, so that at the canyon bottom along the Colorado River, you may experience daytime highs between 60 and 70 in winter, but well over 100 in summer. Occasionally, trailheads at the South Rim can be quite icy in winter. It's a good idea to wear instep crampons on the upper reaches of some trails. All overnight stays in the inner canyon require backcountry permits, which are available up to four months in advance.

For purposes of clarity, this guide divides the Grand Canyon National Park trail system into South Rim Trails and North Rim Trails. Only the major trails in either section are described. Experienced hikers may want to explore some of the less-travelled secondary trails on their own.

SOUTH RIM TRAIL
DAY HIKE: RIM TRAIL
One-way length: 9.0 miles
Low and high elevations: 6,640 to 7,120 feet
Difficulty: easy

The trailhead for this excellent introductory hike to the Grand Canyon is at Hermits Rest along West Rim Drive. A short 3.5-mile section of the Rim Trail is paved; the rest is a dirt path that travels through piñon-juniper and Gambel oak woodland. Highlights along the trail include Pima, Mohave, Hopi, and Maricopa points, and the storied buildings of the Grand Canyon Village Historic District. The trail ends at the Yavapai Observation Station at Mather Point, which was named for the first director of the National Park Service, Stephen T. Mather.

Grand Canyon

TH **610** **TH**

Nankoweap Trail

○ Point Imperial

North Bass Trail

Transept Trail

Widforss Trail

TH

Uncle Jim Trail

Ken Patrick Trail

Little Colorado River

S. Bass Trail

Tonto Trail

Hermit Trail

Widforss Point

North Rim

N. Kaibab Trail

○ Cape Royal

TH

Boucher Trail

River Tr

Phantom Ranch

Clear Creek Tr

S. Kaibab Trail

Beamer Trail

TH   **TH**

Dripping Springs

Dripping Springs Trail

Indian Garden

Tonto Trail

Rim Tr

Colorado River

Tanner Tr

TH

TH

Bright Angel Trail

S O U T H   R I M

TH   **TH**

64

Grandview Trail

New Hance Trail

TOROWEAP POINT

TH

Lake Mead National Recreation Area

Lake Mead National Recreation Area

○ Lava Falls

Hualapai Reservation

18

Colorado River

○ Diamond Creek

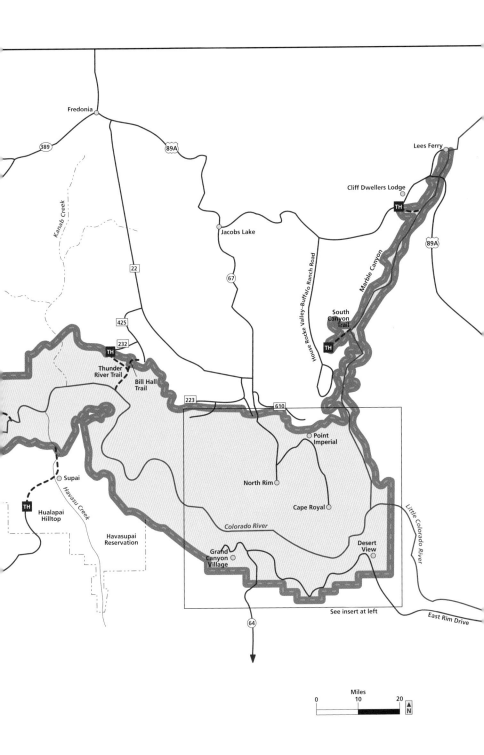

Fredonia

389

89A

Lees Ferry

Cliff Dwellers Lodge

TH

Kanab Creek

Jacobs Lake

Marble Canyon

89A

22

67

House Rocke Valley–Buffalo Ranch Road

425

South
Canyon
Trail

232

TH

TH

Thunder
River Trail

Bill Hall
Trail

223

610

Point
Imperial

North Rim

Cape Royal

Supai

Havasu Creek

TH

Hualapai
Hilltop

Colorado River

Little Colorado River

Havasupai
Reservation

Grand
Canyon
Village

Desert
View

See insert at left

East Rim Drive

64

Miles

0   10   20

N

SOUTH RIM TRAIL
DAY HIKE: GRANDVIEW TRAIL
One-way length: 4.8 miles
Low and high elevations: 3,760 to 7,400 feet
Difficulty: moderate

The trailhead is at Grandview Point along the East Rim Drive. After leaving Grandview Point, the trail descends into an area known as Horseshoe Mesa, where it is intersected by the Tonto Trail. Other trails in the Horseshoe Mesa area offer some great views of Hance Rapids and Vishnu Temple.

SOUTH RIM TRAIL
DAY HIKE: RIVER TRAIL
One-way length: 1.5 miles
Low and high elevations: 2,800 feet level
Difficulty: easy

For hikers who enter the canyon on one trail and wish to return by another, the River Trail is a connector trail between the Bright Angel and South Kaibab Trails.

SOUTH RIM TRAIL
DESTINATION HIKE: BRIGHT ANGEL TRAIL
One-way length: 9.3 miles
Low and high elevations: 2,480 to 6,860 feet
Difficulty: strenuous

Perhaps the most-used trail in the national park, the Bright Angel Trail is well-maintained over its entire distance from the trailhead in Grand Canyon Village to the Colorado River. It's an old trail. Pictographs on the canyon walls indicate that Indians used it; in fact, until the early 20th century, Havasupai Indians still planted crops at Indian Garden, 4.6 miles down trail. The steeper upper portion descends in a series of switchbacks called Jacobs Ladder. From Indian Garden the trail follows Garden Creek through the Tapeats narrows before descending to the Colorado. At the river the trail continues 1.5 miles along the river to Bright Angel Campground and Phantom Ranch.

SOUTH RIM TRAIL
DESTINATION HIKE: HERMIT TRAIL
One-way length: 9.3 miles
Low and high elevations: 2,400 to 6,640 feet
Difficulty: strenuous

The trailhead is located at Hermits Rest along the West Rim Drive, eight miles west of Grand Canyon Village. Difficult to follow in places, this rocky, steep trail descends into Hermit Canyon before dropping into Hermit Gorge. Trails intersected along the way include the Waldron, Dripping Springs, and Tonto trails. Near the Hermit Creek Campground the trail picks up Hermit Creek and follows it for 1.5 miles to the Colorado River and Hermit Rapid.

SOUTH RIM TRAIL
DESTINATION HIKE: BOUCHER TRAIL
One-way length: 8.0 miles
Low and high elevations: 2,760 to 5,280 feet
Difficulty: strenuous

Named for an old prospector and semi-hermit, Louis Boucher, the Boucher Trail is accessed by hiking the Hermit Trail (see above) to the Dripping Springs Trail junction and continuing west on the Dripping Springs Trail for 1.0 mile. The Boucher Trail is recommended for experienced backcountry hikers only, since it is washed out in many places and is not only difficult to follow but also tough to negotiate. Some very steep, exposed sections may require passage on all fours. As it approaches the Colorado, the trail joins Tonto Creek, but splits off again at Boucher Creek to follow the creek bed 1.5 miles to the river.

SOUTH RIM TRAIL
DESTINATION HIKE: SOUTH BASS TRAIL
One-way length: 7.8 miles
Low and high elevations: 2,250 to 6,650 feet
Difficulty: strenuous

To reach the trailhead, drive south from Grand Canyon Village on U.S. Highway 180 to Rowe Well Road (Forest Route 328) and turn right (west). Drive west on Forest Route 328 to the trailhead, which is about thirty miles west of Grand Canyon Village. A four-wheel-drive vehicle is recommended.

William Bass, a Grand Canyon pioneer and entrepreneur, improved what had been a Cohonina and Havasupai Indian foot trail to enable travel by horseback to and from his mines and camps on the Colorado. Bass was one of the first to operate a tourist camp in the Grand Canyon. The trail, which can be difficult to follow, descends steeply to an esplanade below the cliffs and follows the broad terrace for some distance before dropping off into Bass Canyon. Crossing the canyon many times, the trail ends up above Bass Rapid on the Colorado River.

SOUTH RIM TRAIL
DESTINATION HIKE: SOUTH KAIBAB TRAIL
One-way length: 7.3 miles
Low and high elevations: 2,480 to 7,260 feet
Difficulty: strenuous

The trailhead is located at Yaki Point along the East Rim Drive. This trail, developed by the Park Service in the 1920s, is known for its grand vistas as it descends into the inner gorge. The trail is in excellent condition and shows some very impressive rock work from the days of its construction. After crossing the Colorado River on the Kaibab Suspension Bridge, the trail continues for 1.0 mile to the Bright Angel Campground.

SOUTH RIM TRAIL
DESTINATION HIKE: NEW HANCE TRAIL
One-way length: 8.0 miles
Low and high elevations: 2,600 to 7,000 feet
Difficulty: strenuous

To reach the trailhead, park at Moran Point along the East Rim Drive and walk 1.0 mile south to the trail sign. This trail is called the New Hance because the original trail built along Hance Creek by early canyon guide John Hance washed out. Hance then built a new trail in Red Canyon. The trail descends to the top of a cliff before finding a way down a long talus slope to the bottom of dry Red Canyon, which it follows to the Tonto Trail junction at Hance Rapid on the Colorado River. Loose rock makes this trail somewhat difficult to follow.

SOUTH RIM TRAIL
DESTINATION HIKE: TANNER TRAIL
One-way length: 10.0 miles
Low and high elevations: 2,700 to 7,300 feet
Difficulty: strenuous

The trailhead is just east of Lipan Point along the East Rim Drive. Like so many trails leading into the inner gorge of the Canyon, the Tanner Trail is an improved Indian footpath. Seth Tanner, a Mormon pioneer, developed the trail to lead pack horses to his mining claims along the river. The only water source for this rough and somewhat difficult-to-follow trail is the Colorado River, so you may want to stash water along the trail for your return to the rim. The route descends via some steep switchbacks to the head of the west branch of Tanner Canyon. After leaving the drainage, it circles the base of Escalante and Cardenas buttes, then drops into Tanner Canyon to the Colorado.

At the river the Escalante Route heads west for 11 miles to the New Hance Trail. This is an extremely difficult route and should be tried only by expert backcountry hikers.

Heading east from its intersection with the Tanner Trail at the river is the Beamer Trail, which travels 9.5 miles to the mouth of the Little Colorado River.

SOUTH RIM TRAIL
DESTINATION HIKE: TONTO TRAIL
One-way length: 9.5 miles
Low and high elevations: 2,100 to 4,200 feet
Difficulty: strenuous

Traveling parallel to the Colorado River from Red Canyon to Garnet Canyon, the Tonto Trail is the major east-west route through the inner gorge of the Grand Canyon. As such, it is an important link with main trails descending into the canyon from the South Rim. These trails include Boucher, Hermit, Bright Angel, South Kaibab, Grandview, and New Hance. Because it wanders into some of the most remote portions of the inner Canyon, the Tonto Trail is ideal for extended backpacks. The trail can be tough to follow, particularly where it crosses tributary creeks. Good route-finding skills are necessary.

NORTH RIM TRAIL
DAY HIKE: UNCLE JIM TRAIL
One-way length: 2.5 miles
Low and high elevations: 8,250 level
Difficulty: easy

Named for Uncle Jim Owens, a North Rim hunting guide, this easy introduction to the mixed conifer forests of the Canyon's North Rim begins at the Ken Patrick Trailhead (see page 55). Like all of the North Rim's shorter hiking trails, the Uncle Jim Trail affords scenic views of the inner gorge of the Grand Canyon itself as it winds along the head of Roaring Springs Canyon and around the rim of Bright Angel Canyon and the North Kaibab Trail.

NORTH RIM TRAIL
DAY HIKE: WIDFORSS TRAIL
One-way length: 5.0 miles
Low and high elevations: 7,900 to 8,100 feet
Difficulty: easy

To reach the trailhead, drive 2.0 miles north from the Grand Canyon Lodge on the North Rim Parkway to the North Kaibab Trail parking lot and turn left for 0.25 mile on the gravel road across from the parking area.

Named for Gunnar M. Widforss, well-known for his paintings of western landscapes, including the Grand Canyon, this route cruises through shady, mixed conifer forests along the Canyon rim as it gradually descends to Widforss Point. Viewpoints at several locations along the way, and at the point itself, provide glimpses of the Transept, a side drainage of Bright Angel Canyon.

NORTH RIM TRAIL
DAY HIKE: THUNDER RIVER TRAIL
One-way length: 15.0 miles
Low and high elevations: 2,000 to 6,400 feet
Difficulty: strenuous

To reach the trailhead, drive north from the National Park on State Route 67 (North Rim Parkway) to Forest Route 22 (at Kaibab Lodge) and turn left (west) toward Dry Park. Continue west for 18 miles to Forest Route 425. Turn left (south) for approximately 10 miles to Forest Route 232. Turn left (west) to the Indian Hollow Campground and trailhead. Although State Route 67 is plowed by mid-May, forest routes on the North Rim may be impassable until much later in the season. Check road conditions with National Park rangers or Forest Service personnel.

From the trailhead, the Thunder River Trail drops to the Esplanade and turns east. After approximately 4.0 miles it is joined by the Bill Hall Trail which descends steeply from Monument Point. Marked in places by cairns, the trail crosses several drainages before dropping into Surprise Valley and heading east toward Thunder River. The trail then drops along a series of steep switchbacks to the confluence of Thunder River and Tapeats Creek. Here the trail moves downstream past the Upper Tapeats Campground, crossing the creek twice before reaching the Lower Tapeats Campground at the Colorado River.

Thunder River, featuring a 100-foot waterfall, flows for just one-half mile to enter Tapeats Creek, making it one of the world's shortest rivers.

NORTH RIM TRAIL
DAY HIKE: NORTH BASS TRAIL
One-way length: 14.0 miles
Low and high elevations: 2,200 to 7,500 feet
Difficulty: strenuous

To reach the trailhead at Swamp Point, drive north from the National Park on State Route 67 (North Rim Parkway) to Forest Route 22 (at Kaibab Lodge) and turn left (west). Follow Forest Route 22 a short distance to Forest Route 270 and turn left to Forest Route 223. Drive west on Forest Route 223 for several miles to Forest Route 223A and turn west to Swamp Ridge Road and Swamp Point. Forest routes may require a four-wheel-drive vehicle, especially after spring snowmelt. Check road conditions with Forest Service and Park Service personnel.

Descending more than 5,000 feet, remote, rugged, strewn with rockslides and washouts, the North Bass Trail is for seasoned Grand Canyon hikers only. from the trailhead the route descends about 1,000 feet along a series of switchbacks to Muav Saddle where the trail branches. The right fork takes you to an old cabin, the middle one to Powell Plateau, and the left one to a continuation of the North Bass Trail.

From the saddle the trail moves east down a talus ridge into White Canyon and White Creek which it follows to Shinumo Creek. Steep drops in White Creek's streambed require negotiating difficult-to-follow bypasses. Route-finding skills are paramount; watch closely for trail markers.

After reaching Shinumo Creek, the trail follows the stream bed for one mile, leaves the streambed briefly, then drops to the Colorado River upstream from the mouth of Shinumo Creek.

William Bass, for whom the trail is named, operated a tourist business out of a camp along Shinumo Creek, where he cultivated a garden and orchard. Artifacts from Shinumo Camp—old tools, utensils, personal belongings—sometimes turn up in the area. These historic items are protected by law. Do not disturb them.

NORTH RIM TRAIL
DESTINATION HIKE: NORTH KAIBAB TRAIL
One-way length: 14.2 miles
Low and high elevations: 2,400 to 8,250 feet
Difficulty: strenuous

The trailhead is at a parking lot off the paved North Rim Parkway two miles north of the Grand Canyon Lodge. Although it is currently one of the best-maintained and frequently used trails in the National Park, the North Kaibab Trail, like many Canyon routes, probably started out as a game trail before being discovered by Indians as a route into the inner gorge. Subsequently, prospectors, explorers, and adventurers adapted these trails to their needs. In time, owing to modern surveying equipment, the routes of major Canyon trails, including the North Kaibab, were improved.

Mule trains, which have the right of way, share the North Kaibab Trail with hikers as it descends nearly 6,000 feet to Phantom Ranch. If you should encounter a mule train, stand aside and follow instructions from the wrangler. To reach the trailhead, drive north from the National Park on State Route 67 (North Rim Parkway) to Forest Route 22 (at Kaibab Lodge) and turn left (west) toward Dry Park. Continue west for 18 miles to Forest Route 425. Turn left (south) for approximately 10 miles to Forest Route 232. Turn left (west) to the Indian Hollow Campground and trailhead. Although State Route 67 is plowed by mid-May, forest routes on the North Rim may be impassable until much later in the season. Check road conditions with National Park rangers or Forest Service personnel.

From the trailhead the North Kaibab Trail drops nearly 3,000 feet in 4.7 miles to the confluence of Roaring Springs Canyon and Bright Angel Canyon. Seasoned hikers may want to try an alternate route, the Old Bright Angel Trail, that descends from the Ken Patrick Trail (see page 55) to Roaring Springs. This seldom-used route is washed out and difficult to follow, especially in its upper reaches. In fall, bigtooth maples in the upper portions of canyons spilling off the North Rim turn vivid red.

After leaving Roaring Springs, the North Kaibab Trail follows Bright Angel Creek as it gradually descends another 1,000 feet to the Cottonwood Campground (open May through October). About 1.5 miles below Cottonwood, a short spur, the Ribbon Falls Trail, leads to a beautiful waterfall.

Leaving the Cottonwood Campground area, the North Kaibab Trail travels through The Box, a sheer-walled gorge. Just before reaching the Bright Angel Campground at the Colorado River, the trail passes Phantom Ranch, a tourist lodge.

NORTH RIM TRAIL
DESTINATION HIKE: CLEAR CREEK TRAIL
One-way length: 8.7 miles
Low and high elevations: 2,640 to 3,600 feet
Difficulty: moderate

This trail, developed by the Civilian Conservation Corps in 1933, can be reached by hiking 0.3 mile north of Phantom Ranch on the North Kaibab Trail. Traveling east from Bright Angel Creek, the Clear Creek Trail climbs 1,500 feet to the base of Sumner Butte, then descends to the Tonto Platform, which it follows northeast before descending into Clear Creek.

Cheyava Falls, the highest waterfall in Grand Canyon, is about five miles north of the Clear Creek Campground along Clear Creek. Several creek crossings are required along this undeveloped route. Since Cheyava Falls is fed by snowmelt, the best time to see it is early spring.

NORTH RIM TRAIL
DESTINATION HIKE: NANKOWEAP TRAIL
One-way length: 14.5 miles
Low and high elevations: 2,760 to 8,800 feet
Difficulty: strenuous

To reach the upper trailhead for the Nankoweap Trail, drive south 26.5 miles from the North Kaibab Visitor Center on State Route 67 and turn left (east) on Forest Route 611. Drive 1.4 miles to Forest Route 610 and turn right (south) for 12.3 miles to the end of the road and the trailhead

To access the lower trailhead drive 20 miles east on U.S. Highway 89A from the North Kaibab Visitor Center to the House Rock Valley-Buffalo Ranch Road (Forest Route 445). Turn right (south) and drive 27 miles to the trailhead. Near the end Forest Route 445 forks; stay on the right fork.

In 1881, John Wesley Powell and Dr. Charles D. Walcott, director of the U.S. Geological Survey, blazed a horse trail down an old Indian pathway into the

Nankoweap Basin. Nankoweap is a Paiute word meaning "singing" or "echo" canyon. The path developed by Powell and Walcott eventually became the Nankoweap Trail. Splendid views of Marble Canyon are a prime feature of the Nankoweap Trail.

The trail begins outside the National Park as Forest Service Trail 57, a four-mile, easy-going trail along the Canyon rim. The National Park portion of the Nankoweap Trail is extremely difficult and is best attempted only by veteran Grand Canyon hikers.

From the rim, the Nankoweap Trail descends to a narrow ledge and travels east to Tilted Mesa. With dramatically steep drop-offs, the trail is only about a foot wide in places. Beyond Tilted Mesa, the trail climbs down a series of tricky ledges. Many parts of the trail have eroded, leaving slopes covered with loose rock. Footing is very difficult and in some places hikers may actually have to crawl. Upon reaching Nankoweap Creek, the trail continues downstream to the Colorado River.

> **NORTH RIM TRAIL**
> **SHUTTLE HIKE: KEN PATRICK TRAIL**
> One-way length: 10.0 miles
> Low and high elevations: 8,250 to 8,803 feet
> Difficulty: moderate

The trailhead for this 10-mile ramble along the North Rim begins at the Ken Patrick Trailhead, 2.0 miles north of the Grand Canyon Lodge on the North Rim Parkway. Traveling through heavily forested terrain, the route approaches the rim at several points. In places where it skirts deadfall or traverses ravines, the trail may be somewhat difficult to follow. The trail ends at Point Imperial, at 8,803 feet the highest among the North Rim viewpoints. Hikers who want to avoid a 20-mile roundtrip may arrange for a shuttle to meet them at the Point Imperial Viewpoint parking area or where the Ken Patrick Trail crosses Cape Royal Road.

3 Grand Wash Cliffs Wilderness

Tom Till

Joshua trees in the western end of Grand Canyon

LOCATION: 50 miles south of St. George, Utah

SIZE: 37,300 acres

ELEVATION RANGE: 2,800 to 6,700 feet

MILES OF TRAILS: 12

HABITATS: Mohave Desert

ADMINISTRATION: BLM, Arizona Strip Field Office

TOPOGRAPHIC MAPS: Cane Springs SE, St. George Canyon, Olaf Knolls, Last Chance Canyon, Grand Gulch Bench, Mustang Point; also Arizona Strip District Visitor Map

LYING ALONG THE WESTERN TERMINUS of the Colorado Plateau north of the Grand Canyon, the twelve-mile long Grand Wash Cliffs Wilderness is situated on some of the loneliest terrain on the Arizona Strip. A look at a geologic cross-section of the colorful sandstone and limestone formations layering the cliffs reveals that they are actually an extension of the Grand Canyon itself.

The craggy escarpments, rugged canyons, and sandstone cliffs, mesas, and buttes of the wilderness are actually a transition zone between the Colorado Plateau and Basin and Range provinces. Botanically, the wilderness is also in a transition zone between the Mohave and Great Basin deserts. Joshua tree, the signature tree of the Mohave, grows in the lower elevations of the wilderness, while the piñon-juniper woodland, characteristic of colder desert regions, occupies the heights. Desert shrubs such as sagebrush, annual grasses, blackbrush, yucca, prickly pear, and winter fat thrive in the wilderness.

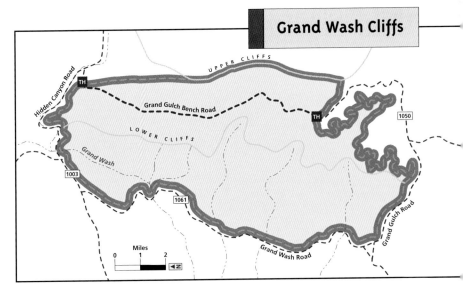

Grand Wash Cliffs

The cliffs are vital habitat for desert bighorn sheep, mountain lion, golden eagle and other raptors, desert tortoise, rock squirrel, black-tailed jack rabbit, and Gila monster.

Summer can be extremely hot in the Grand Wash Cliffs Wilderness and winter quite cold. Occasional accumulations of heavy snow create chancy road conditions. Spring and fall are the best times to enter the Grand Wash Cliffs Wilderness. No water is available; carry plenty.

DAY HIKE: GRAND GULCH BENCH ROAD
One-way length: 12.0 miles
Low and high elevations: 4,000 to 4,800 feet
Difficulty: easy

A distance of nearly fifty miles south of St. George, Utah via a number of interconnecting roads, makes getting to either the northern or southern trailheads of the Grand Gulch Bench Road a bit of a job that is best attempted in a four-wheel-drive vehicle. To find the easiest route check in with the Bureau of Land Management's (BLM) Arizona Strip Field Office in St. George where you can not only learn the latest about weather and road conditions but also purchase the excellent Arizona Strip Visitor Map. Traveling along the base of the cliffs, the Grand Gulch Bench Road is an excellent hiking trail that offers good beginning points for side-canyon explorations.

CROSS-COUNTRY HIKING

There are secret canyons in the isolated Grand Wash Cliffs Wilderness that may have been last explored many years ago by Paiute Indians. The best access to these places is the west and south sides of the wilderness along the Grand Wash and Grand Gulch roads. The shortest routes into these roads start in Mesquite, Nevada. Again, for advice on road conditions and most direct routes, check with the Arizona Strip Field Office.

4 Kachina Peaks Wilderness

Kachina Peaks Trail winds through conifers

LOCATION: 10 miles north of Flagstaff

SIZE: 18,960 acres

ELEVATION RANGE: 7,400 to 12,643 feet

MILES OF TRAILS: 29.2

HABITATS: Ponderosa pine and Gambel oak; spruce, fir, aspen; Arctic-alpine

ADMINISTRATION: Coconino National Forest, Peaks Ranger District

TOPOGRAPHIC MAPS: Humphreys Peak, White Horse Hills, Sunset Crater West

VISIBLE FOR MILES AROUND and in some years clad with a mantle of snow through the month of June, 12,643-foot Humphreys Peak, Arizona's highest, is the centerpiece of the Kachina Peaks Wilderness in the San Francisco Mountains just outside Flagstaff. Humphreys, along with three other high peaks—Doyle (11,460 feet), Fremont (11,969 feet), and Agassiz (12,365 feet)—comprise the Kachina Peaks, sacred to the Hopi and Navajo people, and to the Havasupai and Zuni as well. In Hopi mythology, Kachina deities descend from the high peaks to visit the Hopi mesa-top villages each year at the time of the winter solstice. In the months that follow, they bring rain to the fields and orchards below the mesas and preside over the production and distribution of the harvest. When their work is finished, around the time of summer solstice, the kachinas return to the peaks.

According to Navajo legend the *Dineh,* "ordinary people," traveled through three different worlds before emerging into the present—the fourth, or Glittering World. To remind them of this passage, the Holy People created four sacred mountains in four different directions to establish the boundaries of Navajoland. The San Francisco Peaks define the western boundary.

Standing at the center of a 2,200-square-mile volcanic field in the southwest corner of the Colorado Plateau, the San Francisco Peaks last erupted 2 million years ago. Nearby Sunset Crater (see Strawberry Crater Wilderness, p. 89), which erupted 900 years ago, is the youngest volcano in Arizona, coming at the end of a period of volcanism that had already lasted for several million years. Geologists also point out that lateral and medial moraines and former stream beds in the San Francisco Mountains offer the best examples of Ice-Age glaciation in Arizona.

It was here, in the San Francisco Mountains in the 1880s, that biologist C. Hart Merriam did much of his pioneering work in how plant and animal life alters with elevation. Merriam discerned a pattern, continental in scope, that he named "life zones." Noting that mosses and other plants growing near the summit of Humphreys Peak also grew in Arctic regions, he dubbed the above-timberline summit, Arctic-alpine, the only such habitat in Arizona. Lower down he found trees and plants characteristic of boreal forests in Canada and the Hudson Bay, and thus named these life zones Canadian and Hudsonian. In a transition zone he noted the scrub oak, piñon-juniper, and ponderosa pine that in Arizona occupy a broad belt around 7,000 feet in elevation. Lower down Merriam observed plants that were the same as those growing in Sonora, Mexico, which he divided into two categories—Lower and Upper Sonoran.

Plants, like birds and mammals, can and do migrate between life zones; thus Douglas fir, a high-elevation tree, may be found at lower elevations in cooler, north-facing canyons, or even along riparian corridors, and certain cacti may migrate upslope on a mountain's warmer, sun-drenched south flank. Although birds and mammals prefer to rear their young in life-zone niches where climate, food, and shelter are favorable to their survival, they may also follow the change of seasons through life zones.

Saw-whet owl, common flicker, Western bluebird, pygmy nuthatch, chickadee, raven, Clark's nutcracker, hermit thrush, white-throated swift, wild turkey, Steller's jay, blue grouse, American robin, black bear, porcupine, mountain lion, gray squirrel, bobcat, elk, Abert squirrel, and deer are a few of the many birds and mammals that inhabit the Kachina Peaks Wilderness.

For hikers the preferred times to visit the wilderness are summer and fall. Snow begins in the higher elevations as early as October and may stay on the ground through June. Mid-June through July are the peak blooming periods for high-elevation annuals, such as Rocky Mountain iris; late September and October are the best times to see aspens turn golden.

Cross-country skiing and snowshoeing are excellent within the wilderness, particularly in the Inner Basin and along the Kachina Trail. The Kachina Trail is easy to access via the Snow Bowl Ski Area. Unplowed roads leading to the Inner Basin, however, may be impassable to vehicles in winter, requiring a 4.5-mile ski or snowshoe to Lockett Meadow.

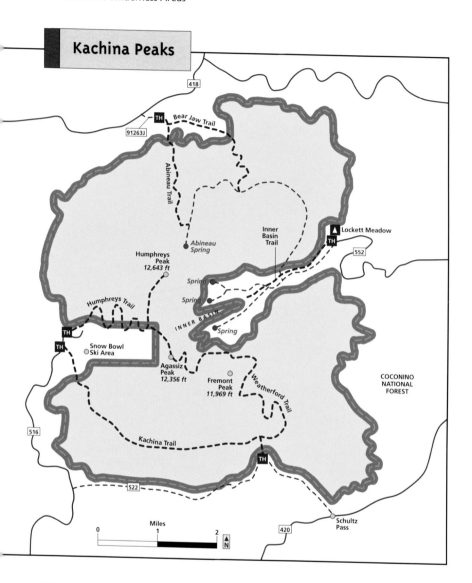

Kachina Peaks

418

TH
91263J
Bear Jaw Trail

Abineau Trail

Abineau Spring

Inner Basin Trail

Lockett Meadow
TH
552

Humphreys Peak
12,643 ft

Spring

Spring

Humphreys Trail

INNER BASIN

Spring

TH
TH

Snow Bowl
Ski Area

Agassiz Peak
12,356 ft

Fremont Peak
11,969 ft

Weatherford Trail

COCONINO
NATIONAL
FOREST

516

Kachina Trail

TH

522

Miles
0   1   2
N

420

Schultz Pass

DAY HIKE: HUMPHREYS TRAIL
One-way length: 4.5 miles
Low and high elevations: 8,800 to 12,643 feet
Difficulty: strenuous

This steep, rocky trail, which gains 4,000 feet in less than five miles, is strenuous, completely exposed, and subject to the vicissitudes of nature above 11,000 feet. It may snow during any season of the year and the unwary are sometimes overtaken by sudden summer thunderstorms, with high winds and lightning.

To reach the trailhead, drive 7.0 miles north from Flagstaff on U.S. Highway 180 to the paved Snow Bowl Road (Forest Route 516). Turn right and drive 7.5 miles to the Snow Bowl Ski Area. After leaving the trailhead at the ski area, the route follows the ski lift upslope before turning into the forest. A little more than halfway to Humphreys Peak, the trail arrives at Agassiz Saddle and an intersection with the Weatherford Trail. With altitude the vegetation begins to show more evidence of harsh environmental conditions. Among trees, only the bristlecone pine, twisted by wind and cold, survives near treeline. Above treeline, tundra-dwelling shrubs and wildflowers cling to life. The tundra environment is so fragile that above 11,000 feet, off-trail hiking is strictly prohibited by the Forest Service in an effort to preserve native plants, among them an endangered groundsel endemic to the Kachina Peaks Wilderness called *Senecio franciscanus*.

The view from the top is a 360-degree panorama. On a clear day you can see north to the Grand Canyon, the Hopi Mesas, the Painted Desert, and Navajo Mountain; east to the White Mountains; and south to Oak Creek Canyon and the Verde Valley.

DAY HIKE: INNER BASIN TRAIL
One-way length: 2.0 miles
Low and high elevations: 8,600 to 9,400 feet
Difficulty: moderate

This short trail into the remnants of an ancient caldera that once spewed fire and lava over an immense area begins in beautiful Lockett Meadow. Aspens and high peaks now encircle the blurred outline of the old caldera and, in spring, wildflowers carpet its floor.

To reach the trailhead, drive 12.5 miles north from Flagstaff on U.S. Highway 89 just past the Sunset Crater turnoff to Forest Route 552. Turn left (west) on Forest Route 552. After 1.0 mile, bear right at the Lockett Meadow sign to the trailhead.

The Inner Basin, which is cherry-stemmed out of the wilderness, contains a number of springs that provide water to Flagstaff, so you may encounter city-owned trucks and other vehicles along this route.

Beginning in Lockett Meadow, the trail climbs for about 2.0 miles to the Inner Basin, where a number of side trails take off to higher elevations. The Inner Basin, where snow may linger into early summer, is a favorite destination for cross-country skiers.

LOOP HIKE: ABINEAU – BEAR JAW TRAILS
One-way length: 6.0 miles
Low and high elevations: 8,500 to 10,500 feet
Difficulty: strenuous

To reach the trailhead, travel 14 miles north from Flagstaff on U.S. Highway 89 to Forest Route 418. Turn left (west) on Forest Route 418 for 7.0 miles to Forest

Route 9123J (about 1.0 mile east of Reese tank). Turn left (south) on Forest Route 9123J for 1.2 miles to the trailhead.

Beginning in Abineau Canyon, the trail follows a dry creek through ponderosa forest that gradually gives way to aspen, Douglas fir, and limber pine. Climbing steeply, the trail enters avalanche-stripped open country affording views of the upper reaches of Abineau Canyon and the north flank of Humphreys Peak. The trail ends after about three miles in a large open meadow at Abineau Canyon Road.

From the meadow, hike east on the Abineau Canyon Road, which runs along the base of a long talus slope, for approximately 1.0 mile to the Bear Jaw Trail, then descend into Bear Jaw Canyon and return to the trailhead.

Because the Abineau and Bear Jaw trails are among the least used in the wilderness, your chance of encountering wildlife, especially black bears, is quite good.

LOOP HIKE: HUMPHREYS – WEATHERFORD – KACHINA TRAILS
One-way length: 16.7 miles
Low and high elevations: 8,600 to 12,000 feet
Difficulty: moderate

This hike can be done as a long day hike or overnighter. Starting at the Snow Bowl ski lift trailhead, Humphreys Trail climbs 3.0 miles to the Weatherford Trail junction at Agassiz Saddle. The Weatherford Trail is an old motorcar road bed, built in the 1920s as a route from the base of the mountain to a scenic overlook about 0.2 mile south of the trail junction. The Weatherford Trail follows the old road to its terminus at Schultz Pass, some 8.7 miles down trail.

The trail drops into a camping area at Fremont Saddle between Agassiz and Fremont peaks. Because the saddle, at 11,200 feet, is still in a zone of fragile alpine vegetation, you should not build a campfire; use a camp stove instead. No water is available on this hike, so you will have to carry sufficient water for two days or plan your trip for late spring or early summer when snow is still available for melting over a camp stove. Allen Doyle, a hunting guide and the man for whom Doyle Peak is named, had a camp here in the late 19th century. You may find some weathering lumber and other artifacts lying around.

From Fremont Saddle the route descends a series of switchbacks 2.0 miles to Doyle Saddle. As you traverse them, you will notice that some of the slopes are devoid of trees, evidence of winter avalanches.

Leaving Doyle Saddle, the trail descends 4.0 miles to the wilderness boundary where it crosses a meadow to the junction with the Kachina Trail, which travels 5.0 miles west to the trailhead at the Ski Bowl parking lot.

Built in the 1980s, the Kachina Trail ascends an easy gradient, and some of the most beautiful scenery in the Kachina Peaks Wilderness lies along its path. There are large meadows, aspen groves, stands of mixed conifers, and open areas affording great views of the surrounding terrain and the city of Flagstaff. In the fall, aspen leaves turn golden and the air is filled with the sounds of bull elk bugling to attract females.

Kanab Creek Wilderness 5

Weathered canyon walls

SOME OF THE RICHEST URANIUM DEPOSITS on the Arizona Strip are located along the Kanab Creek's spectacular gorge. Setting portions of it aside as wilderness, therefore, required some give-and-take among mining interests and wilderness advocates. In the end, some of the less scenic areas were left out of the 1984 Arizona Wilderness Act, thereby allowing exploration and drilling to continue on the fringes of the wilderness.

One of the major tributaries of the Colorado River, Kanab Creek rises fifty miles north in southern Utah and cuts a network of deep vertical gorges across the Kanab and Kaibab plateaus. Its steep canyon walls conceal intricate weather-sculpted knobs, fins,

LOCATION: 30 miles south of Fredonia

SIZE: 75,300 acres

ELEVATION RANGE: 3,500 to 6,200 feet

MILES OF TRAILS: 50

HABITATS: Riparian, piñon-juniper, sagebrush flats

ADMINISTRATION: Kaibab National Forest, North Kaibab Ranger District, BLM, Arizona Strip Field Office

TOPOGRAPHIC MAPS: Toothpick Ridge, Gunsight Point, Grama Spring, Jumpup Point, Sowats Spring, Fishtail, Kanab Point, Big Springs; Arizona Strip District Visitor Map

potholes, obelisks, niches, and other carved forms. Lying along the western edge of the Kaibab Plateau, the Kanab Creek Wilderness, consisting of 68,600 acres administered by the Forest Service and 6,700 acres under Bureau of Land Management (BLM), is rugged, inhospitable terrain, subject to extreme weather conditions. Water is scarce or non-existent, and during summer months temperatures may soar to 120 degrees Fahrenheit.

The Southern Paiute Indians succeeded the Anasazi who themselves came after paleo-Indian hunter-gatherers who were here as early as 7,000 B.C. Scatterings of interesting Indian rock art attest to their existence in what is now wilderness. Many of the region's surviving native-American place names are Paiute. Kaibab means "mountain lying down" in the Paiute language; Kanab means "willow," probably for the willows growing along the upper reaches of the creek.

The dominant plant of the Kanab Creek Wilderness is desert shrub black-brush, a transitional plant that lives on the margins of the Great Basin and Mohave Deserts and on the Colorado Plateau. Spiny though it may be, it is a significant browse plant for bighorn sheep and mule deer. In the lower elevations, you will find occasional clumps of Indian ricegrass and needle-and-thread grass. Piñon-juniper grow in the higher elevations along with sagebrush, some cacti, tumbleweed, and prickly poppy. Cottonwood, ash, red bud, and desert almond grow along creek bottoms. The exotic tamarisk is beginning to invade some riparian areas.

With the advent of snow and deep cold, mule deer migrate from the higher elevations of the Kaibab Plateau to winter in the Kanab Creek Wilderness. Bobcat, mountain lion, fox, coyote, rabbit, rock squirrel, porcupine, and mice also inhabit the wilderness. Almost the entire Arizona population of chukar partridge occur here, and other birds include raven, peregrine falcon, various sparrows, red-tailed hawk, and scrub jay. The only known poisonous snake occurring in the wilderness is the rattlesnake, but several other non-toxic species are found. Toads, frogs, and lizards are also at home in the wilderness.

Too dry and hot for comfort in the summer, the weather in Kanab Creek Wilderness is most favorable from October through April. Although the lower elevations may be free of snow in winter, snow on roads leading into the wilderness may block access.

DAY HIKE: HACK CANYON
One-way length: 5.0 miles
Low and high elevations: 3,900 to 5,100 feet
Difficulty: easy

To reach the trailhead, drive west from Fredonia on U.S. Highway 89A to the Toroweap Point turnoff. Follow this road south for 23 miles to the sign for Hack Reservoir. Turn left and follow this road 9.5 miles to the end and the Willow Springs trailhead. The last few miles before the trailhead are extremely rough, so you will need to drive a four-wheel-drive vehicle or park and hike to the trailhead.

Situated in the smaller BLM portion of the Kanab Creek Wilderness, the Hack Canyon Trail offers very quick access to Kanab Creek itself. From Willow Springs the trail follows Hack Canyon down to its junction with Kanab Creek, the turnaround for this short day hike and a good beginning point for other wilderness excursions.

DAY HIKE: JUMPUP-NAIL TRAIL
One-way length: 6.0 miles
Low and high elevations: 4,200 to 6,170 feet
Difficulty: strenuous

Because this hike is in a remote, waterless, rugged area, I recommend that you check with the Visitor Center at Jacob Lake for current information on trail access. From the Visitor Center drive 0.25 mile south on State Route 67 to Forest Route 461 and turn right (west). Drive west on Forest Routes 461 and 462 for about 9.0 miles to Forest Route 422. Turn left (south) and drive 11.5 miles (5.0 miles beyond Big Springs) to Forest Route 425. Turn right (west) and drive about 8.0 miles to Forest Route 233. Turn right (west) on Forest Route 233 about 9.0 miles to the trailhead. The trail descends 2,000 feet from Sowats Point into Sowats and Jumpup canyons. Vermilion cliffs, natural rock sculptures, isolated stands of piñon-juniper, and steep sandstone walls are among the scenic features of this hike.

At the base of Sowats Point, the trail crosses Sowats Canyon, winds around the point, and enters Jumpup Canyon. After 6.0 miles the trail meets the Ranger Trail coming in from the north. This is the turnaround point.

Hikers who wish to extend their distance may proceed up the Ranger Trail for an additional distance of 4.0 miles to Forest Route 423.

The descent from Sowats Point is steep and narrow and not recommended for equestrian use except by the most experienced trail horses.

DESTINATION HIKE: RANGER TRAIL TO KANAB CREEK
One-way length: 10.0 miles
Low and high elevations: 2,600 to 5,699 feet
Difficulty: moderate

To reach the trailhead, drive about 25 miles east of Fredonia on U.S. Highway 89A to Forest Route 422A. Turn right (south) on Forest Route 422A for about 12 miles to Forest Route 423. Turn right (west) and continue to the end of the road. Watch the road signs carefully to avoid getting lost in a series of twists and turns. An old cabin is at the trailhead.

The trail descends into Jumpup Canyon and reaches Jumpup Spring (not a reliable source of water) after about 1.0 mile. After this point an indistinct trail travels down the canyon bottom to Lower Jumpup Spring where reliable water can usually be found.

Kanab Creek

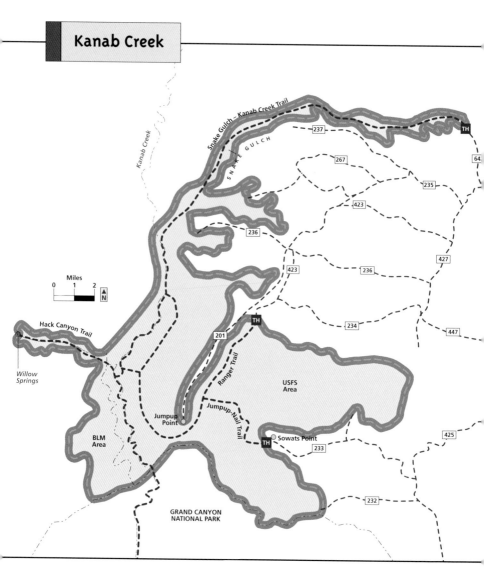

Below the spring, the creek is often running and the going is somewhat trickier. Sowats Canyon comes in from the east after approximately 1.0 mile. As you round Jumpup Point, two interesting side canyons—Kwagunt Hollow and Indian Hollow—intersect Jumpup Canyon from the east. Within one mile of each other, these two beautiful canyons invite exploration.

Consisting of steep red-limestone walls, the section of trail between Sowats Canyon and Kanab Creek passes through a spectacular narrows. The turnaround for this hike is Kanab Creek near the mouth of Hack Canyon, but adventurous hikers may extend their distance by traveling upstream or down in Kanab Creek.

DESTINATION HIKE: SNAKE GULCH – KANAB CREEK TRAIL
One-way length: 21.5 miles
Low and high elevations: 2,600 to 5,860 feet
Difficulty: moderate

To reach the trailhead from the Visitor Center at Jacob Lake, drive 0.25 mile south on State Route 67 to Forest Route 461. Turn right (west) and drive 9.0 miles on Forest Routes 461 and 462 to Forest Route 422. Turn left (south) and drive 2.0 miles to Forest Route 423. Turn right (west) and drive 1.3 miles to Forest Route 642. Turn right (north) on Forest Route 642 for about 2.0 miles to the end of the road and trailhead.

Before joining Kanab Creek, the Snake Gulch Trail travels past many-hued cliffs, a few old homesteads, and some Indian pictographs painted in red and yellow. After joining the Kanab Creek you head downstream in the canyon bottom of wide sandy beaches, cottonwoods, oaks, and red-walled cliffs. After passing Jensen Canyon, the trail leaves Kanab Creek and becomes the Ranger Trail.

Although unmarked and unmaintained, it is possible to follow Kanab Creek downstream another ten miles to the mouth of Jumpup Canyon and the boundary of Grand Canyon National Park. To continue your hike into the park itself, you are required to obtain a backcountry permit from the National Park Service.

6 Kendrick Mountain Wilderness

Aspen grove

LOCATION: 21 miles northwest of Flagstaff

SIZE: 6,510 acres

ELEVATION RANGE: 7,800 to 10,418 feet

MILES OF TRAILS: 13.5

HABITATS: Ponderosa pine, oak, spruce, fir, aspen

ADMINISTRATION: Coconino National Forest, Chalendar Ranger District

TOPOGRAPHIC MAPS: Kendrick Peak, Moritz Ridge

PART OF THE VAST SAN FRANCISCO MOUNTAIN volcanic field extending east and west of Flagstaff, the Kendrick Mountain Wilderness, although small, is a favorite among hikers. The heart of the wilderness is Kendrick Mountain, at 10,418 feet the second highest summit in northern Arizona. Three trails of varying degrees of difficulty lead to the top of the mountain. All offer panoramic views of the surrounding volcanic field, of the red rock country of Oak Creek and Sycamore canyons to the south, and of the cliffs of the Grand Canyon's North Rim, more than fifty miles north.

All routes to Kendrick Peak travel through forested terrain. Gambel oak and ponderosa pine at the lower elevations give way to Douglas fir, white fir, Engelmann spruce, and aspen as you approach the summit. Small meadows along the way are lush with ferns and wildflowers in the spring and

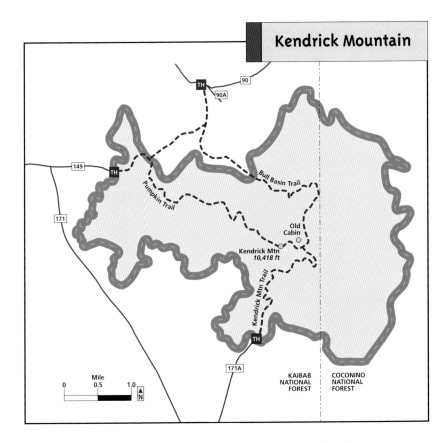

Kendrick Mountain

early summer. In the fall aspen groves within the wilderness and on the upper slopes of the nearby San Francisco Mountains become a palette of vivid yellow tinged here and there with red.

Although the Kendrick Mountain Wilderness was logged in the past, some of the steeper, less accessible slopes still contain old growth forest—prime habitat for the Mexican spotted owl and the Northern goshawk. Mountain lion, mule deer, elk, and black bear also find excellent habitat within the wilderness area. The pine-fir forest is prime habitat for a number of birds, among them the Steller's jay, mountain chickadee, pygmy nuthatch, and Western flycatcher. The red-faced warbler is sometimes observed in the higher regions.

A fire lookout at the summit is operated in summer. Visitors are usually welcomed by the tower lookout, but forest protocol requires that you ask permission before ascending the stairs. An old cabin situated about a quarter-mile east of the summit housed fire lookout crews from about 1912 until the 1930s. It is now listed on the National Register of Historic Places.

Carry plenty of water while hiking in the Kendrick Mountain Wilderness, especially during the warmer months. No permanent water sources are available within the wilderness.

DAY HIKE: KENDRICK MOUNTAIN TRAIL
One-way length: 4.0 miles
Low and high elevations: 8,000 to 10,418 feet
Difficulty: moderate

The most direct route to the Kendrick Mountain trailhead is 15.0 miles north from Flagstaff on U.S. Highway 180 to Forest Route 245. Drive west on Forest Route 245 for approximately 3.0 miles to Forest Route 171. Turn right on Forest Route 171 and continue another 3.0 miles to Forest Route 171A. Turn right 0.6 mile to the trailhead.

Constructed to maintain the fire lookout tower, the Kendrick Mountain Trail is the best maintained of the three trails to the summit. Although it gains 2,418 feet in elevation, its gentle switchbacks make it a surprisingly easy hike.

After about 2.0 miles, Kendrick Peak and the lookout tower come into view. The Bull Basin Trail, coming in from the north, joins the Kendrick Mountain Trail just below the summit. From this junction it is a 0.3-mile hike to the top.

As mentioned, mountain-top views are splendid from the summit of Kendrick Peak and even better from the lookout tower. Remember to announce your arrival to the tower lookout and ask permission before going up.

LOOP HIKE: PUMPKIN – BULL BASIN TRAIL
One-way length: 11.0 miles
Low and high elevations: 7,300 to 10,418 feet
Difficulty: strenuous

To reach the Pumpkin Trailhead, drive north from Flagstaff for 15 miles on U.S. Highway 180 to Forest Road 245. Drive west on Forest Route 245 for approximately 3.0 miles to Forest Route 171. Turn right and drive 9.3 miles to the marked trailhead.

Gaining more than 3,000 feet in a little more than 5.0 miles, the Pumpkin-Bull Basin Trail to the summit of Kendrick Peak is quite steep and strenuous. Leaving the trailhead at Pumpkin Center, the route follows an old road through ponderosa pine forest before beginning to climb. After about 1.5 miles the Pumpkin Trail ascends to a saddle where it joins a connector trail to the Bull Basin Trail. The Connector Trail turns east and traces the wilderness boundary to cross a saddle into Bull Basin. After 2.0 miles the Connector Trail ends at its junction with the Bull Basin Trail.

The Bull Basin Trail heads southeast through dense forest and alpine meadows before climbing precipitously toward the east flank of Kendrick Mountain. At its junction with the Kendrick Peak Trail and close to the site of the old lookout-tower cabin, the Bull Basin Trail ends. From here it is a short distance to the summit. The return route via the Pumpkin Trail begins on the west side of the lookout tower.

Although there are no reliable water sources within the wilderness, the Pumpkin-Bull Basin Trail loop can become an overnighter in early spring when snow lying in drifts near the summit can be melted for water.

Mount Trumbull Wilderness 7

Tom Till

An isolated but beautiful landscape

REMOTE AND RATHER SMALL, with limited hiking opportunities, the Mount Trumbull Wilderness in the Uinkaret Mountains at the southern end of the Uinkaret Plateau is one of Arizona's seldom-visited wilderness areas. And that may be one of its charms. Like much of the backcountry on the Arizona Strip, north of the Grand Canyon, getting to the Mount Trumbull Wilderness takes some doing. But once there, you may just have it to yourself, all 7,880 acres of it.

LOCATION: 61 miles south of Fredonia

SIZE: 7,880 acres

ELEVATION RANGE: 5,600 to 8,029 feet

MILES OF TRAILS: 2.7

HABITATS: Piñon-juniper to ponderosa pine and oak

ADMINISTRATION: BLM, Arizona Strip Field Office

TOPOGRAPHIC MAPS: Mount Trumbull NW, Mount Trumbull NE, Mount Trumbull SE

Actually a large basalt-capped mesa, Mount Trumbull was named after United States Senator Lyman Trumbull of Connecticut by John Wesley Powell during Powell's exploration of the Arizona Strip in the 1870s.

The principal vegetative communities of the Mount Trumbull Wilderness are cliff rose, mountain mahogany, piñon-juniper, Gambel oak, and isolated aspen groves. The mesa's summit is overspread by ponderosa pine. Kaibab squirrels, native to the North Rim of the Grand Canyon, were introduced to the Mount Trumbull Wilderness in the 1970s. Other wildlife includes wild turkey, mountain lion, and mule deer. Birds of prey, including golden eagles, also inhabit the wilderness.

In the early 1900s, homesteaders ran large herds of cattle and sheep on the Arizona Strip. But drought made homesteading a gamble, and most of the small communities that sprouted around homesteads have vanished, although their remains can still be found here and there. One such homestead was the small town of Mt. Trumbull, which survived into the 1960s.

Evidence of lumbering still exists in the region of the Mount Trumbull Wilderness. Seven former sawmill locations are known on Mount Trumbull alone. And Nixon Spring, just north of the Mount Trumbull trailhead, was the site of a steam-powered sawmill built by Mormon pioneers in the 1870s. Lumber for the construction of the Mormon Temple in St. George, Utah was milled from ponderosa pine at Nixon Spring and hauled eighty miles to the temple site by teams of oxen.

> **DAY HIKE: MOUNT TRUMBULL**
> One-way length: 2.7 miles
> Low and high elevations: 6,400 to 8,029 feet
> Difficulty: easy

To reach the Mount Trumbull Trailhead, drive 8.0 miles west from Fredonia on State Route 389. Turn south on County Road 109 (Mount Trumbull Loop), a well-graded gravel road, and continue southwest for about 46 miles to County Road 5. Turn right and drive 7.0 miles northwest to the trailhead.

Initially the trail to the summit follows the route of a former wooden flume that channeled water to a sawmill site. After about 1.5 miles the trail peters out, but finding your way to the summit through the open ponderosa forest is

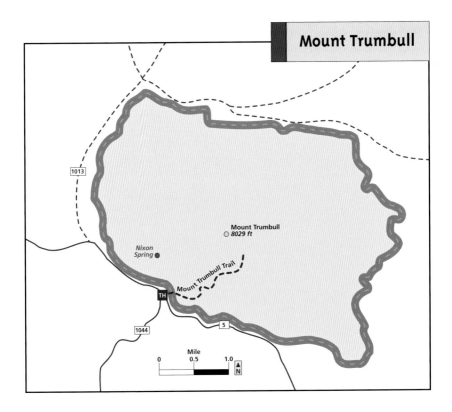

Mount Trumbull

fairly easy. At the summit, you will find a United States Geological Survey marker and the remains of a weather station.

The view from the Mount Trumbull summit not only offers a great survey of the Arizona Strip, including Mount Logan to the south, but also of portions of the Grand Canyon. And, if you avoid hiking during hunting season, you will be utterly alone in the wilderness.

8 Paiute Wilderness

Steve Bruno

Paiute Mountains rising from the desert, northwestern Arizona

LOCATION:
16 miles southwest of
St. George, Utah

SIZE: 87,900 acres

ELEVATION RANGE:
2,000 to 8,012 feet

MILES OF TRAILS: 15.5

HABITATS: Mohave and
Great Basin deserts to
ponderosa pine and fir

ADMINISTRATION:
BLM, Arizona Strip Field
Office

TOPOGRAPHIC MAPS:
Littlefield, Mountain
Sheep Spring, Elbow
Canyon, Mount Bangs,
Jacobs Well, Cane Springs,
Purgatory Canyon, Wolf
Hole Mtn. W., Mustang
Knoll

IN ITS LOWER ELEVATIONS the Paiute Wilderness,
located in the Virgin Mountains about sixteen miles southwest
of St. George, Utah, merges with the Beaver Dam Mountains
Wilderness along the Virgin River Gorge. In addition to this
river-gorge border, it shares with its sister wilderness the over-
lapping of two great desert biomes—the Mohave and Great
Basin. The Paiute is more than four times the size of its sister
wilderness, however, and, with a far greater elevation range,
the Paiute is much more diverse in topography and biology.

Sagebrush, creosote bush, banana yucca, Mormon
tea, range ratany, barrel cactus, prickly pear cactus, and Joshua
tree are the dominant plants in the lower portions of the Paiute
Wilderness, named for the Southern Paiute Indians whose
native ground includes the Arizona Strip region. At the middle elevations piñon-juniper dominate, and from 7,000 feet
up to the 8,012-foot summit of Mount Bangs, the wilderness

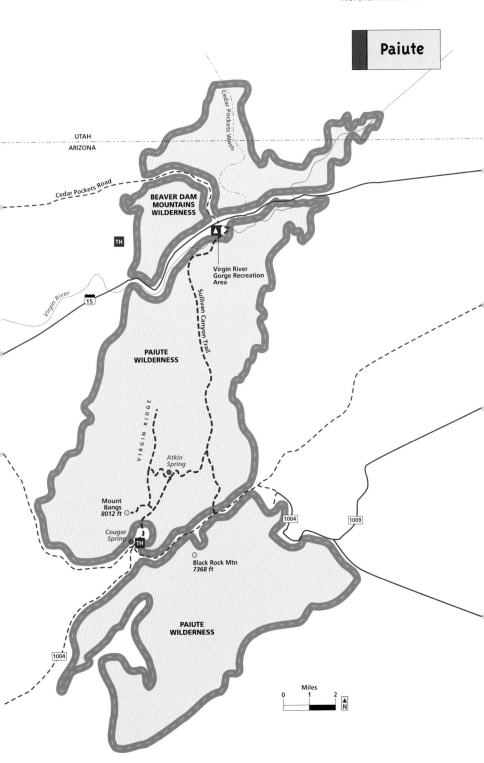

Paiute

UTAH
ARIZONA

Cedar Pockets Wash

Cedar Pockets Road

BEAVER DAM
MOUNTAINS
WILDERNESS

TH

Virgin River
Gorge Recreation
Area

Virgin River

15

Sullivan Canyon Trail

PAIUTE
WILDERNESS

VIRGIN RIDGE

Atkin
Spring

Mount
Bangs
8012 ft

Cougar
Spring

TH

Black Rock Mtn
7368 ft

1004

1009

PAIUTE
WILDERNESS

1004

Miles
0   1   2

N

is forested with ponderosa pine, Gambel oak, Douglas fir, and white fir. In some of the watered canyons, plants typical of a riparian association can be found.

More than 250 animal species inhabit the Paiute Wilderness, including desert bighorn sheep, mountain lion, raven, cliff swallow, mule deer, assorted birds of prey, and desert tortoise.

> **DAY HIKE: SULLIVAN CANYON TRAIL**
> One-way length: 13.0 miles
> Low and high elevations: 2,700 to 8,012 feet
> Difficulty: moderate

Access to the Sullivan Canyon Trail begins at the Virgin River Gorge Recreation Area, 16 miles southwest of St. George, Utah on Interstate 15 from the recreation area, ford the stream to the south side of the Virgin River. Use great caution, especially if you are carrying a pack. Swift moving water only a few inches deep can knock you off your feet. The first time I visited the wilderness, the river was swollen to flood stage with heavy spring runoff and I was unable to cross.

Once across the river, walk downstream about 1.5 miles to the mouth of Sullivan Canyon, then turn south into the drainage, which is rocky and rough and requires some boulder-hopping. About 8.0 miles up the canyon, you will come to a fork. Stay to the right and continue another 2.0 miles to Atkin Spring. The trail then climbs to the head of the canyon, tops a ridge, and proceeds for about another mile to the summit of Mount Bangs, which not only stands between the Colorado Plateau geologic province to the east and the Basin and Range to the west, but also verges on the Mohave and Great Basin deserts. The views from up top are splendid.

There is another shorter route to the summit, but it's at the end of a grueling drive over unimproved back roads. I don't recommend it. But for those who want to try, the directions follow:

From St. George, Utah drive a few miles southwest on I-15 to Black Rock Road (BLM Road 1009). Follow BLM 1009 south 19.6 miles to its intersection with BLM 1004. Drive west on BLM 1004 about 13.3 miles to a right turn into a side canyon and the Cougar Springs Trailhead. From Cougar Spring, a trail climbs about 2.0 miles to the summit of Mount Bangs. BLM 1004 is a cherry-stem road dividing the Paiute Wilderness as it passes between Black Rock Mountain and Mount Bangs. The road is rough and may be impassable in bad weather, even for four-wheel-drive vehicles. Always check with the BLM Arizona Strip Office in St. George about weather conditions.

Paria Canyon – Vermilion Cliffs Wilderness   9

Vermilion cliffs with clearing clouds west of Lees Ferry

JUSTLY FAMOUS for the Grand Canyon, Arizona also contains many spectacularly beautiful, lesser-known canyons. Three—Paria, Buckskin Gulch, and Wire Pass—are in the 112,500-acre Paria Canyon–Vermilion Cliffs Wilderness, established in 1984 under the Arizona Wilderness Act. Paria Canyon has soaring, multi-colored sandstone walls streaked with a tapestry of desert varnish. Hanging gardens adorn seeps and springs, carved arches and amphitheaters, and wooded terraces. Three zones of riparian vegetation line the Paria River, a year-round stream. Aquatic plants such as cattail, sedge, reed, rushes, and horsetail grow close to the stream. Seedlings of cottonwood, willow, and ash also sprout in this zone. Farther from the river, ash, cottonwood, willow, and tamarisk saplings have gained a foothold. And on the wooded terraces up away from the river, in a transition zone between desert and riparian habitat, tall, sturdy trees provide shelter and shade for wildlife and hikers.

LOCATION: Approximately 30 miles west of Page

SIZE: 112,500 acres

ELEVATION RANGE: 3,200 to 7,300 feet

MILES OF TRAILS: 55.7

HABITATS: Great Basin Desert

ADMINISTRATION: BLM, Arizona Strip Field Office and National Park Service

TOPOGRAPHIC MAPS: Pine Hollow Canyon, West Clark Bench, and Bridger Point, Utah; Wrather Arch, Water Pockets, Ferry Swale, Lees Ferry, Arizona

Paria is a Paiute Indian word meaning "elk water" or "salty water," depending on the source. The human presence on the Paria Plateau and in Paria Canyon itself goes back at least 10,000 years, when paleo-Indians occupied the region.

The white-throated swift and violet-green swallow inhabit the deeply incised canyons of the Paria Plateau, as do the flycatcher, black-throated sparrow, great horned owl, red-tailed hawk, rock wren, great blue heron, canyon wren, and the endangered peregrine falcon. Golden eagles are year-round residents, and bald eagles are seen occasionally in winter. California condors were released in 1997 on the rugged escarpment of the 7,000-foot Vermilion Cliffs portion of the wilderness, but canyon hikers are not likely to see these magnificent birds.

Mountain lion, bobcat, beaver, fox, ground squirrel, coyote, jackrabbit, and mule deer are common in the canyons. On one of my early-spring rambles through Paria Canyon's thirty-eight-mile length, I saw a female porcupine with three small kits. From time to time, desert bighorn sheep, reintroduced to the area in the 1980s, are seen on high ridges and crags in the lower portion of Paria Canyon. The Paria River provides habitat for speckled dace, razorback sucker, flannel-mouth sucker, and blue-head sucker. Red-spotted toads, known for their loud, musical trilling calls during summer mating season, are numerous in the canyons.

Venomous creatures, such as rattlesnakes, scorpions, and conenose bugs, also live in the Paria Canyon–Vermilion Cliffs Wilderness. Scorpions, which roam after dark, seek refuge in brush, under rocks, and occasionally in hikers' boots. Conenose bugs, also called kissing bugs, are parasitical on rodents but also will suck blood from humans. A few people develop a hypersensitivity to their venom and go into shock. Avoid rodent nests when making camp, particularly wood rat nests.

HIKING TIPS FOR PARIA CANYON

• Study maps to learn locations of springs before you leave the White House Trailhead. The best reliable spring is just beyond mile 25. Treat all water.

• In many places, Paria Canyon is full of clinging muck; wear hiking boots that you will not mind discarding after your hike. I purchased inexpensive Army surplus boots, designed for wet terrain.

• Check local weather forecasts before entering any of the canyons in the Paria Canyon-Vermilion Cliffs Wilderness.

DAY HIKE: WIRE PASS
One-way length: 1.7 miles
Low and high elevations: 4,600 to 4,800 feet
Difficulty: easy

Narrower but not as deep as Buckskin Gulch or Paria Canyon, Wire Pass is a short, pleasant hike from the trailhead to its confluence with Buckskin Gulch. In summer months this slot canyon can be more than fifteen degrees cooler than open terrain above. Usually dry except during periods of heavy rain, Wire Pass is a shortcut to Buckskin Gulch, saving more than four miles of walking from the Buckskin Trailhead.

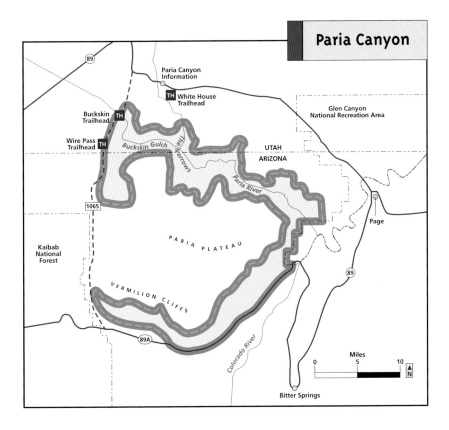

Paria Canyon

DESTINATION HIKE: BUCKSKIN GULCH TO PARIA CONFLUENCE
One-way length: 16.0 miles
Low and high elevations: 4,200 to 4,800 feet
Difficulty: strenuous

Buckskin Gulch is a steep-walled, boulder-strewn, and sometimes water-filled slot canyon. Only the hardiest hikers should undertake its sixteen-mile length to the confluence with the Paria. Flash flooding during rainy seasons is a serious danger in this narrow canyon. Once you have entered, there is virtually no way out of the canyon except one difficult climbing route to the plateau at mile 10.5.

Footing is unstable throughout the canyon, and log and boulder jams present tricky obstacles. One boulder-choked area at mile 14.5 may require the use of ropes. Depending on recent water flows in the gulch, hikers may come upon deep pools of cold water that require swimming. Campfires are not allowed in Buckskin Gulch, and no springs or other sources of drinking water exist, so bring warm clothes and carry plenty of extra water (at least four quarts per person in summer).

> **LOOP HIKE:** BUCKSKIN – PARIA LOOP
> One-way length: 23.0 miles
> Low and high elevations: 4,400 to 4,800 feet
> Difficulty: strenuous

An alternative to hiking back up Buckskin Gulch (very hard) from its confluence with the Paria is to hike seven miles upstream in Paria Canyon to the White House Trailhead. Just upstream from the Buckskin-Paria confluence, Paria Canyon's 500-foot-high walls narrow to fifteen feet. A few tenths of a mile farther on, you come to Slide Rock Arch, a huge, intact slab of sandstone that broke away from the cliff face and slid down in one piece. The route back to the trailhead travels through Navajo sandstone, the same kind of rock that surrounds Lake Powell in the Glen Canyon National Recreation Area nearby.

> **LOOP HIKE:** WIRE PASS – BUCKSKIN – PARIA LOOP
> One-way length: 20.5 miles
> Low and high elevations: 4,400 and 4,800 feet
> Difficulty: strenuous

This hike through Wire Pass to Buckskin Gulch, down Buckskin to the Paria, then upstream to the White House Trailhead is a variant of the hike described above.

> **SHUTTLE HIKE:** PARIA CANYON
> One-way length: 38 miles
> Low and high elevations: 3,200 and 4,400 feet
> Difficulty: strenuous

This hike, from the White House Trailhead to Lees Ferry on the Colorado River, is the icing on the cake for any visit to the Paria Canyon-Vermilion Cliffs Wilderness. Depending on your pace, the weather, and volume of water in the river, it should take from four to five days. During spring runoff, you will be hiking through cold, muddy, ankle-deep water. Quicksand danger is highest during times of heavy creek flow or following flash flooding. During the dry months of May and June the creek bed is sometimes dry until the Paria's confluence with Buckskin Gulch. Once, while hiking the canyon in mid-June, a hot, dry time when daytime temperatures approach 100 degrees Fahrenheit, I fought off dehydration and heat exhaustion by logging many miles during early morning and twilight hours. In the afternoons, the hottest part of the day, I rested in the shade. Summer rains begin in July and August, increasing the risks of lightning and flash flooding, especially in the narrows.

Until mile 28, where large boulders obstruct the way, hiking Paria is in the stream bed, crisscrossing the river many times. Most hikers leave the river at mile 28 and hike along the south side. The fourteen-day parking lot at Lees Ferry, where you can leave a vehicle, is a short distance past the registration box at mile 38. Although river water is non-potable, drinking water is available at springs along the way.

For fee and group size information, contact the BLM's Arizona Strip Office (see Appendix 2).

Petrified Forest Wilderness

Balanced log

WHEN ARMY LIEUTENANT AMIEL WEEKS WHIPPLE surveyed what is now the Petrified Forest Wilderness in 1853, he was so astonished at all the recently exposed chips, nuggets, blocks, and enormous segments of petrified log that had spilled from multi-layered cones and eroding cliffs that he named the wide arroyo running through here Lithodendron—literally, "stone-tree."

    Established as a national monument in 1906, the Petrified Forest contains the world's largest concentration of petrified wood. It's dense stuff: a piece the size of an orange has the heft of a shot-put ball, and a cubic foot of the material weighs in the neighborhood of 170 pounds. And it's beautiful. Pick up a chunk, wipe it clean of the sticky reddish clay that covers everything

LOCATION:
In Petrified Forest National Park, approximately 115 miles east of Flagstaff on I-40

SIZE: 50,260 acres

ELEVATION RANGE: 5,413 to 6,234 feet

MILES OF TRAILS:
No marked or maintained trails

HABITATS: Great Basin Desert

ADMINISTRATION:
National Park Service

TOPOGRAPHIC MAPS: Agate House, Kachina Point, Little Lithodendron Tank, North Mill Well, Pinta, Chinde Mesa, Adamana

in the Painted Desert, turn it to the sun, and watch its faceted surface reflect rainbow hues.

Navajo mythology teaches that it's the bones and other body parts—toes, scales, bits of feather, claws—of monsters long ago killed by twin heroes, Monster Slayer and Child Born For Water, that lie exposed across the Painted Desert, and that the blood of these creatures stains the ground an indelible red.

The geologic record is no less fantastic. Today's petrified logs are the remnants of monstrous tropical trees buried here more than 200 million years ago. Over time the wood cells were replaced by multi-colored mineral crystals, transforming the trees into polychromatic stone. During ensuing eons, erosion gradually exposed the petrified forest.

National park status was conferred on the monument in 1962. On October 23, 1970, 50,260 acres—comprising two separate units of the Petrified Forest National Park—were designated as the Petrified Forest National Wilderness. It was the first wilderness area created in Arizona since passage of the Federal Wilderness Protection Act of 1964, and the first wilderness area established in the National Park System under the provisions of the 1964 act. The larger of the two Petrified Forest Wilderness units covers the northern portion of the National Park. Access to a primitive trail descending into the wilderness is at Kachina Point, north of park headquarters (where no-fee backcountry permits may be obtained).

DAY HIKE: KACHINA POINT TO LITHODENDRON WASH
One-way length: approximately 2.5 miles
Low and high elevations: 5,492 to 5,823 feet
Difficulty: easy

Descending from Kachina Point onto the Painted Desert's basin, this trail allows you to see Lithodendron Wash in the near distance. The area below Kachina Point is crisscrossed by a number of foot trails, most of which give out after a short distance. You can either follow one of those trails or head west or north cross-country to strike Lithodendron Wash. Once on the wash, you can follow its bed as it winds across the desert, taking side excursions to explore other arroyos draining into Lithodendron. Check your orientation occasionally by locating Kachina Point.

Although the national park is open year round, the best times for day hikes in the Petrified Forest Wilderness are spring and fall. Use caution while hiking in extremely hot weather. Carry plenty of water at all times of the year; there are no water sources in the wilderness area. And a word of warning: it is illegal to remove petrified wood, even the tiniest chip. Park Service officials estimate that more than twelve tons are stolen from the wilderness each year. The minimum fine for stealing petrified wood is $275.00.

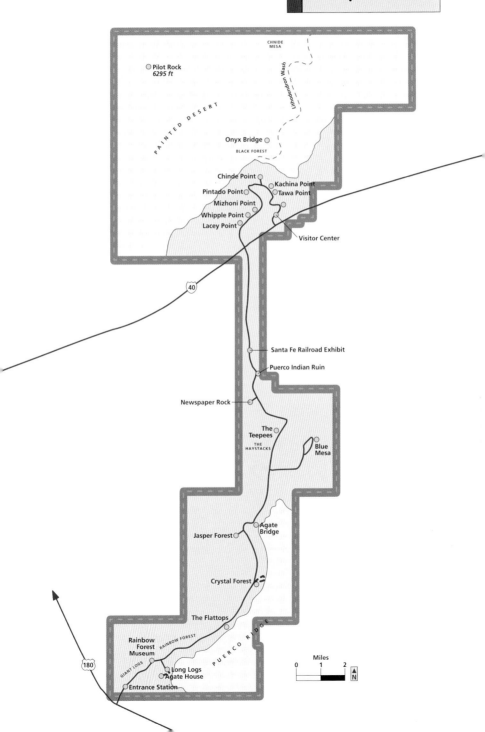

Petrified Forest

CHINDE MESA

Pilot Rock
6295 ft

Lithodendron Wash

P A I N T E D   D E S E R T

Onyx Bridge

BLACK FOREST

Chinde Point
Kachina Point
Pintado Point
Tawa Point
Mizhoni Point
Whipple Point
Lacey Point
Visitor Center

40

Santa Fe Railroad Exhibit

Puerco Indian Ruin

Newspaper Rock

The Teepees
THE HAYSTACKS
Blue Mesa

Agate Bridge
Jasper Forest

Crystal Forest

The Flattops

PUERCO RIDGE

Rainbow Forest Museum
RAINBOW FOREST
GIANT LOGS
Long Logs
Agate House
Entrance Station

180

Miles
0   1   2

N

DESTINATION HIKE: KACHINA POINT TO POINTS NORTH
One-way length: not available
Low and high elevations: 5,400 to 5,800 feet
Difficulty: moderate

Because there are no water sources and no developed trails in the wilderness, a multi-day backpack presents obstacles. One solution to the water problem is to hike in ahead of time and cache water along your intended route—a bit of work. Another is to return to the trailhead daily—a lot of work. A third solution, my preference, is to backpack in winter after a moderately heavy snowfall. One year in January, a friend and I camped in the wilderness for three days, melting snow for all our water needs. It was cold (night-time temperatures dropped to near zero degrees Fahrenheit), but we avoided lugging in a lot of water.

We set up base camp in an area called the Black Forest where large chunks of petrified logs lie exposed on the surface. In three days of off-trail hiking, we observed close-up the processes that continue to shape the Painted Desert— freezing, thawing, wind (which can exceed 80 miles per hour), rain, and snow. The snow was a bonus, adding another hue to the terrain's iridescent geometry. Another bonus was that we were absolutely alone in this wide expanse of harsh, hauntingly beautiful land.

Dry most of the year, Lithodendron Wash flowed with a cold, mixed slurry of red clay, ice, and snow, which froze solid overnight. When the ground thawed by mid-day, we slogged through gooey red mud. On some days we hiked along the wash before venturing overland to points of interest, such as Onyx Bridge.

Although air temperatures remained cold, the winter sun had melted most of the snow by the end of our third day, so we had to break camp and head back to Kachina Point.

Saddle Mountain Wilderness ‖

A bright autumn morning

NAMED FOR A DISTINCTIVE RIDGELINE that resembles a saddle, horn and all, the Saddle Mountain Wilderness lies along the eastern edge of the Kaibab Plateau. The main feature of its spectacularly rugged terrain is its central ridge, which falls off sharply to the south to form the sheer walls of the Nankoweap Rim. From trails within the wilderness, hikers are treated to magnificent views of the Grand Canyon, Marble Gorge, Cocks Comb, House Rock Valley, and the Vermilion Cliffs. Rocky and steep throughout, the Saddle Mountain Wilderness is bounded on three sides by deep, steep-walled canyons.

The lower reaches of the wilderness are dominated by piñon-juniper woodland, sagebrush, cliff rose, and a variety of grasses, such as blue grama, mutton grass, and squirreltail. As you gain elevation, you move through ponderosa pine, Gambel oak, aspen, and spruce-fir forest.

LOCATION: 57 miles south of Fredonia

SIZE: 40,610 acres

ELEVATION RANGE: 6,000 to 8,800 feet

MILES OF TRAILS: 19.5

HABITATS: Piñon-juniper, ponderosa pine Gambel oak, spruce-fir

ADMINISTRATION: Kaibab National Forest, North Kaibab Ranger District

TOPOGRAPHIC MAPS: Dog Point, Cane, Point Imperial Little Park Lake

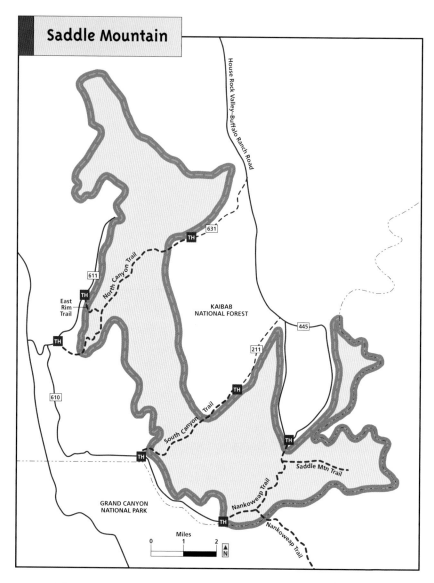

When snow is heavy on the plateau, mule deer migrate to the lower elevations of the wilderness to browse in the sagebrush prairie. Buffalo from a state run game farm and pronghorn sometimes wander from the House Rock Valley onto slopes along the east flank of the wilderness. Cottontail rabbit, jackrabbit, kangaroo rat, pocket gopher, bobcat, coyote, rock squirrel, badger, porcupine, Kaibab squirrel, badger, wood rat, ringtail, and mountain lion are among the mammals resident in the Saddle Mountain Wilderness. Birds found there include American kestrel, blue grouse, turkey, peregrine falcon, band-tailed pigeon, cedar waxwing, Steller's jay, raven, rufous-sided towhee, common poorwill, meadowlark, American robin, Western and mountain bluebird, and pygmy nuthatch.

A perennial mountain brook below the rim in North Canyon supports a threatened population of Apache trout. Frogs, toads, lizards and snakes, including rattlers, also inhabit the wilderness.

Snow comes early to the Kaibab Plateau and stays late, often to mid-May. The best times to explore the higher elevations of the Saddle Mountain Wilderness are May through October. Although road closures prevent access to high-elevation trailheads after the first winter snowfall, low-elevation hiking is possible throughout the year.

DAY HIKE: NORTH CANYON TRAIL
One-way length: 7.0 miles
Low and high elevations: 6,130 to 8,800 feet
Difficulty: strenuous

This trail can be accessed by either an upper or lower trailhead. To reach the upper trailhead, drive south 26.5 miles on State Route 67 from the North Kaibab Visitor Center at Jacob Lake to Forest Route 611. Turn left (east) on Forest Route 611. After 1.4 miles, Forest Route 611 crosses Forest Route 610 and continues east 1.3 miles to the trailhead.

To access the lower trailhead, drive 20 miles east from the North Kaibab Visitor Center on U.S. Highway 89A to the House Rock Valley-Buffalo Ranch Road (Forest Route 445) and turn right (south). Drive 17.5 miles to Forest Route 631 and turn right (west) 1.3 miles to the trailhead. These roads are best attempted in a high-clearance pickup or four-wheel-drive vehicle.

From the upper trailhead, the North Canyon Trail descends through mixed conifer and oak into North Canyon. A short distance below the rim it intersects the 1.5-mile East Rim Trail which originates along the rim about one mile north of the North Canyon Trailhead. The trail reaches a small stream where endangered Apache trout lurk in some of the deeper pools. Crisscrossing the stream, the trail drops some 2,600 feet over its seven-mile distance to the lower trailhead at Forest Route 631. As you descend you move from mixed conifers to sagebrush desert. Along the creek bottom, the crimson leaves of bigtooth maples are a special treat for fall hikers.

DAY HIKE: SOUTH CANYON TRAIL
One-way length: 2.5 miles
Low and high elevations: 6,500 to 8,800 feet
Difficulty: moderate

To reach the upper trailhead for the South Canyon Trail, drive south 26.5 miles on State Route 67 from the North Kaibab Visitor Center to Forest Route 611 and turn left (east). Drive 1.4 miles to Forest Route 610 and turn right (south). Continue south for 7.5 miles to the trailhead.

To access the lower trailhead, drive 20 miles east on U.S. Highway 89A from the North Kaibab Visitor Center to the House Rock Valley-Buffalo Ranch Road (Forest Route 445). Turn right (south) and drive 23 miles to Forest Route 211. Turn right (southwest) and drive 2.0 miles to the end of the road. From this point you must hike another 2.0 miles to the beginning of the South Canyon Trail.

From the upper trailhead the South Canyon Trail descends steeply into South Canyon, then follows the canyon bottom. Traveling through aspen, fern, and mixed conifer in its upper portion, the trail affords splendid views of Marble Canyon. Eventually, the trail becomes the above-mentioned old road which served a pipeline supplying water to Buffalo Ranch.

DAY HIKE: NANKOWEAP TRAIL
One-way length: 4.0 miles
Low and high elevations: 6,480 to 8,800 feet
Difficulty: moderate

To reach the upper trailhead for the Nankoweap Trail, drive south 26.5 miles from the North Kaibab Visitor Center on State Route 67 and turn left (east) on Forest Route 611. Drive 1.4 miles to Forest Route 610 and turn right (south) for 12.3 miles to the end of the road and the trailhead

To access the lower trailhead drive 20 miles east on U.S. Highway 89A from the North Kaibab Visitor Center to the House Rock Valley-Buffalo Ranch Road (Forest Route 445). Turn right (south) and drive 27 miles to the trailhead. Near the end Forest Route 445 forks; stay on the right fork.

In 1881, John Wesley Powell and Dr. Charles D. Walcott, director of the U.S. Geological Survey, blazed a horse trail down an old Indian pathway into the Nankoweap Basin. That path eventually became the Grand Canyon National Park's Nankoweap Trail that joins the Saddle Mountain Wilderness's Nankoweap Trail on National Forest lands. Nankoweap is a Paiute word meaning "singing" or "echo" canyon.

For the first mile or so from the upper trailhead, the Nankoweap Trail descends through an area burned off in 1960 by the Saddle Mountain fire. Locust and aspen now populate this area. Below this point, ponderosa pine is the dominant tree. Splendid views of Marble Canyon are a prime feature of the Nankoweap Trail.

After a short distance along the rim, the trail intersects the Grand Canyon National Park portion of the trail which drops south to the Colorado River. This trail is very difficult and should be attempted by seasoned hikers only. About a mile above the lower trailhead, the Nankoweap Trail is met by the Saddle Mountain Trail, coming in from the south.

DAY HIKE: SADDLE MOUNTAIN TRAIL
One-way length: 6.0 miles
Low and high elevations: 6,500 to 6,700 feet
Difficulty: easy

To reach the Saddle Mountain Trail, follow directions for the upper Nankoweap Trailhead described above. Maintaining an even grade, this easy trail travels along a bench of piñon-juniper woodland, with panoramic views of the Kaibab Plateau, House Rock Valley, Marble Canyon, and the Vermilion Cliffs. Although the trail ends about a mile short of the Marble Canyon Rim, it's an easy cross-country hike to the rim. Your reward is a great view of the Colorado River from rim's edge.

Strawberry Crater Wilderness 12

Sunset colors the eastern rim of Strawberry Crater

FOR GEOLOGY ENTHUSIASTS, the Strawberry Crater Wilderness is a wonderland. Part of the San Francisco Mountains volcanic field, intermittently active for the past 1.8 million years, Strawberry Crater itself resulted from recent eruptions that University of Arizona tree-ring researchers believe started in A.D. 1064 and probably continued until A.D. 1220—virtually yesterday in geologic time.

The biggest blast was in nearby Sunset Crater (now a national monument), but more than 400 volcanoes and hundreds of mini-volcanoes, known as fumaroles and spatter cones, were active. The earth trembled, hot gases seethed from cracks and vents, and clouds of ash swirled in the air. Farmers of the Sinagua culture (meaning "no water") may have escaped in time to save themselves from the volcano's devastation. In the 1930s, excavations of pit houses

LOCATION: 20 miles northeast of Flagstaff

SIZE: 10,141 acres

ELEVATION RANGE: 5,500 to 6,653 feet

MILES OF TRAILS: No marked or maintained trails

HABITATS: Gambel oak, piñon-juniper, ponderosa pine

ADMINISTRATION: Coconino National Forest, Peaks Ranger District

TOPOGRAPHIC MAPS: Strawberry Crater

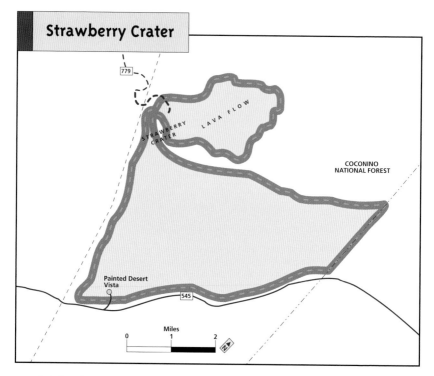

revealed that those who fled Sunset Crater's explosion removed not only their belongings but also timbers from their homes. Clearly, they intended to rebuild elsewhere.

Prior to Sunset Crater's eruption, a very small population had managed hardscrabble subsistence farming on land in the vicinity. Ironically, although it uprooted many people, the volcanic explosion produced a cultural explosion as well. The volcano laid waste to everything near its epicenter, scorching the vegetation and smothering the land beneath layers of lava or ash. Survivors apparently moved just beyond the volcano's circle of devastation and resettled.

Away from the cone, however, a light dusting of ash and cinders helped the soils absorb and hold moisture. Plants thrived. Soon, farmers of diverse cultures began to move back, and this fertile, now well-watered agricultural zone became a melting pot of Sinagua, Hohokam and Anasazi traditions.

This promising civilization was cut short by a drought that began in 1150 A.D. and lasted for an estimated thirty years. By A.D. 1170, many of the region's inhabitants began leaving the area in search of more hospitable terrain. Most moved south to the Verde Valley or to the northeast where they lived with the Hopi.

An exploration of the Strawberry Crater Wilderness might well begin at the Visitor Center of the Sunset Crater Volcano National Monument north of Flagstaff where displays help explain the lava flows, the cindered terrain, and the flora and fauna of the wilderness.

Dominant vegetation in the wilderness is piñon-juniper and Gambel oak. Shrubby plants tend to be widely spaced, owing to lack of soil moisture.

Barren though it may appear, the Strawberry Crater Wilderness is nonetheless home to the raven, mountain lion, deer, elk, red-tailed hawk, and other raptors.

HIKING THE WILDERNESS

Perhaps the easiest access to the Strawberry Crater Wilderness is from the Painted Desert Vista within the Sunset Crater Volcano National Monument. A paved road, Forest Route 545, runs along the southeastern boundary of the wilderness for several miles. The Painted Desert Vista provides entry for cross-country hiking across the entire expanse of the wilderness lying to the north and northeast. From the heights of some of the low cones in the area there are excellent views of the Painted Desert, the Hopi Mesas, and the Little Colorado River Valley.

The best times for hiking the Strawberry Crater Wilderness are spring and fall. Winters are too cold, as a rule, and temperatures in summer are searing. No water is found in the wilderness; carry plenty.

Rim Country:
Mogollon Rim to the Salt River

The Mogollon Rim, otherwise known as Arizona's Central Highlands or the Colorado Plateau's Tonto Section, defines the southern terminus of the Colorado Plateau. A wide belt across Arizona's midsection, the Rim is also a demarcation line between the Colorado Plateau and the Basin and Range land areas. Fifty to one hundred miles wide and heavily forested, the rim is oriented southeast to northwest along a line from the White Mountains near the New Mexico border, up through Flagstaff, and beyond to the Grand Canyon.

The ponderosa pine thrives in a narrow band of elevation between 6,500 and 8,000 feet where annual rainfall averages between eighteen and twenty-six inches, a description that sounds like a topographical and meteorological summary of the Mogollon Rim. Thus, it should come as no surprise that the Mogollon Rim and other portions of the Colorado Plateau contain the largest ponderosa pine forest in the world. Extending in a nearly unbroken but narrow 300-mile band from the Kaibab Plateau north of the Grand Canyon, down through Flagstaff, and southeast along the Rim into New Mexico, this ponderosa forest encompasses 20 million acres, roughly one fourth of the entire state.

As it falls away to the south and west toward the Salt and Verde rivers, Mogollon Rim country is very steep, rugged terrain, incised by deep-walled canyons. Some of Arizona's roughest, and most beautiful, backcountry is located in this region.

Courthouse Butte under blustery skies, Munds Mountain Wilderness

13 Bear Wallow Wilderness

Bear Wallow Creek

LOCATION: 30 miles south of Alpine

SIZE: 11,080 acres

ELEVATION RANGE: 6,700 to 9,000 feet

MILES OF TRAILS: 18

HABITATS: Pine, fir, spruce forests, and riparian

ADMINISTRATION: Apache-Sitgreaves National Forest, Alpine Ranger District

TOPOGRAPHIC MAPS: Baldy Bill, Hoodoo Knoll

MOST BACKCOUNTRY REGIONS I've hiked or backpacked in have at least one bear wallow, a wet, boggy place where black bears wallow in mud to rid themselves of vermin or to fend off biting insects. Pioneer settlers found so many wallows along this tributary creek of the Black River that they named it Bear Wallow Creek. And in 1984, more than 11,000 acres of the territory surrounding it became the Bear Wallow Wilderness.

Bordered on the west by the San Carlos Indian Reservation, on the south by the rugged Mogollon Rim, and with the Blue Range Primitive Area lying only a few miles to the east, the Bear Wallow Wilderness lies amid some of the most truly wild terrain in Arizona. The centerpiece of the wilderness is Bear Wallow Creek itself. Lined with Arizona ash, oak, box elder, and alder and flowing year round, the

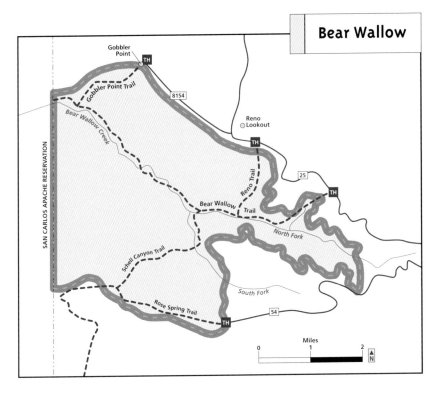

creek provides habitat for the native Apache trout, the survival of which is threatened by habitat degradation and hybridizing with rainbow trout. Conservation efforts to protect the Apache trout include the construction of stream barriers along Bear Wallow Creek to prevent the upstream migration of rainbows.

The wilderness contains some of the most extensive acreage of virgin ponderosa pine in the Southwest. Aspen, Colorado blue spruce, Engelmann spruce, and Douglas fir are among the other trees found in the Bear Wallow Wilderness.

Black bears do, indeed, roam the wilderness area. The wildlands along the Black River on the adjacent San Carlos Indian Reservation may very well harbor the largest concentration of black bears within Arizona. Elk, deer, bobcat, coyote, squirrel, fox, wild turkey, spotted owl, and blue grouse also inhabit the wilderness.

> **DAY HIKE: BEAR WALLOW TRAIL**
> One-way length: 7.6 miles
> Low and high elevations: 6,700 to 8,700 feet
> Difficulty: moderate

To reach the trailhead, drive 6.0 miles south from Hannagan Meadow on U.S. Highway 191 to Forest Route 25. Turn west for 3.0 miles to the trailhead. Starting out as an old logging path that soon becomes a foot trail, the Bear Wallow Trail follows the North Fork of Bear Wallow Creek all the way to the San Carlos Indian Reservation. Crossing the creek many times as it drops 2,000 feet over its 7.6-mile length, the trail intersects three other trails, inviting side explorations north or south. The first of these, 2.0 miles in, is the two-mile Reno Trail, which starts on the north side of the wilderness along Forest Route 25.

The second trail encountered, about 3.5 miles in, is the Schell Canyon Trail which moves south to the Rose Spring Trail which begins along Forest Route 54. Combined the Schell Canyon and Rose Spring Trails cover a distance of 5.8 miles. Finally, about 0.5 mile from the San Carlos Indian Reservation boundary fence, the Bear Creek Trail connects with the Gobbler Point Trail which climbs some 2,000 feet to scenic Gobbler Point in slightly less than 3.0 miles.

Blue Range Primitive Area 14

An expansive view

THE BLUE RIVER HEADS up in Catron County just across the border in New Mexico, flows into Arizona near Alpine, then bisects the Blue Range Primitive Area as it flows south to the San Francisco River. The Blue River, known locally by the diminutive "the Blue," is the likely landscape feature that lent its name to this remote backcountry region along Arizona's eastern border, although some have argued that the name derives from a bluish tinge cast over the spruce-fir forest terrain when the light is just right at dawn or dusk.

LOCATION: 14 miles south of Alpine

SIZE: 173,726 acres

ELEVATION RANGE: 4,500 to 9,346 feet

MILES OF TRAILS: 200

HABITATS: Piñon-juniper, oak woodland, ponderosa pine, spruce-fir forest

ADMINISTRATION: Apache-Sitgreaves National Forest, Alpine Ranger District

TOPOGRAPHIC MAPS: Hannagan Meadow, Beaverhead, Bear Mountain, Strayhorse, Dutch Blue Creek, Alma Mesa, Maness Peak, Rose Peak, Fritz Canyon, Maple Creek

When originally designated as a Primitive Area in 1933, the Blue Range consisted of more than 200,000 acres, but with the passage of the 1980 New Mexico Wilderness Act, a 29,304-acre portion within the State of New Mexico was split off as the new Blue Range Wilderness. Of the seventy-five primitive areas set aside for protection in the 1930s, the Arizona Blue Range alone has not yet been reclassified as wilderness. Standing in the way of wilderness status are powerful ranching and mining interests who fear that wilderness designation for the Blue would eliminate grazing allotments and mineral exploration.

The Blue has it all. There are emerald-green alpine meadows carpeted with spring wildflowers, endless ponderosa pine, spruce-fir and aspen forests, and miles of perennial streams, beaver ponds, and native trout. Its lowest elevations are dominated by piñon-juniper, scrub oak, manzanita, and mountain mahogany. Its riparian habitats feature New Mexico locust, box elder, bigtooth maple, velvet ash, Arizona walnut, and cottonwood.

The bald eagle is at home in the Blue, as are the black bear, elk, beaver, wild turkey, spotted owl, mountain lion, Rocky Mountain bighorn sheep, peregrine falcon, coyote, squirrel, and blue grouse. The grizzly bear used to inhabit this wild ground, the last one having been killed in the nearby Mount Baldy Wilderness in 1939. And, as of March 29, 1998, the Mexican gray wolf once again roams wild in the Blue, which was selected over several other possible release sites. Despite the opposition of cattle growers who fear wolf depredation on livestock, eleven captive-bred wolves—released in three family groups—were reintroduced to the Blue. Although one pregnant female had to be recaptured after her mate was shot and killed by a camper, wildlife biologists believe that at least one other female has given birth in the wild.

CROSS-COUNTRY SKIING

Although snow impedes hiking in winter, excellent snowshoeing and cross-country skiing are available in the Blue starting at the Hannagan Meadow and KP Campground trailheads.

HIKING THE AREA

With more than 200 miles of trails, the Blue offers some outstanding wilderness hiking experiences. At the lower elevations, hiking is possible throughout the year. Spring, summer, and fall are ideal for hiking in the upper elevations. Some of the main hiking routes across the primitive area are described below.

DAY HIKE: A.D. BAR TRAIL
One-way length: 11.9 miles
Low and high elevations: 5,900 to 6,500 feet
Difficulty: strenuous

The trailhead lies along U.S. Highway 191, thirty-six miles north of Clifton and one-half mile north of milepost 200. This hike begins and ends outside the primitive area, traveling through ponderosa pine in its upper reaches. In the first few miles it travels along Squaw Creek and, as it descends, crosses Thomas Creek and Benton Creek near Benton Falls before reaching the Blue River on private property at the H.U. Bar Ranch.

For a multi-day trip, consider hiking north along the Blue River Trail and linking with either the Strayhorse Canyon or Raspberry trails (see page 104) to return to trailheads along U.S. 191.

DAY HIKE: BLUE CABIN TRAIL
(also known as BLUE LOOKOUT TRAIL)
One-way length: 3.5 miles
Low and high elevations: 6,500 to 8,900 feet
Difficulty: moderate

To reach the trailhead, drive 28.5 miles south from Alpine on U.S. Highway 191 to Forest Route 84 (Blue Lookout Road), which is just south of the KP Cienega Campground on the east side of the highway. Drive east on Forest Route 84 about 6.5 miles to where the road is closed at a parking area. Hike the closed road to within 0.5 mile of the Blue Lookout Fire Tower. From that point the Blue Cabin Trail descends steeply on a series of switchbacks to the remains of Blue Cabin that once housed lookout crews. Continuing down the drainage in which the cabin is located, the trail joins the KP Trail at KP Creek.

An aspen and mixed conifer forest near the trailhead give way to ash, maple and other hardwoods along the riparian areas.

Blue Range Primitive Area

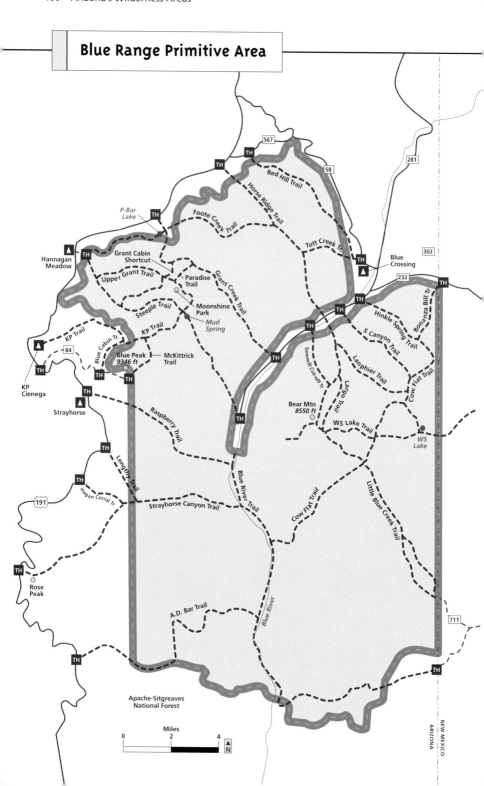

Red Hill Trail

Horse Ridge Trail

Foote Creek Trail

Tutt Creek Tr.

P-Bar Lake

Grant Cabin Shortcut

Hannagan Meadow

Upper Grant Trail

Paradise Trail

Grant Creek Trail

Blue Crossing

Steeple Trail

Moonshine Park

Mud Spring

Hinkle Spring Trail

Bonanza Bill Tr.

KP Trail

KP Trail

Blue Cabin Tr.

Blue Peak 9346 ft

McKittrick Trail

S Canyon Trail

Lanphier Trail

Cow Flat Trail

Sawmill Cutoff Tr.

Largo Trail

KP Cienega

Strayhorse

Raspberry Trail

Bear Mtn 8550 ft

WS Lake Trail

WS Lake

Lengthy Trail

Blue River Trail

Hagan Corral Tr.

Strayhorse Canyon Trail

Cow Flat Trail

Little Blue Creek Trail

Rose Peak

A.D. Bar Trail

Blue River

Apache-Sitgreaves
National Forest

NEW MEXICO

ARIZONA

Miles
0   2   4
N

DAY HIKE: McKITTRICK TRAIL
One-way length: 5.9 miles
Low and high elevations: 6,700 to 9,346 feet
Difficulty: moderate

Beginning at the end of Forest Route 84 (see hike description above), hike the old road to the McKittrick Trailhead. Passing near the summit of Blue Mountain, before descending across a series of ridges and feeder creeks, the trail drops into KP Creek Canyon where it intersects the KP Trail. Some of the best views in the primitive area are available from this trail, including a good look at Sawed Off Mountain. To extend your hiking distance, you can return to U.S. 191 at the KP Cienega Campground via a six-mile section of the KP Trail.

You can also do a loop by hiking about 1.0 miles up the KP Trail to the Blue Cabin Trail junction and then 3.5 miles back to the trailhead.

DAY HIKE: BONANZA BILL TRAIL
One-way length: 12.1 miles
Low and high elevations: 7,040 to 8,400 feet
Difficulty: moderate

To reach the trailhead, drive about 3.5 miles east of Alpine on U.S. Highway 180 to Forest Route 281 (Blue River Road) and turn right (south). Continue south on Forest Route 281 for 20.7 miles to Forest Route 232 and turn left (east). Drive 4.7 miles to the trailhead.

The Bonanza Bill Trail, which travels the eastern boundary of the Blue Range along the Arizona-New Mexico border, offers access to a number of other routes in the primitive area. Winding along a divide that separates the canyons of the Blue and San Francisco rivers, the Bonanza Bill Trail affords excellent views of the Steeple Creek watershed, the San Francisco Valley, and Bonanza Bill Point. When it reaches Bonanza Flat, the Bonanza Bill Trail links up with the Cow Flat Trail.

DAY HIKE: COW FLAT TRAIL
One-way length: 12.15 miles
Low and high elevations: 4,800 to 7,760 feet
Difficulty: moderate

There are other routes that provide access to the Cow Flat Trail (check your topo maps), but the trailhead access for this hike is from the Bonanza Bill Trail at Bonanza Flat (see description above). Initially the Cow Flat Trail is well-defined as it crosses Cow Flat, but it becomes indistinct and difficult to follow as it traverses Bear Valley and Government Mesa. As you cross Bear Valley keep an eye out for some old buildings and a broken-down wagon, artifacts of a time when the valley was farmed around the turn of the century. The Cow Flat Trail is intersected by the 11.3-mile WS Lake Trail and the 10-mile Little Blue River Trail, which offer opportunities for some loop hikes in the vicinity of Bear Mountain. Ladron Spring gushes to the surface at the base of a large walnut tree not far from trail's end at the Blue River, and as you approach the river you pass several small waterfalls. Below Ladron Spring, there's a traverse of a steep bedrock chute that can be somewhat dicey to cross with pack animals.

> **DAY HIKE: HINKLE SPRING TRAIL**
> One-way length: 4.5 miles
> Low and high elevations: 5,700 to 7,520 feet
> Difficulty: moderate

To reach the trailhead, drive 3.5 miles east from Alpine on U.S. Highway 180 to Forest Route 281 (Blue River Road). Continue 21.3 miles south on Forest Route 281 to the trailhead on the left (east) side of the road.

Beginning along the Blue River, the Hinkle Spring Trail climbs to the canyon's east rim. Initially the trail heads up Cow Canyon, a major side drainage along the Blue. Leaving the canyon for the high ground between the Cow Creek and Steeple Creek drainages, the trail offers splendid views of the primitive area and Blue River Canyon. The trail was built to move cattle between pastures and is named for the spring near its terminus at the Bonanza Bill Trail that provides a dependable water source.

For longer hikes and backpacks, the Hinkle Spring Trail can be combined with other trails in this remote section of the primitive area.

> **DAY HIKE: HORSE RIDGE TRAIL**
> One-way length: 5.0 miles
> Low and high elevations: 6,400 to 8,100 feet
> Difficulty: moderate

To reach the trailhead drive about 14.5 miles south from Alpine on U.S. Highway 191. The trailhead is 0.5 mile past Forest Route 567 on the east side of the road.

Before dropping into the Foote Creek drainage, the Horse Ridge Trail offers an excellent view of some of top landmarks of the Blue Range Primitive Area. Castle Rock, Bell Rock, Bear Mountain, and Whiterock Mountain all stand out. The trail descends into Foote Creek where it ends at the junction with the Foote Creek Trail.

For a longer hike or backpack, you could drop south on the Foote Creek Trail to the Tutt Creek Trail. Go east on the 4.2-mile Tutt Creek Trail to the 9.7-mile Red Hill Trail, which returns north to Forest Route 567 just 1.0 mile from U.S. 191.

> **DAY HIKE: RED HILL TRAIL**
> One-way length: 9.7 miles
> Low and high elevations: 5,790 to 8000 feet
> Difficulty: strenuous

To reach the trailhead drive 14 miles south of Alpine on U.S. Highway 191 to Forest Route 567, then east 1.0 mile to the trailhead.

Like the Horse Ridge Trail, the Red Hill Trail provides outstanding views of some of the primitive area's most scenic features, Red Bluff, Foote Creek Canyon, Blue River Canyon, Bear Mountain, and Whiterock Mountain among them. The Red Hill Trail, which begins just outside the primitive area boundary, follows a stairstep course into Blue River Canyon, dropping down steep slopes and alternately crossing broad benches. The trail drops into and follows the Bush Creek drainage to its end near the Blue Crossing Campground.

> **DESTINATION HIKE: STEEPLE TRAIL TO THE BLUE RIVER**
> One-way length: 13.2 miles
> Low and high elevations: 5,280 to 9,200 feet
> Difficulty: strenuous

The trailhead is located in Hannagan Meadow. To reach the Hannagan Meadow Trailhead drive about 23 miles south of Alpine on U.S. Highway 191 to Forest Route 29A. The trailhead is a short distance east of the highway on Forest Route 29A. A great introduction to the habitat diversity of the Blue Range, the Steeple Trail begins at an elevation of 9,200 feet as it travels through aspens and mixed conifers, opening periodically into marshy high-country meadows called cienegas, prime habitat for elk, deer, and black bear. Dropping into Steeple Creek the trail passes through ponderosa pine, alligator juniper, ash, walnut, and maple. At Mud Springs the Steeple Trail intersects the KP Trail. From this point on, it loses elevation rapidly as it descends to the Blue River.

> **DESTINATION HIKE: KP TRAIL TO MUD SPRINGS**
> One-way length: 9.4 miles
> Low and high elevations: 6,560 to 8,960 feet
> Difficulty: moderate

To reach the trailhead, drive 28 miles south from Alpine on U.S. Highway 191 to the road leading to the KP Cienega Campground. Turn left (east) 1.3 miles to the trailhead.

This trail follows the meandering course of KP Creek as it descends toward the Blue River. About three miles from the trailhead, the route drops steeply to where the South Fork and North Fork unite to form KP Creek. Ten-foot waterfalls cascade into KP Creek from these two tributaries creating pools containing fairly large native trout. From this point the trail crosses the creek many times as it winds through steep rock walls. About 3.0 miles before it ends at its junction with the Steeple Trail at Mud Springs, the KP Trail leaves the canyon for higher ground and high desert vegetation consisting of scrub oak, yucca, and cholla.

LOOP HIKE: S CANYON TRAIL – LANPHIER TRAIL
One-way length: 12.4 miles
Low and high elevations: 5,600 to 7,800 feet
Difficulty: moderate

To reach the trailhead, drive 3.5 miles east from Alpine on U.S. Highway 180 to Forest Route 281 (Blue River Road). Continue 23 miles south on Forest Route 281 to the Blue Administrative Site. The Foote Creek, Lanphier, and S Canyon trailheads are all located here.

From the trailhead, hike upriver to the mouth of S Canyon. As it climbs 5.8 miles from the river bottom to the canyon rim to intersect the Cow Flat Trail, the S Canyon Trail provides great views of the Blue River Canyon area, one of which is an overlook into a narrow, sheer-walled section of the Blue. The canyon takes its name from the s-shape it describes as it plunges from the east rim down to the Blue.

At the intersection with the Cow Flat Trail, hike south about 1.0 mile to the junction with the Lanphier Trail, which descends 5.6 miles to the Blue River and the Trailhead. Along the way the Lanphier Trail passes through verdant riparian areas of Lanphier and Indian Creeks. Bear Mountain, Lanphier Peak, and Lanphier Canyon are among the scenic highlights of this trail.

SHUTTLE HIKE: RASPBERRY – BLUE RIVER – STRAYHORSE CANYON TRAILS
One-way length: 27.0 miles
Low and high elevations: 5,000 to 8,200 feet
Difficulty: strenuous

To begin this hike, drive approximately 32 miles south of Alpine on U.S. Highway 191 to the Strayhorse Campground and walk one-quarter mile east to the Raspberry Trailhead. The 9.4-mile Raspberry Trail descends into Raspberry Creek Canyon and follows the stream all the way down to the Blue River. Along the upper stretches of the trail you can see Bear Mountain and Maple Peak, east of the Blue River, and Whiterock Mountain beyond the border in New Mexico. South you can see all the way to Mount Graham in the Pinaleños.

The trail descends through piñon-juniper woodlands until it reaches Raspberry Creek, lined with conifers and wild raspberry bushes. Lower down the conifers give way to alder, ash and other typical riparian trees. Before reaching the Blue, the trail travels along a ridge that separates Raspberry and McKittrick Canyons, then returns to the riparian habitat of Raspberry Creek.

At the Blue River, continue south on the Blue River Trail for approximately 3.0 miles to the lower Strayhorse Canyon Trailhead. The 12.7-mile Strayhorse Canyon Trail climbs more than 3,000 feet along the narrow Strayhorse Canyon to a trailhead near the Rose Peak Lookout on U.S. 191. The trail is indistinct in places and, in the last mile alone, it climbs some 800 feet to the Rose Peak Trail among ponderosa pines.

Hikers who prefer a shorter loop may return to U.S. 191 by the 3.3-mile Lengthy Trail or the 3.1-mile Hagan Corral Trail, which intersect the Strayhorse Canyon Trail just before it leaves the primitive area to climb toward the highway.

SHUTTLE HIKE: HAGAN CORRAL – STRAYHORSE – LENGTHY TRAILS
One-way length: 6.5 miles
Low and high elevations: 5,700 to 7,200 feet
Difficulty: moderate

To reach the Hagan Corral Trailhead, drive 47 miles north of Clifton on U.S. Highway 191. The trailhead is on the east side of the road. Beginning among ponderosa pine and Gambel oak, the Hagan Corral Trail descends 1,500 feet along its length to join the Strayhorse Trail just inside the primitive area. Continue east on the Strayhorse Trail for about one mile to its junction with the Lengthy Trail. Return via the Lengthy Trail to U.S. 191, 3.0 miles north of the Hagan Corral Trailhead. The Hagan Corral Trail is rocky in places and the Lengthy Trail contains areas of side-sloping slickrock.

SHUTTLE HIKE: FOOTE CREEK – GRANT CREEK TRAILS
One-way length: 26.0 miles
Low and high elevations: 5,440 to 9,200 feet
Difficulty: strenuous

Beginning at the Hannagan Meadow Trailhead (see page 103), the 16-mile Foote Creek Trail follows an old logging road along a ridge for roughly 4.5 miles through a cool canopy of spruce, fir, and aspen. Past P-Bar Lake it drops into the upper reaches of Foote Creek and follows the drainage through riparian habitat all the way to Blue Administrative site at the Blue River. Along-the-trail treats are views of Castle Rock, some red rock cliffs, and long-distance vistas of the Blue River. You will need to have a second vehicle parked at Blue Camp or otherwise arrange for a shuttle to transport you south along Forest Route 281 to the lower Grant Creek Trailhead. The 10-mile Grant Creek Trail climbs nearly 4,000 feet to its intersection with the Foote Creek Trail near P-Bar Lake. From this point you return to Hannagan Meadow via the Foote Creek Trail.

15 Castle Creek Wilderness

Stunning view of the desert valley

LOCATION: 35 miles south of Prescott

SIZE: 29,770 acres

ELEVATION RANGE: 2,800 to 7,000 feet

MILES OF TRAILS: 26.5

HABITATS: Upper Sonoran, desert grassland, chaparral, ponderosa

ADMINISTRATION: Prescott National Forest, Bradshaw Ranger District

TOPOGRAPHIC MAPS: Crown King, Bumble Bee, Battle Flat, Cleator

AS YOU DRIVE NORTH on Interstate 17 just beyond Black Canyon City, a long, rugged escarpment, looming some 4,000 feet above the desert floor, comes into view to the west. You are looking into the folded canyons of the Castle Creek Wilderness, located along the eastern flank of the Bradshaw Mountains overlooking the Agua Fria River. Castle Creek, the wilderness area's namesake creek, derives its own name from the castellated rock walls through which it flows before empting into the Agua Fria. Prospectors once sought gold and silver in the Bradshaws and numerous defunct mines dot the wilderness landscape—the Crown King, Bill Arp, Lincoln, Tiger, Button, Gazelle, Howard, Boaz, Pacific, and Algonquin, the remains of which lie along the Algonquin Trail.

At its lower elevations the Castle Creek Wilderness is dominated by desert-dwelling plants, including saguaro, palo verde, mesquite, acacia, ocotillo, prickly pear, creosote bush, and various species of cholla. The plant succession as you move higher is typical: manzanita, century plant, mountain mahogany, scrub oak, and juniper, giving way to a ponderosa-Gambel oak forest in the higher elevations.

Mule deer, and the deer's chief predator, the mountain lion, are abundant in the Castle Creek Wilderness. Also inhabiting the wilderness are black bear, coyote, rock squirrel, porcupine, desert cottontail, javelina, ringtail, striped skunk, bobcat, and gray fox. Birds of the wilderness include scrub jay, curve-billed thrasher, cactus wren, pygmy nuthatch, Gila woodpecker, great horned owl, and many others.

A rule of thumb: If you avoid the lower elevations in summer and the heights in winter, it is possible to comfortably visit the Castle Creek Wilderness during twelve months of the year.

> **DAY HIKE**: ALGONQUIN TRAIL
> One-way length: 5.0 miles
> Low and high elevations: 4,600 to 6,850 feet
> Difficulty: moderate

Like many of the trails in the Castle Creek Wilderness, the Algonquin Trail, which leads to the old Algonquin Mine, was developed to move mining supplies and equipment. It ends at the ruins of several cabins, an old mine shaft, and other mining artifacts. To reach the trailhead, exit Interstate 17 at Bumblebee, north of Black Canyon City, and drive about 30 miles west on Forest Route 259 to Crown King. Continue south on Forest Route 259 beyond Crown King for 0.5 mile to Forest Route 52 and turn left (south) for 2.5 miles to the trailhead.

From the trailhead, the route follows Juniper Ridge for about one mile before dropping steeply into Horsethief Canyon, a reputed hideout for horse rustlers. The Algonquin Trail then meets the Horsethief Canyon Trail near the site of the Algonquin Mine. This is the turnaround point for this hike although you can extend your distance and elevation by hiking 2.0 miles up the Horsethief Canyon Trail to Horsethief Basin, some 2,000 feet above.

> **DAY HIKE**: CASTLE CREEK TRAIL
> One-way length: 7.7 miles
> Low and high elevations: 4,400 to 6,700 feet
> Difficulty: moderate

A two-wheel drive road leads to a spur trail that connects with the Castle Creek Trail midway along its route. To reach the spur trailhead from Interstate 17, take the Bumblebee exit and drive 5.0 miles north on Crown King Road to the Forest Route 684 turnoff. Take Forest Route 684 to the end and the trailhead.

Along its one-mile length, the spur trail climbs 1,000 feet before connecting with the Castle Creek Trail. A left turn at this trail junction takes you west along the Castle Creek Trail to the trailhead in Horsethief Basin, just outside the wilderness area. In four miles, this route climbs more than 2,000 feet.

A right turn at the spur-Castle Creek trail junction takes you north for 3.0 miles to the Twin Peaks Trail.

Castle Creek

DAY HIKE: TWIN PEAKS TRAIL
One-way length: 8.0 miles
Low and high elevations: 4,000 to 6,700 feet
Difficulty: moderate

The Twin Peaks Trailhead is located in Horsethief Basin, 7.0 miles south from Crown King on Forest Route 52. This route descends nearly 3,000 feet as it travels north across the wilderness to the Bill Arp Mine near Forest Route 101. You can also access the Twin Peaks Trail from this northern trailhead, but it requires a four-wheel-drive vehicle.

By hiking the Castle Creek Trail (see page 107) and a portion of the Twin Peaks Trail, you can describe a loop from Horsethief Basin of nearly 12 miles. An old road at Horsethief Basin separates the Castle Creek and Twin Peaks trailheads by less than two miles.

HIKING THE WILDERNESS

Also beginning in Horsethief Basin are three other trails. The quite easy East Fort Trail travels east for less that one mile to an abandoned 1880s U.S. Army post called the East Fort. The 4.0-mile Willow Creek Trail and the 2.0-mile Jim Creek Trail drop south from Horsethief Basin. Both are steep, rough, and difficult to follow.

Escudilla Wilderness 16

A serene August sunrise

IN *A SAND COUNTY ALMANAC,* Aldo Leopold writes eloquently and regretfully about a government trapper's killing of what may have been one of the last grizzly bears in Arizona. Although Leopold and other foresters had never actually seen the grizzly, they had seen bear signs: huge tracks beside muddy springs and a grizzly-killed cow, its head reduced to pulp, "as if she had collided head-on with a fast freight." Mourning the grizzly's loss, Leopold writes: "Escudilla still hangs on the horizon, but when you see it you no longer think of bear. It's only a mountain now."

Mexican gray wolves have been reintroduced to Arizona in the Blue Range Primitive Area not far from the Escudilla Wilderness, and at some distant future time the grizzly may be restored to the wildlands along the Arizona-New Mexico border. In the meantime, all we've got is a mountain, but what a mountain it is. The Escudilla, meaning

LOCATION: 8 miles north of Alpine

SIZE: 5,200 acres

ELEVATION RANGE: 8,700 to 10,912 feet

MILES OF TRAILS: 3

HABITATS: Pine, fir, and spruce forest

ADMINISTRATION: Apache-Sitgreaves National Forest, Alpine Ranger District

TOPOGRAPHIC MAPS: Escudilla

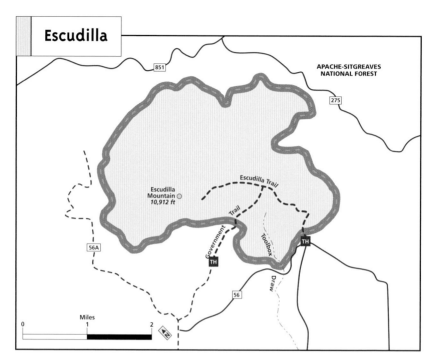

"bowl" in Spanish and possibly referring to the extinct volcanic crater that forms its summit, is the third highest peak in Arizona. From its fire lookout, the highest in the state, you can sometimes see all the way to the San Francisco Peaks near Flagstaff and to the Pinaleño Mountains near Safford.

Douglas fir, white fir, Colorado blue spruce, Engelmann spruce, aspen, and ponderosa pine interspersed with lovely subalpine meadows grace the mountain. In spring and summer the meadows come alive with wildflowers. Wildlife supported by the Escudilla Wilderness include elk, deer, black bear, mountain lion, wild turkey, pygmy nuthatch, and Clark's nutcracker.

Hiking and cross-country skiing are the main recreational activities in the Escudilla Wilderness. The Forest Route to the Escudilla Trailhead is not plowed in winter, so skiers will have to ski the five miles from U.S. Highway 191 to reach the trail.

> **DAY HIKE: ESCUDILLA TRAIL**
> One-way length: 3.0 miles
> Low and high elevations: 9,480 to 10,876 feet
> Difficulty: easy

To reach the trailhead, drive 5.5 miles north from Alpine on U.S. Highway 191 to Forest Route 56 and turn right (east) 5.0 miles to the trailhead. This easy 1,400-foot climb travels through a meadow at the head of Toolbox Draw and after 2.0 miles joins the Government Trail, a steep, unmaintained trail coming up from the west side of the wilderness that originally served as a supply route to the fire lookout. The Escudilla Trail ends at the fire lookout, just short of the summit.

Fossil Springs Wilderness 17

Early morning sun reflected in rushing water

EVEN BELOW THE MOGOLLON RIM, where many Arizona wildlands support perennially flowing creeks, the Fossil Springs Wilderness is unique. Two small tributaries, Sandrock and Calf Pen, come together to form a basin that narrows sharply before widening into a stunning oasis. Widely spaced springs gush into the creek, producing a flow of 20,000 gallons per minute at a constant temperature of 72 degrees Fahrenheit. Opened up by the springs, the creek flows down into large pools overhung by alder, sycamore, netleaf hackberry, cottonwood, Arizona walnut, bigtooth maple, and oak. Canyon grape intertwines tree branches; ferns cascade from rock crevices; blackberry bushes crowd the banks. In warm seasons, monkeyflower and columbine sprout along the creek bottom. On the faces of the sheer cliffs above the springs, tangled thickets of manzanita discourage hikers with any notion of bushwhacking into the oasis.

LOCATION: 10 miles west of Strawberry

SIZE: 11,550 acres

ELEVATION RANGE: 3,800 to 6,800 feet

MILES OF TRAILS: 9.5

HABITATS: Riparian canyons and mesas

ADMINISTRATION: Coconino National Forest, Beaver Creek Ranger District

TOPOGRAPHIC MAPS: Strawberry, Pine

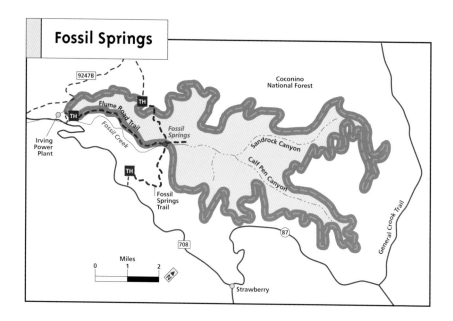

More than one hundred species of birds have been identified in the Fossil Springs Wilderness, which also provides habitat for elk, white-tailed and mule deer, bald eagle, Arizona black rattlesnake, ringtail, and black bear. Two endangered fish species, the round-tailed chub and the Gila topminnow, survive in Fossil Creek.

In 1916 the water below the springs was dammed and run by flume ten miles to the Irving Power Plant along the Verde River. Still in use, the flume is on the National Register of Historic Places. In the 1920s and early '30s, before the repeal of Prohibition, a number of illegal whiskey stills were operated in the remote canyons within the wilderness. The remains of these stills are occasionally discovered by canyon explorers.

Although winters are fairly mild in the vicinity of the Fossil Springs Wilderness, the best times to visit are spring and fall. The spring brings magnificent wildflower displays; the fall an exhibition of changing colors, especially of the bigtooth maple leaves.

Bushwhacking the creek bottom is rigorous, with many boulder chokes, deep pools, and narrows impeding progress. But for the intrepid, that is the preferred method of wilderness travel. Be aware, however, that spring snowmelt and heavy summer rains can produce flash flooding in these narrow canyons.

DAY HIKE: MAIL TRAIL – FOSSIL SPRINGS TRAIL
One-way length: 3.9 miles
Low and high elevations: 3,800 to 5,100 feet
Difficulty: easy

To reach the Mail Trailhead, drive east from Camp Verde on State Route 260 to Forest Route 9247B. Turn right (south) to the trailhead at Stock Tank #2. Forest Route 9247B is suitable for high-clearance two-wheel-drive vehicles. When early ranchers in the territory discovered it, they called it the Indian Trail. Later the route was used to transport mail between Payson and Camp Verde, and its name was changed to the Mail Trail. Scarcely three miles long, the Mail Trail drops 1,300 feet from the Mogollon Rim to where it joins the lower end of Fossil Springs Trail coming in from the south. From this intersection, it is just a short distance east to Fossil Springs. The trailheads for the Fossil Springs Trail and the Flume Road Trail, both of which lie outside the wilderness, can be reached by traveling west from Strawberry on Forest Route 708. The Fossil Springs Trailhead is five miles west of Strawberry, the Flume Road Trail ten miles.

18 Granite Mountain Wilderness

Rugged country along the Granite Mountain Trail

ASK ANYBODY IN PRESCOTT where Granite Mountain is and they will likely point to an enormous granite outcrop, a familiar local landmark, just beyond the city limits. When you view the wilderness close-up, though, you notice that it consists of many weathered and rounded freight-car-size boulders stacked one atop the other. Some two billion years old, they have been molded over eons by wind and water.

Arroyos running through the wilderness are vegetated by a fairly typical riparian association: willow, alligator juniper, Fremont cottonwood, Arizona walnut, ash, and Arizona grape. In the upland landscape around the

LOCATION: 7 miles north of Prescott

SIZE: 9,700 acres

ELEVATION RANGE: 5,000 to 7,626 feet

MILES OF TRAILS: 3.5

HABITATS: Piñon-juniper, oak, ponderosa pine

ADMINISTRATION: Prescott National Forest, Bradshaw Ranger District

TOPOGRAPHIC MAPS: Iron Springs, Jerome Canyon

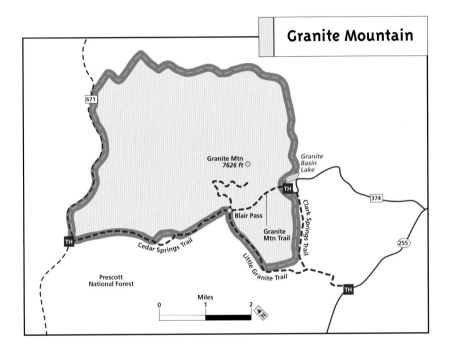

Granite Mountain

5,000 foot mark, piñon-juniper and oak dominate. Higher, thickets of manzanita grow beside the footpaths, interspersed with colonies of Parry's Century Plant. The highest elevations of the Granite Mountain Wilderness are covered with ponderosa pine.

The precipitous cliff faces of the wilderness are prime nesting sites for the endangered peregrine falcon. Other raptors include the American kestrel, red-tailed hawk, and a variety of owls. The tassel-eared Abert's squirrel is numerous in the oak woodlands as is the ubiquitous and noisy acorn woodpecker. Mule deer, fox, bobcat, and scrub jay also inhabit the wilderness.

Granite Mountain Wilderness is a favorite hiking destination, but rock-climbing the solid granite cliff faces may be an even more popular recreation. Climbers should be aware, however, that between February and July, when peregrine falcons are nesting, the Forest Service closes some of the best climbing routes. Because wilderness weather is moderate year-round, hiking is pleasant during all seasons. Note, however, that winter storms occasionally bring snow and cold weather. During thunderstorms, lightning danger is especially high due to the great amount of exposed rock. No water is available in the wilderness.

DAY HIKE: GRANITE MOUNTAIN TRAIL
One-way length: 3.5 miles
Low and high elevations: 5,300 to 7,626 feet
Difficulty: easy

Although three other trails skirt the wilderness perimeter, the Granite Mountain Trail, which begins near Granite Basin Lake, is the only one that actually enters the Granite Mountain Wilderness. To reach the trailhead from Prescott, drive approximately 5.0 miles west from town on the Iron Springs Road to Granite Basin Lake Road (Forest Route 374). Turn right and drive approximately 4.0 miles to Granite Basin Lake.

The Granite Mountain Trail climbs through oak woodland and across some exposed ridges for about a mile to Blair Pass, where it turns north toward the Granite Mountain Saddle. Steeper in this section, the route climbs some 800 feet in slightly more than one mile. From the saddle, the trail turns in a southeasterly direction to climb about 1.5 miles to the summit.

Three worthy trails trace the wilderness boundary—the Cedar Springs (2.7 miles), Clark Springs (1.5 miles), and Little Granite (3.3 miles). On these particular trails you might encounter mountain bikes, which are permitted on National Forest lands outside the wilderness.

Hellsgate Wilderness

Tonto Creek just below Hellsgate Wilderness

KNIFING DOWN OFF THE MOGOLLON RIM to the Salt River, Tonto Creek is the centerpiece of the Hellsgate Wilderness. Cutting deeply into granite, Tonto and its main tributary, Haigler Creek, have carved deep canyons that rise in places to more than 1,500 feet above the stream bottoms. The wilderness derives its name from the turbulent confluence of Tonto and Haigler Creeks, which pioneer settlers dubbed Hells Gate.

The southern portion of the wilderness, near a settlement called Gisela, was inhabited during the twelfth and thirteenth centuries by a native

LOCATION: 18 miles east of Payson

SIZE: 36,780 acres

ELEVATION RANGE: 3,000 to 6,400 feet

MILES OF TRAILS: 24

HABITATS: Riparian, desert, chaparral, pine-fir forest

ADMINISTRATION: Tonto National Forest, Payson Ranger District

TOPOGRAPHIC MAPS: Diamond Butte, McDonald Mountain, Sheep Basin Mountain, Buzzard Roost Mesa, Payson South, Gisela

group that archaeologists call the Salado. Their artifacts indicate that these people were essentially farmers who raised crops in the bottomlands along the creeks draining into the Salt River. They were also active traders with other groups throughout the Southwest. Several hundred years later, Apache Indians migrated to the area from the Great Plains and stayed until they were driven out by Anglo ranchers and miners.

Plants associated with the Sonoran Desert—saguaro cactus, ocotillo, agave, and cholla—grow in the lower elevations of the wilderness. The riparian gallery features willow, sycamore, cottonwood, ash, and Arizona walnut. At mid-level elevations you find scrub oak, alligator juniper, piñon, and manzanita. Ponderosa pine and Douglas fir grow in the higher, cooler elevations.

Intrepid fishermen bushwhack to Tonto Creek's deeper pools where lunker brown and rainbow trout lurk. Mammals living in the wilderness include beaver, black bear, ringtail, mountain lion, hog-nosed skunk, and deer. The red-tailed hawk, American robin, Northern flicker, canyon wren, and Western bluebird are among the birds that inhabit Hellsgate.

November through April are the best months to hike in the Hellsgate Wilderness, although heavy snowmelt runoff in spring can make for dangerous creek crossings.

DAY HIKE: HELLSGATE TRAIL
One-way length: 11.0 miles
Low and high elevations: 3,984 to 5,655 feet
Difficulty: strenuous

To reach the north trailhead, drive eleven miles east from Payson on State Route 260 just past Little Green Valley. Turn right (south) onto Forest Route 405A and continue for about one-quarter mile to the trailhead near a concrete water trough.

What makes the Hellsgate Trail strenuous is a more than 1,500-foot drop to Tonto Creek going in and a similar climb to the opposite rim going out. The payoff is the cool, shaded canyon bottom with its perennial stream and deep pools. It may be possible to extend your hike by bushwhacking upstream or down, but impassable waterfalls make a hike-swim-float along the drainage very nearly impossible.

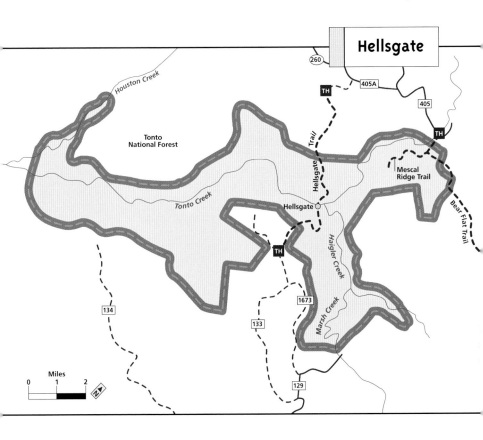

The Hellsgate Trail may also be accessed from the town of Young by driving west on Forest Route 129 for 7.5 miles to Forest Route 133, a four-wheel-drive route. Turn left on Forest Route 133 and drive approximately 8.0 miles to the south trailhead.

> **DAY HIKE: BEAR FLAT TRAIL**
> One-way length: 9.25 miles
> Low and high elevations: 5,200 to 5,800 feet
> Difficulty: easy

To reach the trailhead for this short but scenic wilderness route, drive about 14 miles east from Payson on State Route 260 to Forest Route 405. Turn right (south) and drive 4.5 miles to the Tonto Creek crossing. Park here and wade the creek to start up the trail.

For nearly one-quarter mile, the trail climbs steeply through a grove of mixed conifer to a ridgeline, then heads off in an easterly direction for approximately 1.0 mile before leaving the wilderness. You may extend your hike beyond the wilderness boundary by hiking another 8.0 miles to Forest Route 200 near the base of Oxbow Mountain.

DAY HIKE: MESCAL RIDGE TRAIL
One-way length: 3.0 miles
Low and high elevations: 5,400 to 5,580 feet
Difficulty: easy

The Mescal Ridge Trail connects with the Bear Flat Trail within the first mile of the latter. At the intersection, the Mescal Ridge Trail moves west-southwest into the wilderness; the Bear Flat Trail heads east. The Mescal Ridge is short but it affords some excellent views of the countryside. It's a nice introduction to the Hellsgate Wilderness.

Juniper Mesa Wilderness 20

View looking south over rolling hills and mountains

SMALL, RUGGED, AND WATERLESS, the character of the Juniper Mesa Wilderness is just what its name implies: a broad, flat, juniper-clad mesa. Vegetation, which varies with exposure, tends toward piñon pine and Utah juniper on the southern slopes and alligator juniper and ponderosa pine on its north faces. Several varieties of oak also grow in the wilderness along with cliff rose, mountain mahogany, sotol, prickly pear, and agave.

Black bear, deer, Abert's squirrel, white-throated woodrat, deer mouse, coyote, and bobcat are among the mammals found in the wilderness. Birds include Gambel's quail, mourning dove, Cooper's hawk, curve-billed thrasher, roadrunner, Western kingbird, and great horned owl.

The few springs located within the wilderness become dry during periods of prolonged drought, so hikers should

LOCATION: 40 miles north of Prescott

SIZE: 7,640 acres

ELEVATION RANGE: 5,400 to 7,100 feet

MILES OF TRAILS: 16.8

HABITATS: Piñon-juniper, alligator juniper, ponderosa pine

ADMINISTRATION: Prescott National Forest, Chino Valley Ranger District

TOPOGRAPHIC MAPS: Juniper Mesa, Indian Peak

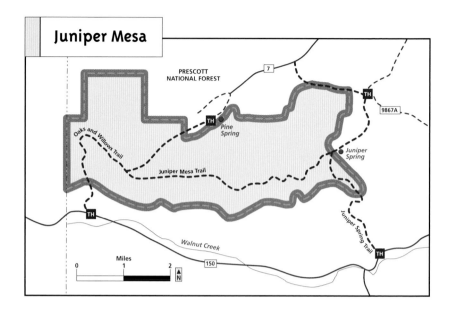

always carry plenty of water. Spring and autumn are the best times to visit the Juniper Mesa Wilderness. Winter hiking is also pleasant, depending on weather and road conditions. Summers are often too hot for hiking.

> ## DAY HIKE: OAKS AND WILLOWS TRAIL
> One-way length: 6.6 miles
> Low and high elevations: 6,000 to 7,000 feet
> Difficulty: moderate

To reach the trailhead for the Oaks and Willows Trail, drive 36 miles north from Prescott on Williamson Valley Road (which becomes Forest Route 6) to Forest Route 95. Turn left on Forest Route 95 and drive 1.5 miles to the Forest Service Work Station at Walnut Center. Just beyond the work station, turn right (west) onto Forest Route 150 and drive 6.0 miles to the trailhead.

Starting outside the wilderness boundary, the Oaks and Willows Trail travels across part of the western portion of the Juniper Mesa Wilderness. After entering George Woods Canyon, the trail ascends the south slope of the mesa. Although steep, the hiking is moderate. After reaching the mesa top, the route turns northeast and gradually drops toward Pine Spring, which lies just outside the wilderness boundary at the end of Forest Route 7.

DAY HIKE: JUNIPER MESA TRAIL
One-way length: 6.5 miles
Low and high elevations: 5,300 to 7,000 feet
Difficulty: moderate

The Juniper Mesa Trail is accessed via its junction with the before-mentioned Oaks and Willows Trail about two miles from the trailhead. From this point, the Juniper Mesa Trail takes off in an easterly direction along the rim of the mesa, affording the best views of the surrounding terrain.

As the route approaches Juniper Spring, it is joined by the Juniper Spring Trail which comes in from near the Walnut Creek Center to the south. Climbing more than 1,000 feet in 3.7 miles, the Juniper Spring Trail is outside the wilderness boundary for most of its length. Just beyond Juniper Spring, the Juniper Mesa Trail leaves the wilderness and descends steeply to Forest Route 9867A, a four-wheel-drive road.

21 Mazatzal Wilderness

Delicate columbine

NOT COUNTING THE GRAND CANYON, with its 1.2 million acres, only three other Arizona backcountry areas—Organ Pipe Wilderness, Cabeza Prieta Refuge Wilderness, and Kofa Refuge Wilderness—exceed the Mazatzal Wilderness in size. Originally established as a Forest Reserve in 1908, the Mazatzal was changed to a Primitive Area in 1938 and upgraded to wilderness classification in 1940. The 1964 Wilderness Act confirmed its wilderness status; then in 1984 the Arizona Wilderness Act added 35,000 acres, increasing the Mazatzal to its present quarter-million acres.

LOCATION: 25 miles northeast of Carefree

SIZE: 252,500 acres

ELEVATION RANGE: 2,100 to 7,904 feet

MILES OF TRAILS: 240

HABITATS: Sonoran, grassland, riparian, piñon-juniper, pine-fir

ADMINISTRATION: Tonto National Forest, Payson Ranger District

TOPOGRAPHIC MAPS: Mazatzal Peak, North Peak, Cypress Butte, Table Mountain, Horseshoe Dam, Lion Mountain, Reno Pass, Chalk Mountain, Wet Bottom Mesa, Verde Hot Springs, Cane Springs Mountain, Buckhead Mesa

The name is something of a mystery. Pronounced *MAH zat sall,* it is a Nahuatl (Aztec) word meaning "land of the deer." Apache and Yavapai Indians inhabited the range until the late 1800s, and before them, a paleo-Indian group called the Salado Culture. Aztecs, of course, were never in this area. Is the name accidental? A corrupted spelling or pronunciation of some other name? No one knows.

One of the first Anglo-American trappers to enter the area was Kit Carson, who in 1829 trapped fur-bearing animals down the Salt River and up the Verde. Indian resistance curtailed further explorations of the region until the 1870s, when troops led by General George Crook expelled the Yavapai and Western Apaches. The last war chief to surrender was Delshay, a leader of a Tonto Apache band holed up in the Mazatzals.

Cattle and sheep were introduced to the region around the same time, and by the early twentieth century the area was heavily stocked. Ten grazing allotments are still under permit within the Mazatzal Wilderness. If you wish to experience the wilderness without encountering cattle, check with the local ranger for areas free of livestock. Like it or not, cattle grazing in the wilderness is legal by virtue of provisions in the 1964 Wilderness Act. Close all gates behind you and do not deny cattle access to water.

Stretching from the Salt River on the south all the way north to the Mogollon Rim, the Mazatzal Wilderness spans sixteen miles at its widest. The Verde River, Arizona's only Wild and Scenic River, flows nearly twenty-eight miles through the northwestern portion of the wilderness before meandering just outside its southwestern boundary. Draining the basin to the west of the wilderness is Tonto Creek, which spills off the Mogollon Rim to flow south into the Salt River.

Lower Sonoran Desert vegetation dominates the Mazatzal's low-elevation western margin along the Verde River. Saguaro cacti, ocotillo, cholla, palo verde, creosote, brittlebush, mesquite, triangle-leaf bursage, acacia, and range ratany are among the desert trees and shrubs found there. Above this desert scrub region is a small grassland zone. The succession of plants as elevation increases goes from scrub oak, mountain mahogany, and manzanita to piñon-juniper at mid-level, and ponderosa and Gambel oak in the wilderness heights. A few colonies of Douglas fir are also found in cooler regions high up. Along canyon creeks and streams in the wilderness, trees and shrubs are typical of riparian zones: Arizona sycamore, canyon ragweed, wolfberry, desert hackberrry, fremont cottonwood, desert honeysuckle, ash, and Arizona walnut.

Desert bighorn sheep, which, along with deer, provide a prey base for mountain lions, inhabit some of the craggiest heights of the Mazatzal Wilderness. Black bear, ringtail, porcupine, raccoon, bobcat, javelina, kit fox, gray fox, black-tailed jackrabbit, rock squirrel, desert cottontail, white-throated wood rat, hog-nosed skunk, badger, and many species of bats are among the numerous mammals inhabiting the wilderness.

Raptors include golden eagle, peregrine falcon, red-tailed hawk, and zone-tailed hawk. Other birds include cactus wren, canyon wren, house finch, canyon towhee, rufous-sided towhee, curve-billed thrasher, dark-eyed junco, black-throated sparrow, scrub Jays, Gila woodpeckers, Western tanager, Northern flicker, white-crowned sparrow, Scott's oriole, and many others. The wilderness is also home to many reptiles and amphibians, including diamondback rattlesnake, gopher snake, Gila monster, short-horned lizard, coachwhip, red-spotted toad, and canyon treefrog.

Overall, fall and spring are the prime seasons to visit the Mazatzal Wilderness, regardless of elevation. Avoid low elevations in summer, particularly on the west side of the wilderness where there is very little shade and temperatures may soar as high as 110 degrees Fahrenheit. Snow in winter may make some of the higher elevations inaccessible.

RIVER RUNNING

You will not encounter any Class III or IV rapids on the Verde River, but when the river's volume is swelled by spring runoff or summer thunderstorms, kayaking or rafting from the point sixty miles outside of Camp Verde to the take-out at Sheep Bridge can generate a few thrills and chills. Canoeing the Verde is also possible during times of moderate stream flow. The best boating season on the Verde is from January through mid-May.

HIKING THE WILDERNESS

The Forest Service lists 240 miles of "system" trails within the Mazatzal Wilderness and contiguous areas. In addition to developed trails there are many "wildcat" trails, some of them old foot trails, others jeep roads. The terrain is rough and forbidding, however, so use caution while hiking on unmaintained trails. Listed below are some of the principal trails across the Mazatzal Wilderness.

DAY HIKE: BARNHARDT TRAIL
One-way length: 6.0 miles
Low and high elevations: 4,200 to 6,000 feet
Difficulty: moderate

To reach the Barnhardt Trailhead, drive 14.5 miles south from Payson on State Route 87 to Forest Route 419. Turn right (west) on Forest Route 419 for 4.7 miles to the trailhead. The Barnhardt Trail, one of the most heavily used, climbs steeply toward the vicinity of 7,904-foot Mazatzal Peak, the highest point in the wilderness. The Barnhardt Trail reaches a junction with the Mazatzal Divide Trail after 6.0 miles.

DAY HIKE: HALF MOON – ROCK CREEK TRAILS
One-way length: 6.7 miles
Low and high elevations: 4,000 to 4,300 feet
Difficulty: easy

One of the newer trails in the wilderness, the Half Moon Trail is also accessed from the Barnhardt Trailhead. Moving across the eastern foothills, this route stays fairly level as it travels north to intersect the Rock Creek Trail, which climbs west some 3,100 feet over its 3.7-mile length before reaching the Mazatzal Divide Trail near Hopi Spring. The Half Moon Trail is well-constructed and well-maintained, ideal for trail running. The Rock Creek Trail, on the other hand, is very steep and not recommended for equestrian use.

DAY HIKE: SADDLE RIDGE TRAIL
One-way length: 9.0 miles
Low and high elevations: 3,240 to 5,800 feet
Difficulty: moderate

The trailhead for this hike is located on Hardscrabble Mesa along Forest Route 194 (see directions on page 131). This trail passes through piñon-juniper forest and crosses the East Verde River near the LF ranch before reaching Forest Route 406. After crossing the river, you can connect with the 10-mile Bull Spring Trail, which travels west to intersect the Wet Bottom Trail near the Verde River. Another option is to turn left (east) on Forest Route 406 and walk 3.0 miles to the wilderness boundary where you may arrange to leave a shuttle.

LOOP HIKE: BARNHARDT – MAZATZAL DIVIDE – Y BAR BASIN TRAILS
One-way length: 17.0 miles
Low and high elevations: 4,200 to 7,180 feet
Difficulty: strenuous

This loop around Mazatzal Peak begins at the Barnhardt Trailhead (see directions for Barnhardt Trail). Take the Barnhardt Trail to its junction with the Mazatzal Divide Trail and turn left (south) for approximately 5.0 miles to the Y Bar Basin Trail. Return to the trailhead via the Y Bar Basin Trail. The scenic views along this route are quite good and there are a number of camp sites. Near its terminus at the Barnhardt Trailhead, the Y Bar Trail may be somewhat indistinct.

LOOP HIKE: DEER CREEK – SOUTH FORK TRAILS
One-way length: 16.0 miles
Low and high elevations: 3,400 to 6,040 feet
Difficulty: moderate

The Deer Creek Trailhead is about 17 miles south of Payson at the junction of State Routes 87 and 188. From the trailhead you travel southwest along the north fork of Deer Creek, a deep canyon bottom. The first few miles of trail are outside the wilderness boundary. The trail then crosses a small section of the southeast corner of the wilderness before reaching its terminus at Forest Route 201. Walk south on Forest Route 201 about 1.0 mile to the upper end of the South Fork Trail. Return to the trailhead by the 7.5-mile South Fork Trail, which travels along the south fork of Deer Creek. Both trails cover pleasant riparian habitats.

LOOP HIKE: DAVENPORT WASH – SHEEP CREEK – SEARS TRAILS
One-way length: 19.8 miles
Low and high elevations: 2,000 to 5,500 feet
Difficulty: strenuous

The loop described by these three trails explores the southwestern portion of the Mazatzal Wilderness, a rough, remote section of wilderness where the trails are not always well-defined. Accessing the trailhead for the beginning of this hike requires fording the Verde River, which may be impossible during periods of high water. Drive north from Cave Creek on the Tom Darlington Road (Forest Route 24) for about 10 miles to the Bartlett Road. Turn right (east) on the Bartlett Road for approximately 6.0 miles to Forest Route 205. Turn left (north) on Forest Route 205 for 7.7 miles to Forest Route 161. From this point, it is possible to cross the river, but remember you do so at your own risk. Once across the river, drive northeast on Forest Route 479 about 0.75 mile to Forest Route 474 and turn right for about 3.0 miles to the Davenport Trailhead. A four-wheel-drive vehicle is recommended.

The first leg of the hike is along the Davenport Wash Trail, which travels approximately 6.3 miles northeast to its junction with the Sheep Creek Trail. From the junction, turn right or south on the Sheep Creek Trail and hike about 5.0 miles to its intersection with the Sears Trail. The Sears Trail moves 7.0 miles east to return you to the trailhead.

A cursory scan of your topo maps will indicate other loop-hike possibilities beginning along Forest Route 474 in the remote southwestern corner of the wilderness. One such twenty-four-mile loop would involve the seven-mile Copper Camp Trail in combination with the Sheep Creek and Davenport Wash trails.

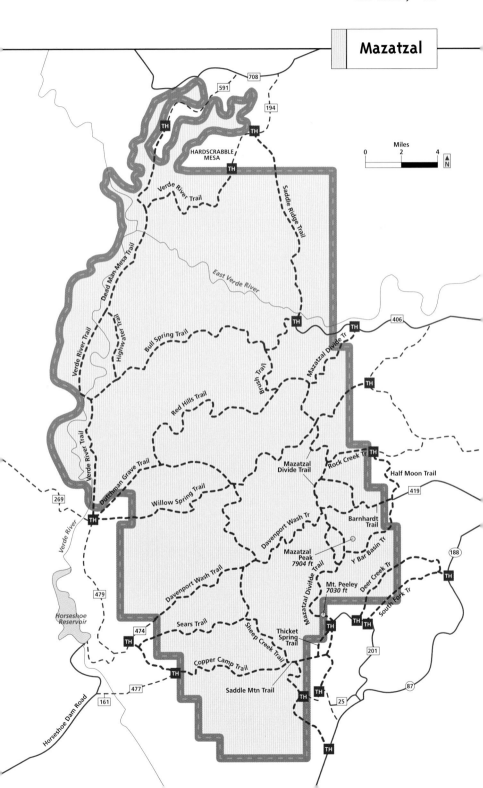

Mazatzal

LOOP HIKE: WILLOW SPRING – DUTCHMAN GRAVE TRAILS
One-way length: 20.0 miles
Low and high elevations: 2,080 to 4,040 feet
Difficulty: strenuous

To begin this loop in the west-central portion of the Mazatzal Wilderness, drive 35 miles northeast from the town of Carefree on the Cave Creek Road (Forest Route 24) to a T-junction with Forest Route 269. Turn right (east) on Forest Route 269 for about 12 miles to the Sheep Bridge Trailhead. Three trails—Willow Spring, Verde River, and Dutchman Grave—can be accessed from this trailhead.

From the trailhead, take the Willow Spring Trail east to its intersection with the upper end of the Dutchman Grave Trail near Mountain Spring, then turn left and return westward along the Dutchman Grave Trail to the Sheep Bridge area. Both trails can be steep in places and somewhat difficult to follow. The Willow Spring Trail is not recommended for horses.

A longer loop that could very well occupy a week is made possible by continuing east on the Willow Spring Trail to the Mazatzal Divide Trail, then north approximately 4.0 miles to the junction of the Mazatzal Divide and Red Hills trails. From this point you can return to the Sheep Bridge area via the Red Hills and Dutchman Grave trails.

SHUTTLE HIKE: MAZATZAL DIVIDE TRAIL
One-way length: 30.0 miles
Low and high elevations: 3,500 to 7,180 feet
Difficulty: moderate

The Mazatzal Divide Trail is the major north-south artery tracking through the eastern portion of the wilderness. It's northern terminus is at the City Creek Trailhead. To reach the trailhead from Payson, drive 11.0 miles west toward the East Verde River on Main Street (Forest Route 406) to a small parking area on the right (north) side of the road. Forest Route 406 is steep and poorly maintained. A four-wheel-drive vehicle is recommended for hauling a horse trailer. Cross to the south side of Forest Route 406 to reach the trailhead.

The Mazatzal Divide Trail is very well maintained and easy to follow. It's a popular trail, though, and gets plenty of use, so don't expect solitude. Along its length the Mazatzal Divide Trail is intersected by a half-dozen east-west trails, opening up the possibility for numerous side excursions or loop hikes of your own design.

The southern terminus of the trail is located along Pine Mountain Road (Forest Route 201), which travels north from State Route 87 about 46 miles north of Mesa near the Slate Creek Divide. Forest Route 201 may require a four-wheel-drive vehicle.

SHUTTLE HIKE: VERDE RIVER TRAIL
One-way length: 28.0 miles
Low and high elevations: 2,080 to 5,900 feet
Difficulty: strenuous

A low-elevation hike that is best set aside for cooler times of the year, the Verde River Trail takes off from the Sheep Bridge Trailhead and travels north along the Verde River, passing through the Mazatzal Wilderness portion of the Verde designated as "wild and scenic." River crossings at Red Creek and Pete's Mesa may be not only difficult to find but also risky. Don't attempt to cross at high-water levels.

To avoid river crossings at flood stage, leave the Verde River Trail at its junction with the Wet Bottom Trail, about 7.0 miles north of Sheep Bridge, and hike a short distance to the Highwater Trail. The 4.5-mile Highwater Trail will return you to the river above the two crossings.

The northern seven miles of the Verde River Trail are fairly easy to follow. As it nears the end, the trail climbs Hardscrabble Mesa and reaches Twin Buttes Road (Forest Route 194) and your shuttle vehicle. To reach this trailhead, take State Route 87 through Payson to Strawberry and turn left onto Forest Route 428 (south) at the Strawberry Lodge. Continue about 5.0 miles to Forest Route 427 and turn left about 0.5 mile to Forest Route 194. Turn right (south) and take Forest Route 194 for about 5.0 miles to the trailhead. A four-wheel-drive or high-clearance vehicle is recommended for these roads.

22 Mount Baldy Wilderness

East fork of the Little Colorado River

LOCATION:
30 miles southwest
of Springerville

SIZE: 7,079 acres

ELEVATION RANGE:
8,700 to 11,000 feet

MILES OF TRAILS: 14

HABITATS:
Boreal forest

ADMINISTRATION:
Apache-Sitgreaves
National Forest,
Springerville Ranger
District

TOPOGRAPHIC MAPS:
Mount Baldy

ALTHOUGH SMALL, the Mount Baldy Wilderness in the White Mountains is one of Arizona's most popular wilderness areas. Slopes heavily forested with corkbark fir, ponderosa pine, white fir, and Engelmann spruce, five miles of trout stream, lovely meadows, abundant wildlife, and a cool, wet climate make Mount Baldy a favorite Rim Country destination among outdoor lovers. So great is its popularity, in fact, that the Forest Service limits the size of hiking and equestrian groups to twelve and overnight camping groups to six.

The 11,403-foot summit of Mount Baldy itself is on the Fort Apache Indian Reservation just outside the wilderness area. Sacred to the White Mountain Apache Tribe for whom the summit is host to mountain spirits, the peak is closed to outsiders. Trespassers may have their equipment confiscated or be arrested and fined.

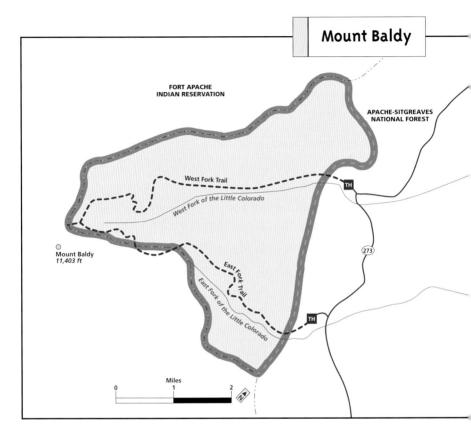

Elk are numerous in the wilderness along with black bear, deer, golden-mantled ground squirrel, mountain lion, blue grouse, gray jay, Audubon's warbler, redbreasted nuthatch, and wild turkey. In spring the meadows are carpeted with Rocky Mountain iris and wild orchids. Portions of both the east and west forks of the Little Colorado River, which pass through the wilderness, harbor gold-bellied brook trout.

Spring, summer, and fall hiking is the main recreational activity within the Mount Baldy Wilderness, but in winter cross-country skiers may want to try ski touring on the fairly easy grades of the West Fork Trail. Roads leading to the trailhead are usually plowed.

DAY HIKE: WEST FORK TRAIL
One-way length: 7.0 miles
Low and high elevations: 9,200 to 11,000 feet
Difficulty: easy

To reach the trailhead for the West Fork Trail, drive about 3.0 miles west from Edgar on State Route 260 to State Route 261. Turn south on State Route 261 for about 23 miles to State Route 273. Turn right about 7.2 miles to the Sheep Crossing Trailhead.

The West Fork Trail follows the West Fork of the Little Colorado, ascending gradually. A little more than halfway up, it moves away from the creek and switchbacks to the top of a ridge which it follows to the boundary marker of Fort Apache Indian Reservation. A sign usually marks the spot. This is the turn-around point.

Near the turn-around, the West Fork Trail joins the East Fork Trail, which moves toward the summit from the Phelps Cabin Trailhead, located on State Route 273 approximately 3.0 miles south of the Sheep Crossing Trailhead. You may define a loop by returning to State Route 273 via the East Fork Trail. A plan to connect the two trailheads via a connecting trail has not yet been implemented, so you will have hike back to your vehicle on the roadway or park a second vehicle at the Phelps Cabin Trailhead.

Both the West and East Fork Trails offer open meadows, deep forest, sparkling streams, spectacular cliffs, lichen-covered boulders, and stunted spruce trees.

Munds Mountain Wilderness 23

Snowstorm near Sedona

LOCATED IN THE HEART of Arizona's Red Rock Country, the Munds Mountain Wilderness offers mesa-top hiking with superb views of the beautiful Coconino and Supai sandstone spires, buttes, mesas, pinnacles, obelisks, and cliffs surrounding Sedona. Sagebrush and desert grasses dominate the lower elevations, giving way to scrub oak and manzanita farther upslope. The broad mesas are dominated by piñon-juniper and groves of Arizona cypress with ponderosa pine, Gambel oak, and a few aspen coming in at the highest elevations. In some of the wetter, north-facing canyons, Douglas fir can be found. Major drainages of the wilderness support riparian associations: Arizona walnut, willow, cottonwood, ash, and Arizona sycamore.

Birds in the Munds Mountain Wilderness include scrub jay, raven, white-throated swift, dark-eyed junco, and

LOCATION: One mile east of Sedona

SIZE: 18,150 acres

ELEVATION RANGE: 3,600 to 6,800 feet

MILES OF TRAILS: 18

HABITATS: Desert grassland, chaparral, piñon-juniper, oak woodland, ponderosa pine, riparian

ADMINISTRATION: Coconino National Forest, Sedona Ranger District

TOPOGRAPHIC MAPS: Munds Mountain

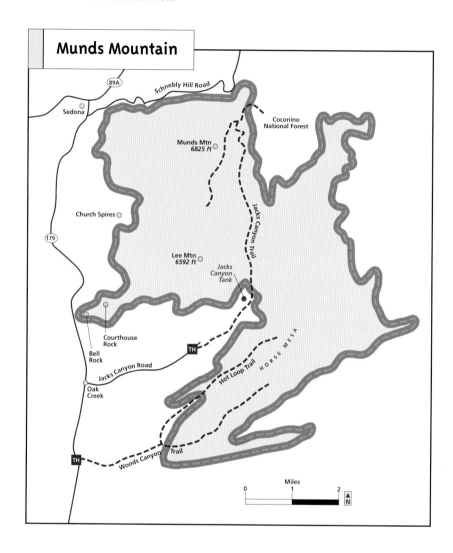

red-tailed hawk. Mountain lions thrive in the wilderness as do the lions' chief prey species, mule deer. Javelina, elk, coyote, fox, and bobcat are also present.

Although hiking, backpacking, and horseback riding are the primary recreational activities in the Munds Mountain Wilderness, rock climbing, bird watching, and even swimming are also possible. Splendid vistas in every direction make the wilderness a popular destination among photographers, amateur and professional alike.

The best seasons for recreation within the Munds Mountain Wilderness are spring and fall. Although overnight temperatures in winter often drop below freezing, sunny days make for pleasant hiking. In summer, daytime temperatures often exceed 100 degrees Fahrenheit.

DAY HIKE: WOODS CANYON TRAIL
One-way length: 4.0 miles
Low and high elevations: 4,000 to 4,500 feet
Difficulty: easy

To reach the trailhead for the Woods Canyon Trail, drive six miles south from Sedona on State Route 179 to the town of Oak Creek. Continue on State Route 179 approximately 1.5 miles south of Jacks Canyon Road to the Woods Canyon Trailhead on the east side of State Route 179.

Beginning outside the wilderness boundary, the trail travels for about 2.0 miles before reaching the junction of the Hot Loop Trail. The Munds Mountain Wilderness begins just beyond this point. The Woods Canyon Trail follows the canyon bottom for about 4.0 miles.

Adventurous hikers may extend the trip by boulder-hopping up the canyon for about another 10 miles and 2,000 feet in elevation to a point near Interstate 17. Except during extremely dry seasons, large pools form behind boulder-chokes and canyon narrows.

DAY HIKE: HOT LOOP TRAIL
One-way length: 6.0 miles
Low and high elevations: 4,000 to 6,000 feet
Difficulty: moderate

The Hot Loop Trail branches off the Woods Canyon Trail about two miles in from the trailhead. The Hot Loop climbs 2,000 feet to the top of Horse Mesa. Once atop the mesa, you can orienteer for miles cross-country on relatively flat terrain. Views into red rock country to the west are splendid from the mesa top.

DAY HIKE: JACKS CANYON TRAIL
One-way length: 6.0 miles
Low and high elevations: 4,000 to 6,825 feet
Difficulty: moderate

To reach the Jacks Canyon Trailhead, drive six miles south from Sedona on State Route 179 to the town of Oak Creek. At the Jacks Canyon Road intersection, turn left (east) and drive about 2.5 miles to the entrance to the Pine Valley subdivision. The trailhead begins at a parking area on the south side of the road.

The trail reaches the wilderness area at Jacks Canyon Tank, about 1.5 miles from the trailhead. After entering the wilderness, the trail continues up the canyon for 4.0 miles before climbing steeply to a saddle at the head of the canyon. A left turn (west) at the saddle will take you about 1.0 mile to the summit of Munds Mountain. A right turn (east) at the saddle follows a ridgeline out to the rim.

Red Rock – Secret Mountain Wilderness

Evening view through tall pine

LOCATION: One mile north of Sedona

SIZE: 43,950 acres

ELEVATION RANGE: 4,500 to 7,196 feet

MILES OF TRAILS: 58

HABITATS: Riparian, piñon-juniper, pine-fir forest

ADMINISTRATION: Coconino National Forest, Peaks and Sedona Ranger Districts

TOPOGRAPHIC MAPS: Loy Butte, Wilson Mountain, Munds Park, Sycamore Basin, Dutton Hill, Mountainaire

DRIVING SOUTH on State Route 89A from Flagstaff, you drop some 1,500 feet off the Mogollon Rim at the southern edge of the Colorado Plateau into an astonishing landscape of vermilion and buff-colored cliffs, mesas, and spires. This is the Red Rock-Secret Mountain Wilderness that sprawls in a northwesterly direction from the City of Sedona. It is among the most oft-visited regions in Arizona. Here, high elevation canyons drain into perennial Oak Creek and the Verde River, Arizona's only waterway with a Wild and Scenic River designation.

Riparian flora, including bigtooth maple, cotton-wood, willow, ash, box elder, and Arizona walnut dominate Oak Creek canyon and other streams in the wilderness. Oak, manzanita, banana yucca, and agave grow at mid-level elevations along with piñon pine and juniper. The ubiquitous ponderosa pine in association with Gambel oak covers the higher mesas and peaks. And pockets of aspen and Douglas fir are found in the cooler, wetter regions.

Elk, black bear, mule and white-tailed deer, mountain lion, javelina, skunk, fox, Abert squirrel, ringtail, badger, and bobcat are among the mammals living in the wilderness. Birds include the raven, red-tailed hawk, rufous-sided towhee, American robin, black phoebe, and hermit thrush. Trout thrive in Oak Creek.

Regional lore suggests that an old cabin encountered by hikers near the summit of Secret Mountain was either a hide-out for horse thieves or a haven for Mormon polygamists during the 1880s. Also of historical note are Indian artifacts, such as the ruins of twelfth-century Sinagua cliff dwellings and the petroglyphs and pictographs found throughout the wilderness.

A good number of trails penetrate the Red Rock-Secret Mountain Wilderness —the shortest less than one mile long, the longest eight miles. Low elevation trails are best avoided during the summer months when temperatures can hit 100 degrees Fahrenheit. Snow and cold in the upper reaches may hinder winter hiking.

> **DAY HIKE: A.B. YOUNG TRAIL**
> **(also known as EAST POCKET TRAIL)**
> One-way length: 2.2 miles
> Low and high elevations: 5,200 to 7,200 feet
> Difficulty: moderate

To reach the trailhead, drive nine miles north of Sedona on State Route 89A to the Bootlegger Campground. To avoid paying a campground fee, park in one of the highway pullouts. Walk through the campground, boulder-hop across Oak Creek, and turn south on a trail that parallels the creek. Watch for a sign that marks the beginning of the A.B. Young Trail.

Gaining elevation quickly, the trail moves out of the pines and other dense riparian vegetation into low-growing manzanita, mountain mahogany, and scrub oak. The trail then becomes a series of switchbacks, winding up the rugged face of the canyon. The splendors of Oak Creek Canyon open up north and south.

White rooftops of posh resort hotels sparkle in the warm sunlight, and a few miles down canyon, the green orchards and lawns of Slide Rock State Park contrast sharply with many-hued sandstone buttes, pinnacles, and cliffs.

It's an old trail, the A.B. Young, going back to settlement days in the late nineteenth century. Back then it was used to move livestock up to summer pasture on the rim. In the 1930s, the trail was improved by Civilian Conservation Corps crews. Today, it's in excellent shape, smooth and gently graded, a bit cobbly only where it crosses rock-slide debris.

Once on top of the mesa, the trail moves along the rim through ponderosa pine. Where the trail becomes indistinct, blaze marks and rock cairns mark its passage. After a short distance, the trail moves west to the East Pocket Lookout, one of few remaining wooden fire-lookout towers in Arizona. Before climbing the tower, call to the person staffing it and ask permission. Up top there are wonderful views of the Mogollon Rim and Oak Creek Canyon.

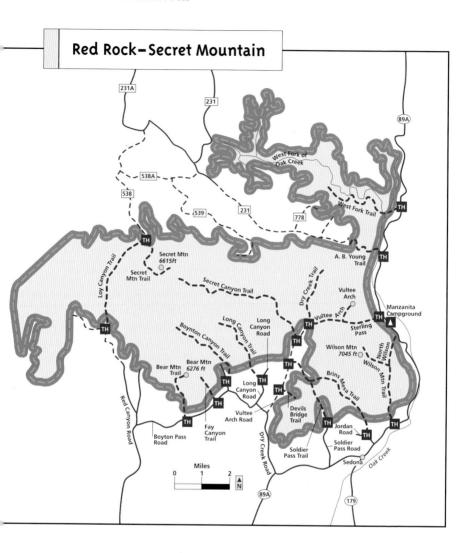

Red Rock–Secret Mountain

DAY HIKE: WEST FORK TRAIL
One-way length: 3.0 miles
Low and high elevations: 5,300 to 5,600 feet
Difficulty: easy

To reach the trailhead for this relaxing hike up the West Fork of beautiful Oak Creek Canyon, drive 11 miles north from Sedona on State Route 89A to the parking area. The marked trailhead is at the west end of the parking lot.

Leaving the parking area, the trail crosses Oak Creek and parallels the stream for a very short distance before turning up into the West Fork of Oak Creek. A trail sign and Forest Service registry are located at this point.

The canyon bottom is cool and shaded by tall pines and fir trees. Soaring sandstone cliffs are in view to the south. Often crossing the creek, the West Fork Trail meanders up the canyon for slightly more than three miles. By traveling up-canyon beyond the end of the trail, adventurous hikers can extend the hike by approximately ten miles to Forest Route 231. It's a bushwhack, though, requiring a lot of boulder hopping and swimming across deep pools. Be careful during rainy seasons, when the danger of flash-flooding is significant.

Don't expect solitude. The West Fork Trail is very popular and, especially on weekends, can be quite crowded. No camping is allowed in the lower portions of the West Fork.

> ### DAY HIKE: LOY CANYON TRAIL
> One-way length: 8.0 miles
> Low and high elevations: 4,700 to 6,400 feet
> Difficulty: moderate

Secret Mountain is the destination for this hike, the longest among the many hikes in the wilderness. To reach the trailhead, drive about 10 miles west from Sedona on State Route 89A to Red Canyon Road (Forest Route 525). Turn right (north) for 10 miles to the trailhead.

The trail travels up Loy Canyon, a normally dry creek, for about five miles before climbing more than 1,500 feet to reach a saddle that connects Secret Mountain and the Mogollon Rim. Less than a mile in, the trail passes an alcove on the left side containing several small Sinagua cliff dwellings. In the lower elevations the vegetation is an interesting mix of scrub oak, Arizona cypress, prickly pear cactus, and yucca, giving way to alligator juniper, ponderosa pine, Gambel oak, and fir.

From the saddle, the trail climbs a short distance to the summit of Secret Mountain. At this point you have hiked about five miles. You can add distance by hiking cross-country on the broad, flat mountaintop to several viewpoints. What's left of Secret Cabin sits in a ponderosa grove near a small spring.

The summit here was dubbed Secret Mountain because its location is half-hidden between the heads of Secret Canyon and Loy Canyon. Loy Canyon was named for an 1870s homesteader, Samuel Loy.

> ### DAY HIKE: BOYNTON CANYON TRAIL
> One-way length: 2.5 miles
> Low and high elevations: 4,500 to 5,100 feet
> Difficulty: easy

To reach the trailhead for one of the most popular hikes in the Sedona area, drive west on State Route 89A to Dry Creek Road (Forest Route 152C). Turn north for 2.8 miles to the junction of Dry Creek and Long Canyon Roads. Stay left, continuing on Dry Creek Road for 1.6 miles to Boynton Canyon Road. Turn right (north) a short distance to the trailhead.

For the first mile, the trail travels past a large resort with lawns, tennis courts, fancy buildings—the works—and you may wonder what kind of wilderness experience you're about to have. But after skirting the resort, the trail drops down into Boynton Canyon, heading northwest. The towering red sandstone walls of the canyon close around you as you move up canyon. Finally, the trail moves into and through a pine-fir forest to a viewpoint and a close-up look at Bear Mountain.

DAY HIKE: LONG CANYON TRAIL
One-way length: 2.0 miles
Low and high elevations: 4,600 to 4,900 feet
Difficulty: easy

To reach the trailhead, follow the directions for the above-described Boynton Canyon Trail, but when you reach the junction of Dry Creek and Long Canyon roads, turn right (north) onto Long Canyon Road (Forest Route 152D) and drive one mile to the trailhead.

The trail starts up an old jeep road passing through piñon-juniper woodland outside the wilderness boundary. After about a mile, it enters Long Canyon. After another mile, the canyon narrows and the trail becomes indistinct. You can turn around at this point or take one of several unmarked spur trails that head toward the white cliffs marking the bases of Secret Mountain and Maroon Mountain.

DAY HIKE: BRINS MESA TRAIL
One-way length: 3.0 miles
Low and high elevations: 4,600 to 5,500 feet
Difficulty: easy

You don't have to go far from downtown Sedona to reach the Brins Mesa Trail. Take Jordan Road north from State Route 89A for about one mile to the marked trailhead. An easy introduction to the wilderness, this route climbs atop Brins Mesa and ends at another trailhead just outside the wilderness on Vultee Arch Road. Another route, the Soldier Pass Trail, joins the Brins Mesa Trail about 1.5 miles in. This trail begins outside the wilderness at the end of Soldier Pass Road in Sedona, and travels for just two miles over its entire length.

DAY HIKE: SECRET CANYON TRAIL
One-way length: 4.0 miles
Low and high elevations: 4,700 to 5,100 feet
Difficulty: moderate

To reach the trailhead, drive a few miles west from downtown Sedona on State Route 89A to Dry Creek Road (Forest Route152C). Turn right (north) and drive 2.0 miles to Vultee Arch Road (Forest Route152). Turn right (northeast) on Vultee Arch Road and drive 3.2 miles to the Secret Canyon Trailhead. If the parking area is full, drive to the end of the road, park, and walk approximately 1.0 mile back to the trailhead.

Starting out as a jeep road for the first couple of miles, the Secret Canyon Trail crosses Dry Creek and enters the wilderness a short distance from the parking area. Crossing the usually waterless lower Dry Creek many times, the trail moves through stands of Arizona cypress and piñon-juniper. After becoming a footpath, the route moves up to the north side of the canyon for a short distance and then back to the streambed. At this point, the narrowing canyon usually contains water. Gradually, about four miles in, the trail becomes faint. You can turn around at this point or camp among the ponderosa pines that now grow in the uplands at streamside.

SHUTTLE HIKE: STERLING PASS – VULTEE ARCH – DRY CREEK TRAILS
One-way length: 8.1 miles
Low and high elevations: 4,800 to 6,600 feet
Difficulty: moderate

To reach the Sterling Pass Trailhead, drive about six miles north from Sedona on State Route 89A to the Manzanita Campground. Park in one of the pullouts along the roadway and locate the trailhead just north of the campground. The Sterling Trail climbs away from the highway through stands of ponderosa pine. Then, ascending a series of short, steep switchbacks—climbing 1,200 feet in less than one mile—it reaches a short saddle between Wilson Mountain and the Mogollon Rim.

The Sterling Pass Trail then connects with the Vultee Arch Trail and a short spur heading north a short distance to Vultee Arch, named for Gerard Vultee, the president of Vultee Aircraft, who died in a plane crash near here.

Backtrack on the spur trail to the main Vultee Arch Trail and hike west to the trailhead at the end of Vultee Arch Road. The Dry Creek Trail begins here, heading north along Dry Creek Canyon for two miles where it ends. Return to the trailhead and a second vehicle at the end of Vultee Arch Road.

25 Salome Wilderness

Sunset above Workman Creek Canyon

LOCATION: 40 miles northwest of Globe

SIZE: 18,530 acres

ELEVATION RANGE: 2,500 to 6,543 feet

MILES OF TRAILS: 12

HABITATS: Riparian, semi-desert grassland, chaparral, pine-fir

ADMINISTRATION: Tonto National Forest, Pleasant Valley Ranger District

TOPOGRAPHIC MAPS: Copper Mountain, Windy Hill, Armer Mountain, McFadden Peak, Greenback Creek

SORT OF SANDWICHED BETWEEN other better-known Rim-Country wildlands, somewhat isolated, and therefore less frequently visited, the Salome Wilderness offers backcountry venturers a chance for real solitude. Salome Creek, which runs the entire east-west length of the wilderness and is a year-round stream in its upper reaches, and Workman Creek, another perennial stream, contain deep pools except during periods of prolonged drought.

The wilderness name is interesting. Spanish-speaking settlers named the creek for the biblical Salome, daughter of Herodias, who was rewarded with the head of John the Baptist after a dance performance. Later, American settlers corrupted the name to "Sally May," supposedly after two daughters of an 1880s pioneer, and an apocryphal legend grew around that contention. When the Tonto National Forest was mapped in 1927, "Salome" was restored.

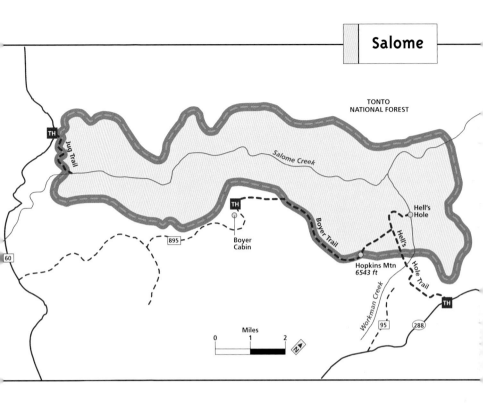

Between A.D. 1200 and 1300, Salome Canyon was inhabited by Salado Indians, the remains of whose dwellings are scattered throughout the wilderness. These areas are protected by Federal law, and, although hikers are allowed to explore them, nothing should be disturbed or removed.

The vegetative communities along Salome and Workman Creeks include bigtooth maple, alder, ash, Arizona sycamore, and box elder, among others. Typical of the upland communities in the lower elevations are saguaro cactus, triangle-leaf bursage, cholla, prickly pear, mesquite, and other desert plants. The succession of plant life as you move higher follows a familiar pattern: scrub oak and piñon-juniper giving way to scattered stands of ponderosa pine and Douglas fir in the higher elevations.

Both Salome and Workman creeks support brown and rainbow trout. Wilderness mammals include badger, ringtail, pocket mouse, striped skunk, white-tailed and mule deer, bobcat, and coyote. Black phoebe, belted kingfisher, phainopepla, cactus wren, wild turkey, broad-billed hummingbird, and American kestrel are among the many birds inhabiting the wilderness.

November through March are the best months to visit the Salome Wilderness. In the lower elevations temperatures routinely top 100 degrees Fahrenheit in summer, and snow may hinder hiking during the winter months. Use caution near creeks during periods of heavy spring snowmelt.

DAY HIKE: HELL'S HOLE TRAIL
One-way length: 5.3 miles
Low and high elevations: 3,920 to 5,480 feet
Difficulty: strenuous

To reach the trailhead from Claypool, drive north for approximately 15 miles on State Route 88 to its junction with State Route 288. Continue north on State Route 288 for about 27 miles to the trailhead located at the Reynolds Creek Group Camp Site.

From the trailhead, the Hell's Hole Trail climbs to a pass between Jack Mountain and a nameless peak to the north before dropping into the Workman drainage. Crossing the creek, it then climbs more than 600 feet. After skirting a knoll, the trail descends very steeply for about 0.5 mile into Hell's Hole. Along the way the route passes through pine forest, chaparral, and a riparian zone.

About 1.0 mile from the Reynolds Trailhead, the trail passes private property. Respect the rights of the property owner; do not trespass.

DAY HIKE: BOYER TRAIL
One-way length: 5.0 miles
Low and high elevations: 4,080 to 5,600 feet
Difficulty: moderate

Reaching the Boyer Trail trailhead requires a four-wheel-drive vehicle. Drive north 15 miles from Claypool on State Route 288 to its junction with State Route 288. Continue north on State Route 288 for 13 miles to A Cross Road (Forest Route 60). Drive west on Forest Route 60 for 9 miles to Forest Route 895 and turn north. Follow Forest Route 895 for 12 miles to Boyer Cabin.

Beginning outside the wilderness boundary, the Boyer Trail parallels Boyer Creek, climbing steadily through semi-desert grassland and chaparral. After topping out, it follows the ridge above Salome Creek before connecting with the Hell's Hole Trail at its terminus. In places the trail is somewhat overgrown and difficult to follow.

For hikers who do not possess a four-wheel-drive vehicle, the Boyer Trail may also be accessed from the north via the Hell's Hole Trail.

DAY HIKE: JUG TRAIL
One-way length: 2.0 miles
Low and high elevations: 4,080 to 5,600 feet
Difficulty: moderate

To reach the A Cross Trailhead for the Jug Trail, drive 15 miles north from Claypool on State Route 88 to its junction with State Route 288. Continue north on State Route 288 for about 12 miles to the A Cross Road (Forest Route 60). Turn west on Forest Route 60 for 17 miles to the trailhead on the north side of the road.

An old jeep road, the Jug Trail follows ridges along the southern boundary of the wilderness south of Salome Mountain, descending gradually to Salome Creek where it ends.

Salt River Canyon Wilderness 26

Afternoon view upstream from Roosevelt Lake

ESTABLISHED IN 1984, the Salt River Canyon Wilderness, a rare Sonoran Desert riparian zone, has it all: a beautiful steep-walled canyon containing thirty-two miles of wild river; spectacular geological formations ranging from the salt banks that give the river its name to black and white granite, sandstone, and quartzite; twenty-seven white-water rapids; numerous side creeks to explore; cliff dwellings; river otter and beaver; eagle, hawk, and osprey; and great botanical diversity.

Although wilderness access is permitted via primitive four-wheel-drive roads at Gleason Flat and Horseshoe Bend, there are no developed hiking trails within the entire wilderness. River

LOCATION: River access at Salt River Gorge Bridge approximately 30 miles north of Globe on U.S. Highway 60

SIZE: 32,100 acres

ELEVATION RANGE: 2,200 to 4,200 feet

MILES OF TRAILS: No marked or maintained trails

HABITATS: Riparian, oak woodland, piñon-juniper, Lower Sonoran

ADMINISTRATION: Tonto National Forest, Globe Ranger District

TOPOGRAPHIC MAPS: Salt River Peak, Medlee Wash, Dagger Peak, Haystack Butte, Rockinstraw Mountain

travel by raft or kayak during the short late winter to early spring river-running season is the only way to truly see the wilderness area. Dropping 1,234 feet along its 52-mile length, the river features a series of splendid rapids, such as Ledges, Rat Trap, Maytag, Bump and Grind, Eye of the Needle, Reform, and Black Rock. In the summer of 1994, the Salt's wild character was forever altered when frustrated boating guides, weary of the difficult portage required, dynamited Quartzite Falls, the river's only Class 6 rapids. Although still in the Class 3 to Class 4 category, Quartzite Falls can be run by most river craft.

Numerous primitive camp sites, some located at the mouths of tributary creeks flowing down from the Mogollon Rim, are located along the river.

Commercial rafting companies offer three- and five-day raft adventures through the wilderness. Private trips are also allowed. Between March 1 and May 15, river-runners must obtain permits from the Forest Service to travel through the wilderness portion of the Salt River. Applications for permits are accepted by the Forest Service between December 1 and January 31. For river access from the bridge over the gorge at U.S. Highway 60 down to the beginning of the wilderness at Gleason Flat, permits are also required from the Fort Apache Indian Reservation.

Even at flow rates of 1,000 cubic feet per second and below, the Upper Salt River features many rapids in the Class 3 and Class 4 range. At high water, floating the river can be quite risky and should be attempted only by experienced river runners.

The Forest Service enforces low-impact camping practices throughout the wilderness area. Rafting parties are limited to fifteen persons; all garbage, including human feces and fire ash, must be removed from the wilderness; and fires are allowed only in fire pans. Violators may be fined.

Although the Salt River Wilderness may be visited at any time of the year, it is best avoided during the hottest months from late May through September. Running the river during the July through August summer rainy season, when flash flooding occurs, can be especially risky.

For permit information, contact the Globe Ranger District, Route 1, Box 33, Globe, AZ 85501. Telephone: (520) 425-7189. For Indian reservation permit information, contact White Mountain Game and Fish Department, P.O. Box 220, White River, AZ 85941. Telephone: (520) 338-4385.

For commercial raft adventures, contact Far Flung Adventures, P.O. Box 2804, Globe, AZ 85502. Telephone 1-800-231-7238.

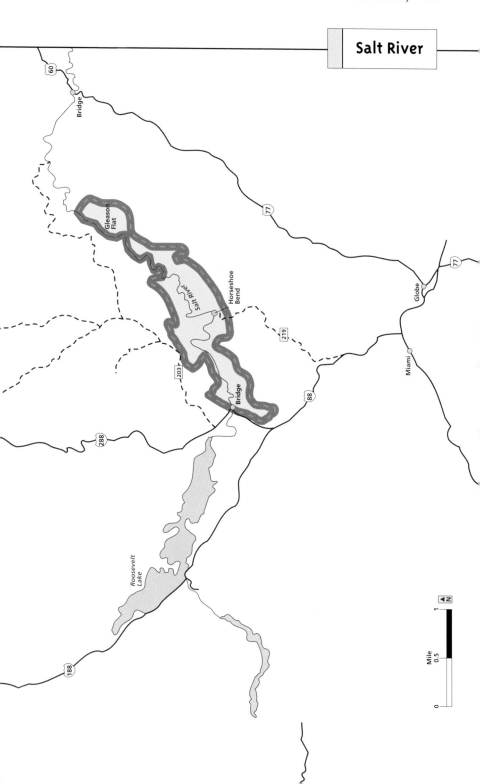

Salt River

27 Sierra Ancha Wilderness

Deeply cut and eroded cliffs

LOCATION: 45 miles northwest of Globe

SIZE: 20,850 acres

ELEVATION RANGE: 4,000 to 7,400 feet

MILES OF TRAILS: 57

HABITATS: Desert scrub, grassland, piñon-juniper, ponderosa pine

ADMINISTRATION: Tonto National Forest, Pleasant Valley Ranger District

TOPOGRAPHIC MAPS: Aztec Peak, McFadden Peak, Meddler Wash, Sombrero Peak

THE HISTORY OF PROTECTION for the Sierra Ancha Wilderness goes back sixty-five years. Established as a 34,000-acre Primitive Area in 1933, the Sierra Ancha was reduced in size and renamed a Wild Area in 1951. In 1964 nearly 21,000 of its acres were set aside as wilderness. For a rather small wilderness area, the Sierra Ancha offers an impressive number of short hiking trails.

In Spanish, Sierra Ancha means "wide mountains," the origin of which is unknown. During the erection of Roosevelt Dam on the Salt River between 1906 and 1911, the Bureau of Reclamation operated a sawmill in the Sierra Ancha to cut timber for the dam's construction.

With steep box canyons and high cliffs, the Sierra Ancha is rough, often inaccessible country. The terrain protects a number of cliff dwellings erected between A.D. 1200 and 1300 by a paleo-Indian culture called the Salado. Indian ruins and artifacts are protected; it is illegal to disturb them. In the 1950s, the Sierra Ancha was thought to contain commercially valuable uranium, and fortune seekers swarmed over what is now wilderness, building roads as they prospected. Now closed, most of these roads are reverting to a natural state.

Vegetation in the higher elevations of the wilderness consists of good stands of ponderosa pine with pockets of mixed conifer. A rare flowering perennial, the threatened Chiricahua dock, is also found at a few sites in the upper Sierra Ancha. Descending the slopes, the parade of plants includes turbinella oak, manzanita, mountain mahogany, and piñon-juniper. Desert scrub and semi-desert grassland dominate the lower reaches.

Mammals common to a desert environment inhabit the lower elevations. These include gray fox, rock squirrel, kangaroo rat, wood rat, javelina, and coyote. Mule deer, mountain lion, bobcat, elk, ringtail, and black bear also inhabit the Sierra Ancha. Birds of the wilderness include cactus wren, red-tailed hawk, wild turkey, canyon wren, phainopepla, black phoebe, pygmy nuthatch, various hummingbirds, and others.

As a general rule, the best time to hike the upper reaches of the Sierra Ancha Wilderness is summer. Spring and fall are good seasons for all-around explorations and winter is the best time to visit the lowlands. Water, which should be treated before drinking, is available at a few springs and, seasonally, in streambed pools.

DAY HIKE: McFADDEN HORSE TRAIL
One-way length: 3.3 miles
Low and high elevations: 6,200 to 7,400 feet
Difficulty: moderate

This is a lightly used trail in the northern portion of the wilderness. To reach the trailhead, drive 15 miles northwest from Claypool (between Miami and Globe) on State Route 88 to State Route 288. Turn right and drive north on State Route 288 for about 29 miles. Watch closely. The trailhead is obscure and easy to miss.

From the trailhead, the McFadden Horse Trail climbs very steeply to a dead end on pine-covered McFadden Horse Mountain. The views from the top are excellent, making the exertion worthwhile.

DAY HIKE: LUCKY STRIKE TRAIL
One-way length: 5.0 miles
Low and high elevations: 4,000 to 6,800 feet
Difficulty: moderate

To reach the upper end of the Lucky Strike Trail at the Billy Lawrence Trailhead, drive 15 miles north from Claypool (between Miami and Globe) on State Route 88 to State Route 288. Turn right on State Route 288 and drive north about 27.5 miles (just past Reynolds Creek). Turn right (east) onto Forest Route 410 and drive about

2.5 miles to Forest Route 235. Turn left (northeast) onto Forest Route 235 for about 2.5 miles to the trailhead. A high-clearance two-wheel-drive or four-wheel-drive vehicle is required for the last 2.5 miles.

This easy-to-follow route on an old jeep road travels through areas of mining activity as it descends 2,800 feet to Cherry Creek Road. At roughly its midpoint, it joins with the southern terminus of the five-mile Grapevine Trail, which travels a steady grade north along an old jeep road to a trailhead on Forest Route 203.

DAY HIKE: CENTER MOUNTAIN TRAIL
One-way length: 2.5 miles
Low and high elevations: 6,700 to 7,500 feet
Difficulty: easy

The route also starts at the Billy Lawrence Trailhead (see directions on page 151). A good summertime hike, the Center Mountain Trail climbs some 800 feet among stands of cool ponderosa pine. Some good viewpoints await at trail's end on top of Center Mountain itself.

DAY HIKE: REYNOLDS CREEK TRAIL
One-way length: 3.7 miles
Low and high elevations: 6,200 to 7,600 feet
Difficulty: moderate

To reach the Reynolds Creek Trailhead, drive 15 miles north from Claypool on State Route 88 to State Route 288. Turn right on State Route 288 and drive about 27.5 miles north (just past Reynolds Creek) to Forest Route 410. Turn east (right) on Forest Route 410 and drive about 4.0 miles to the trailhead. A four-wheel-drive vehicle is recommended.

Climbing 1,400 feet in all, the Reynolds Creek Trail ascends "The Switchbacks" and traverses scenic Knoles Hole before leaving the wilderness to arrive at the private Murphy Ranch. Some early sections of the trail are brushy and somewhat indistinct. As it leaves the wilderness, the trail travels along an old logging road.

DAY HIKE: RIM TRAIL
One-way length: 7.6 miles
Low and high elevations: 6,300 to 6,800 feet
Difficulty: easy

The Rim Trail, along with the Parker Creek Trail and the Coon Creek Trail, is accessed from the Carr Trailhead in the vicinity of Aztec Peak, where a fire lookout is located just outside the wilderness area. To reach the Carr Trailhead, drive 15 miles north from Claypool on State Route 88 to State Route 288. Turn right

Sierra Ancha

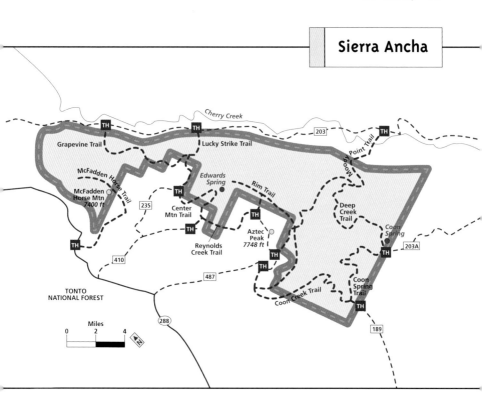

on State Route 288 and drive about 25.5 miles north to Forest Route 484. Turn right (east) on Forest Route 487 and drive 5.5 miles to the trailhead on the right side of the road. Forest Route 487 requires a high-clearance two-wheel-drive or four-wheel-drive vehicle. Between December 15 and March 30, Forest Route 487 is closed for the winter.

From the trailhead, hike a short distance on the Parker Creek Trail to the beginning of the Rim Trail. Climbing only 500 feet in all, the Rim Trail travels through nice stands of ponderosa pine to reach a dead end at Edwards Spring. The views along the way are excellent.

> **DAY HIKE: COON CREEK TRAIL**
> One-way length: 4.4 miles
> Low and high elevations: 4,700 to 7,100 feet
> Difficulty: moderate

The Coon Creek Trail also starts at the Carr Trailhead (see opposite). Descending nearly 2,500 feet over its length, this route drops from the rim through mixed conifer and into chaparral. For much of the way, it parallels Coon Creek and may be washed out in places.

DAY HIKE: MOODY POINT TRAIL
One-way length: 8.6 miles
Low and high elevations: 3,000 to 7,200 feet
Difficulty: strenuous

To reach the trailhead, drive 1.0 mile past the Carr Trailhead (see previous Rim Trail description) on Forest Route 487 to the Moody Point Trailhead on the right side of the road.

The longest and most difficult trail in the Sierra Ancha Wilderness, the Moody Point Trail descends 4,200 feet as it moves west to east across the wilderness. Lightly traveled, the trail may be somewhat difficult to follow in places. Following periods of heavy rainfall, crossing Cherry Creek may be risky. The rewards of this hike are solitude and truly wonderful scenery.

DAY HIKE: COON SPRING TRAIL
One-way length: 4.0 miles
Low and high elevations: 4,400 to 5,100 feet
Difficulty: easy

To reach the Oak Creek Trailhead (for both the Coon Spring Trail and lower Coon Creek Trail), drive 15 miles north from Claypool on State Route 88 to State Route 288. Turn right onto State Route 288 and drive 15 miles north to the junction of Forest Route 189. Turn right (east) on Forest Route 189 and drive five miles to the trailhead. A high-clearance two-wheel-drive or four-wheel-drive vehicle is recommended.

The Coon Spring Trail drops into lower Coon Creek Canyon where it passes through a riparian zone and a very nice grove of Arizona cypress trees. As it approaches its terminus at Deep Creek Trail (see below), the trail arrives at Coon Spring.

DAY HIKE: DEEP CREEK TRAIL
One-way length: 5.0 miles
Low and high elevations: 5,000 to 5,500 feet
Difficulty: easy

The Deep Creek Trail is accessed from the Bull Canyon Trailhead, which can be reached by driving 15 miles north from Claypool on State Route 88 to State Route 288. Turn right on State Route 288 and drive about 6.6 miles north to Cherry Creek Road (Forest Route 203). Turn right (east) on Forest Route 203 for 9.0 miles to Forest Route 203A. Follow Forest Route 203A for approximately 6.5 miles to the trailhead. A high-clearance two-wheel-drive or four-wheel-drive is recommended.

Following an old road for most of its length, the Deep Creek Trail travels through chaparral and grassland to its terminus at the junction of Moody Point Trail. Along the way, it affords good views of the bluffs of the Sierra Anchas.

Sycamore Canyon Wilderness 28

Evening color near Sycamore Pass

ONLY A SHORT POWER-LINE CORRIDOR separates the Sycamore Canyon Wilderness from the Red Rock-Secret Mountain Wilderness to the east. Otherwise, these two adjoining backcountry areas make up nearly 100,000 acres of red sandstone, brown lava, and white limestone wildlands. Although both wilderness areas boast impressive red-rock promontories and deep canyons, there is one big difference between them: close to Sedona, the Red Rock-Secret Mountain Wilderness is very popular and frequently visited, while the more out-of-the-way Sycamore Canyon Wilderness is relatively unknown and seldom visited.

Established in 1935, the defining feature of the Sycamore Canyon Wilderness is the canyon itself, which cuts through the Mogollon Rim and winds for more than twenty miles along Sycamore Creek. Uncommonly broad, Sycamore

LOCATION: 23 miles west of Sedona

SIZE: 55,937 acres

ELEVATION RANGE: 3,600 to 6,500 feet

MILES OF TRAILS: 44

HABITATS: Riparian, piñon-juniper, ponderosa pine

ADMINISTRATION: Coconino, Kaibab, and Prescott National Forests

TOPOGRAPHIC MAPS: Bill Williams Mountain SE, Clarkdale, Loy Butte, Sycamore Basin, Sycamore Point

Canyon spans seven miles rim-to-rim at its widest point. The 1984 Arizona Wilderness Act added 9,000 acres to the wilderness.

There are dozens of place names in Arizona containing the word sycamore, and when you find these places you also find their name sake tree—the ghostly, pale-barked Arizona sycamore. Sycamores grow, of course, along the riparian corridors of the Sycamore Canyon Wilderness along with cottonwood, willow, hackberry, desert honeysuckle, and somota. But the dominant vegetative habitat in the wilderness is piñon-juniper in association with banana yucca and century plant. Ponderosa pine and Gambel oak come in higher up, and in cool, wet niche habitats, a few Douglas fir. At the lowest elevations there are thickets of scrub oak and manzanita.

Wildlife in the Sycamore Canyon Wilderness consists of numerous raptors, including the golden eagle. Mountain lion, bobcat, mule deer, javelina, Common Raven, ringtail, black bear, badger, and gray fox are also at home in the wilderness. Songbirds include the signature bird of canyon country—the canyon wren—along with black-throated sparrow, white-crowned sparrow, Bewick's wren, and Western kingbird.

It's best to avoid the extreme heat of mid-summer in the Sycamore Canyon Wilderness. Winters are usually ideal for extended hikes, but snow and very cold temperatures are possible. The ideal times are late fall and early spring.

> **DAY HIKE: PARSONS TRAIL**
> One-way length: 3.7 miles
> Low and high elevations: 3,600 to 4,000 feet
> Difficulty: easy

To reach the trailhead from the Tuzigoot National Monument near Clarkdale, drive 10.6 miles north from the monument on Forest Route 131. Summers and Parsons springs, in the extreme southern portion of the wilderness, discharge approximately 5,000 gallons of water per minute into Sycamore Creek to turn about three miles of an otherwise dry creek into a perennial stream. The Parsons Trail travels through this beautiful riparian habitat. Needless to say, this is one of the more popular areas in the wilderness—so popular, in fact, that camping is forbidden downstream from Parsons Spring.

> **DAY HIKE: SYCAMORE TRAIL**
> One-way length: 5.0 miles
> Low and high elevations: 4,800 to 5,000 feet
> Difficulty: easy

The trailhead can be reached by way of the five-mile Packard Mesa Trail which begins outside the wilderness at the end of Forest Route 131 (see Parsons Trail above), or by driving east to the end of Forest Route 181, which branches off the Perkinsville Road (Forest Route 354) a few miles north of Perkinsville. While the latter route to the trailhead takes five miles off your hiking distance, it is remote and somewhat difficult to find. Be sure to check your topo maps carefully.

Within its first few miles, the Sycamore Trail encounters two other trails heading northwest. Both are somewhat difficult to follow. The first is the 5.5-mile Yew Thicket Trail. About one mile farther along is the 4.2-mile Cedar Creek Trail.

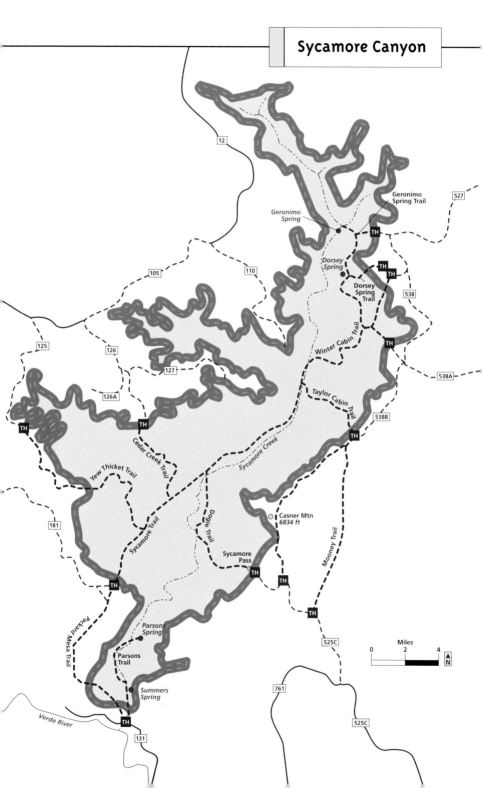

Sycamore Canyon

About 2.0 miles from the lower end of the Cedar Creek Trail, the Sycamore Trail meets the five-mile Dogie Trail which starts at Sycamore Pass to the east. Sycamore Creek, usually dry, is at the junction of these two trails.

This is the turnaround point, although hikers may extend their distance by hiking portions of the aforementioned Yew Thicket and Cedar Creek trails, or by continuing another 5.0 miles upstream to the Winter Cabin and Taylor Cabin trails (see loop hike below).

LOOP HIKE: SYCAMORE CANYON – CASNER MOUNTAIN
One-way length: 19.0 miles
Low and high elevations: 4,300 to 6,400 feet
Difficulty: moderate

This route begins at the Dogie Trail, which can be reached by driving about nine miles northeast from Cottonwood on U.S. Highway 89A to Forest Route 525 (Red Canyon Road). Turn left (north) and drive about 2.6 miles to a left fork at Forest Route 525C. Continue approximately 10 miles on Forest Route 525C to its end at Sycamore Pass.

Geologically, this hike is a mini-Grand Canyon experience, as you encounter some of the same rock as in the big canyon—Kaibab limestone, Toroweap formation, Supai formation, and Redwall limestone.

From Sycamore Pass, the Dogie Trail descends 5.0 miles to Sycamore Creek where it joins the Sycamore Trail. Moving north from this point, the Sycamore Trail arrives at Taylor Cabin after about 3.0 miles.

A National Historic Site, Taylor Cabin, named for John and Ben Taylor, was probably finished in 1931 when four ranchers pooled their resources to hire stonemasons to build it. The cabin's stone chimney leans against a sandstone cliff, which actually forms the back wall. The structure was used as a cowboy line shack when cattle were brought into the canyon for winter range. The brands of the four ranches that used the cabin, along with the names of stonemasons, Despain and Porter, are carved into the cabin's front wall. Tinajas in the creek bed near the cabin may contain seasonal water.

Continue upstream from the cabin for 2.0 miles to a fork. The left branch is the Winter Cabin Trail which continues upstream before climbing east out of the canyon to the Mogollon Rim at the end of Forest Route 538A. Take the right fork, the Taylor Cabin Trail, which climbs nearly 2,000 feet in just 2.0 miles to reach Buck Ridge at the end of Forest Route 538B.

At Buck Ridge, you will find an old jeep road that follows a power line south to Casner Mountain and beyond to Sycamore Pass. This 7.0-mile return to the trailhead is quite scenic, offering views of Sycamore Canyon, Verde Valley, and the San Francisco Peaks. At this point you will actually be traveling along the western margin of the Red Rock–Secret Mountain Wilderness

In late winter, when snowmelt or rainfall have filled some of the tinajas along its course and when natural springs in the wilderness are flowing freely, you could spend several days in Sycamore Canyon, hiking its twenty-one-mile length end to end and exploring a number of side canyons along the way.

West Clear Creek Wilderness 29

Cliffside view

FROM ITS ORIGIN near Clints Well up on the Mogollon Rim to where it enters the Verde River below Camp Verde, West Clear Creek winds for nearly forty miles through some of the most stunningly beautiful terrain in Arizona. In its upper thirty miles, the part that is designated wilderness, West Clear Creek is entirely canyon-bound, offering access to only the few and the hardy. As it travels to the Verde River, West Clear Creek passes through soaring cliffs of creamy Coconino sandstone and vermilion Supai siltstone, which lend their colors to the narrows called the White and Red Boxes. There are hanging gardens of maidenhair fern, red monkeyflower, and scarlet penstemon. There are New Mexico locust, cottonwood, Arizona walnut, willow, alder, Gambel oak, box elder, bigtooth maple, Douglas fir, and ponderosa pine. Century plant grows high on the rim;

LOCATION: 11 miles east of Camp Verde

SIZE: 13,600 acres

ELEVATION RANGE: 3,700 to 6,800 feet

MILES OF TRAILS: 10.2

HABITATS: Riparian gallery forest to ponderosa and Gambel oak

ADMINISTRATION: Coconino National Forest, Long Valley Ranger District

TOPOGRAPHIC MAPS: Buckhorn Mountain, Calloway Butte, Walker Mountain

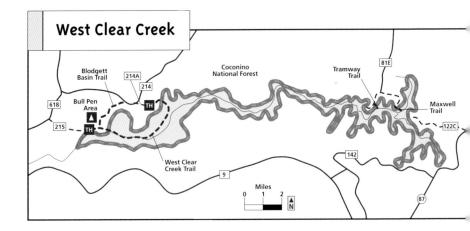

prickly pear in the canyon bottom. In places, water hemlock and poison ivy clog streamside pathways in great profusion. But there are also coneflower, Columbine, and Virginia creeper.

Black bear, elk, white-tailed and mule deer, ring tail, mountain lion, bobcat, badger, and skunk inhabit the wilderness. Bald eagles are sometimes seen there and lunker trout lure fishermen down the canyon's steep walls to fish West Clear Creek's cold, deep pools. Raven, cliff swallow, belted kingfisher, white-throated swift, broad-billed hummingbird, red-tailed hawk, and great horned owl are among the many birds that frequent the wilderness.

Hiking trails at either end of the wilderness provide the only access to the creek. For the remainder of its length, West Clear Creek is a "swim-float" canyon. Some backpackers carry small, inflatable vinyl rafts and paddles; others stuff their gear into heavy-duty trash bags that trap enough air to float a backpack.

Some of the swims are well over 100 yards, and since the sun seldom penetrates the depths of some canyon narrows, the water is cold—very cold—making hypothermia a real risk. Because sheer canyon walls block escape, flash flooding is also a danger during the summer rainy season. But there's no better way to experience pure wilderness solitude than to canyoneer Arizona's West Clear Creek Wilderness. In company, of course; never attempt a solo swim-float trip.

Although the West Clear Creek Wilderness is accessible throughout the year, swim-float trips are advisable only during the warmer months. In winter, road access to higher-elevation trails leading into the canyon may be closed by heavy snowfall.

DAY HIKE: WEST CLEAR CREEK TRAIL
One-way length: 7.7 miles
Low and high elevations: 3,800 to 5,600 feet
Difficulty: moderate

To reach the West Clear Creek Trailhead, travel southeast from Camp Verde for six miles on State Route 260 (General Crook Trail) to Forest Route 618. Turn north for 2.2 miles on Forest Route 618 to Forest Route 215. Turn right (east) on Forest Route 215 for about three miles to the Bull Pen camping area.

The trail leads up the north bank of the canyon for approximately 1.0 mile before making the first of four creek crossings. Except when streamflow is increased by snowmelt or heavy rainfall, crossings are safe and easy. But use caution.

After 5.0 miles, the trail turns north to climb nearly 2,000 feet to the canyon rim and Forest Route 214A. Depending on your fitness, you can hike the 2.5 miles back to the West Clear Creek Trailhead at the Bull Pen Area by way of Forest Route 214A to Forest Route 214 and the Blodgett Basin Trail or arrange for a shuttle to pick you up.

UPPER CANYON ACCESS

The Maxwell Trail provides the easiest access to West Clear Creek Canyon's upper end. To reach the Maxwell Trailhead from Phoenix, drive north on State Route 87 to Clints Well. Turn left (north) onto Forest Route 3 (Lake Mary Road) and continue for about seven miles to Forest Route 81. Turn left (west) on Forest Route 81 for four miles to Forest Route 81E. Take Forest Route 81E to its dead-end and the trailhead. The last few miles may require a high-clearance vehicle.

The difficult Maxwell Trail drops steeply into the canyon, descending more than 700 feet in less than one mile.

Another route into the canyon, the Tramway Trail, descends from the rim in the same general area as the Maxwell Trail. It too is steep and less than one mile in length.

30 Wet Beaver Wilderness

Flowing waters of Wet Beaver Creek

PLUNGING THROUGH LAYERS OF BASALT, limestone, and sandstone on its journey from the Mogollon Rim to the Verde River, Wet Beaver Creek has carved a rugged, high-walled canyon. Trail access is limited to the west end only; otherwise the Wet Beaver Wilderness is essentially trackless.

The riparian canopy that shelters the canyon bottom consists of fremont cottonwood, willow, Arizona sycamore, ash, and walnut. The slopes moving away from the canyon contain piñon-juniper and century plant.

LOCATION: 17 miles south of Flagstaff

SIZE: 6,700 acres

ELEVATION RANGE: 3,800 to 6,500 feet

MILES OF TRAILS: 6.5+

HABITATS: Riparian gallery, piñon-juniper, pine-fir

ADMINISTRATION: Coconino National Forest, Beaver Creek Ranger District

TOPOGRAPHIC MAPS: Casner Butte, Apache Main Mountain

Isolated pockets of ponderosa pine and Douglas fir can be found in some of the cooler, north-facing canyon niches.

Among the fish species inhabiting Wet Beaver Creek are smallmouth bass, trout, and round-tailed chubs. Bald eagles winter along the creek, and the wilderness provides habitat for the belted kingfisher, great blue heron, and canyon wren. Ringtail, deer, black bear, pronghorn, mountain lion, and beaver are also at home in the Wet Beaver Wilderness.

Most hikers see only a small portion of the wilderness where the Bell and Apache Maid trails enter its extreme western edge. You can extend these trails by hiking beyond the wilderness boundary. You may also hike upstream along the canyon bottom. Be forewarned, however, that the terrain is rough and broad pools may require swimming. Exploring the canyon bottom is risky. Always do it in the company of other hikers.

For its good swimming holes, the Wet Beaver Wilderness is a favorite destination during the summer months, but it can be visited year-round.

DAY HIKE: BELL TRAIL
One-way length: 3.0 miles
Low and high elevations: 3,800 to 4,100 feet
Difficulty: easy

To reach the Bell Trailhead, take Interstate 17 to the Sedona Exit (State Route 179) and turn east onto Forest Route 618. Drive southeast on Forest Route 618 for two miles to Forest Route 618A. Turn left on Forest Route 618 a short distance to the end of the road and the trailhead.

For the first couple of miles, the Bell Trail follows an old road. Just before the road becomes a footpath, the Apache Maid Trail comes in from the north. The Bell Trail continues east into the Wet Beaver Wilderness.

The trail travels through lush vegetation on the north side of perennial Wet Beaver Creek, passing some deep pools. After approximately 1.0 mile, the trail crosses the creek at Bell Crossing where there are a number of good campsites. From the crossing, the Bell Trail climbs southeast to the canyon rim, which offers good views

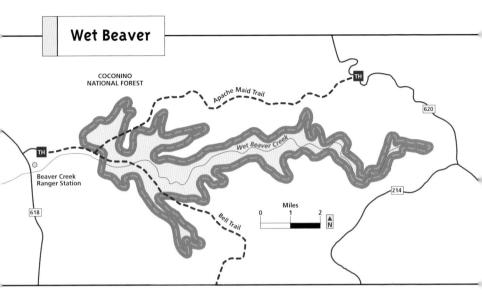

of the area. If you wish to extend the hike beyond the wilderness boundary, you may continue on the Bell Trail all the way to Roundup Basin, some 8.0 miles farther.

DAY HIKE: APACHE MAID TRAIL
One-way length: 3.5 miles
Low and high elevations: 3,900 to 5,100 feet
Difficulty: moderate

To reach the trailhead for the Apache Maid Trail, follow the directions for the Bell Trail. From its junction with the Bell Trail, the Apache Maid Trail climbs the north slope of the canyon through fairly open terrain with fine views into Wet Beaver Creek. After a series of switchbacks, the trail reaches the rim and the base of Casner Butte where it crosses a drainage and starts climbing toward the Mogollon Rim. Views from the rim take in the Verde Valley to the west and the San Francisco Peaks to the north.

From this point the trail is outside the wilderness and becomes quite indistinct and difficult to follow. Hikers who wish to extend the hike may follow rock cairns and other trail indicators that mark the route. After about 2.0 miles, the trail reaches Apache Maid Tanks where it becomes a four-wheel-drive road that proceeds northwest another 4.0 miles to the Apache Maid Mountain area.

HIKE – SWIM – FLOAT LOOP ADVENTURE:
WET BEAVER CREEK
Round-trip length: 23.0 miles
Low and high elevations: 4,000 to 6,000 feet
Difficulty: strenuous

Because this trip involves cross-country hiking, bushwhacking into the canyon, swimming, and pack-floating, it should be planned with the assistance of Beaver Creek Ranger District Forest Service personnel.

This route begins by hiking 3.5 miles on the Apache Maid Trail to the rim of Wet Beaver Canyon. From this point, you hike cross-country in an easterly direction approximately 3.5 miles to the head of Waldroup Canyon, passing Hog Hill slightly more than halfway across.

You enter Wet Beaver Wilderness by bushwhacking about one mile down Waldroup Canyon, which requires climbing down several dry waterfalls. In some places climbing ropes should be used.

When you reach the canyon bottom, hike downstream approximately 0.5 mile to the headwater springs of Wet Beaver Creek. Your trek begins here.

From this point to Bell Crossing and the Bell Trail, you will be in the water almost constantly, so you should carry dry footwear and warm dry clothing for camp. Be prepared to swim at least twenty pools where you will be required to float your pack on a small inflatable raft or air mattress. Some hikers prefer to stuff their packs in heavy-duty garbage bags that trap enough air to float backpacks.

Footing throughout the trip will be slippery and the water cold. Do not try this trip during winter. Plan on being in the canyon at least three days, perhaps longer.

31 Woodchute Wilderness

Evening vista

LOCATION: 10 miles west of Jerome

SIZE: 5,700 acres

ELEVATION RANGE: 5,500 to 7,834 feet

MILES OF TRAILS: 6

HABITATS: Piñon-juniper to ponderosa pine

ADMINISTRATION: Prescott National Forest, Chino Valley Ranger District

TOPOGRAPHIC MAPS: Mundes Draw, Hickey Mountain

NAMED FOR A LONG WOODEN CHUTE once used to deliver ponderosa timbers down the mountain to the mines in Jerome, Woodchute Wilderness is located in the northern portion of the Mingus Mountains. Although fewer than 6,000 acres in size and more of a timbered mesa than a mountain, it is one of the more easily accessible and frequently visited wilderness areas in Arizona.

State Route 89A, winding up from the Sonoran desert through grassland, oak, and piñon-juniper woodland to the ponderosa-Gambel oak forest at Mingus Pass, is interesting for its own sake. In addition to the above-mentioned tree species, the wilderness harbors some very large alligator juniper. Mule deer, rock squirrel, bobcat, and gray fox are at home in the Woodchute Wilderness, along with black-capped

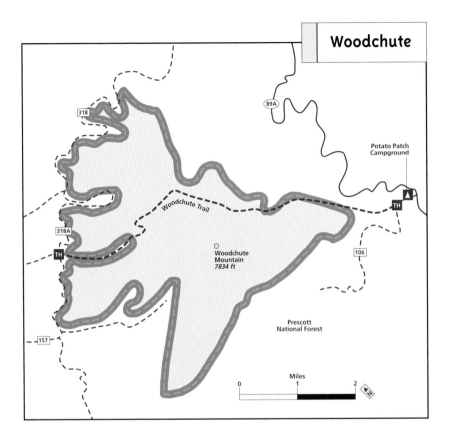

Woodchute

chickadee, pygmy nuthatch, saw-whet owl, scrub jay, and a variety of other birds. The best months for hiking the Woodchute Wilderness are May through October.

> **DAY HIKE: WOODCHUTE TRAIL**
> One-way length: 5.0 miles
> Low and high elevations: 7,000 to 7,700 feet
> Difficulty: easy

To reach the Woodchute Trailhead, drive 8.0 miles southwest of Jerome on State Route 89A, and turn north 0.3 at the Potato Patch Campground at Mingus Pass to Forest Route 106 and the trailhead.

As it travels along ridgelines heading north through a mixed pine forest, the Woodchute Trail looks west into Chino Valley and the Juniper Mountains. As the trail reaches the northern rim of the mountaintop, views open up toward the San Francisco Peaks to the north and to Sedona and red rock country to the east. The northern rim of the mesa is the turnaround point. An indistinct portion of the trail descends a steep slope, heading north approximately 1.0 mile to Forest Route 318.

Southeastern Arizona:
Basin and Range Sky Islands

Fault-block mountain ranges, shaped by cataclysmic upthrusting of enormous chunks of the Earth's crust, run across southeast Arizona's Basin and Range region. Take a look at a relief map of the state, concentrating on the territory southeast of an imaginary line running east and west through Phoenix. You will notice mountains that line up in a rough northwest to southeast orientation. These mountains are steep and craggy on one side and relatively gently sloping on the other, and in between lie flat, sometimes quite broad valleys or basins.

Physiographers call this southeastern portion of Arizona's Basin and Range province the Arizona Upland section. Turn, again, to the relief map. Close your eyes and run the tips of your fingers over it. As your fingertips weave across the map's prominences and depressions toward Arizona's southeast corner, you'll feel the bumps become higher, more broad-backed, and spread out.

Your fingers have been tracing the outlines of Southeast Arizona's "sky islands," soaring giants that from base to summit rise higher than most other mountains in the state. Several peaks push higher than 9,000 feet, with the tallest summit in the region, Mount Graham in the Pinaleño Mountains, topping out at 10,730 feet. And the intermontane valleys— the Santa Cruz, San Rafael, San Pedro, Sulphur Spring, San Bernadino, and San Simon—are higher, wetter, and grassier than those west of Tucson.

The highest and coldest subdivision of the Sonoran Desert, this area is the only Sonoran Desert region where hard winter frosts occur. Because of the climate, trees and shrubs commonly grow on rocky slopes away from arroyos, and the giant saguaro cactus dominates the landscape horizon in most locations.

Many biologists believe that the Arizona Upland, which averages twelve inches of precipitation at its lower elevations and up to thirty inches in the mountainous regions, shouldn't qualify as desert because it's too wet and cool, is heavily vegetated, and has too great a biodiversity. They argue that it should be reclassified as thorn scrub, as it very well may be in the future.

Two rainy seasons are typical in the Arizona Upland region. Summer rains usually begin in late June or early July with the arrival of the monsoon, a change in the wind flow that brings a tropical air mass up from the south, moderating hot, dry temperatures and producing frequent thunderstorms. The second rainy period arrives in winter—December through February.

Majestic rock and blossoming yucca

Although sunny days generally prevail in winter, periodic storms arrive from the Pacific, producing rain, snow, and cooler temperatures. The intervals between these two rainy seasons are often quite hot and dry.

Southeast Arizona's mountains are famous for their biodiversity. Every year, biologists from major American universities arrive to do research in Cave Creek Canyon in the Chiricahua Mountains, Ramsey Canyon in the Huachuca Mountains, Madera Canyon in the Santa Rita Mountains, Sycamore Canyon in the Atascosa Mountains, Guadalupe Canyon in the Peloncillo Mountains, or one of the many other cool, wet, isolated canyons of the region's "sky island" mountain ranges. Needless to say, these mountain ranges also attract bird watchers, other amateur naturalists, and scores of hikers, backpackers, and other recreational users.

32 Aravaipa Canyon Wilderness

Early autumn

LOCATION: 23 miles southeast of Winkelman

SIZE: 19,410 acres

ELEVATION RANGE: 2,600 to 4,900 feet

MILES OF TRAILS: No marked or maintained trails

HABITATS: Riparian and desert uplands

ADMINISTRATION: BLM, Safford Field Office

TOPOGRAPHIC MAPS: Booger Canyon, Brandenburg Mountain, Holy Joe Peak, Oak Grove Canyon

ALTHOUGH SEVERE FLOODING in 1983 and again in 1993 destroyed many mature cottonwood and sycamore trees, Aravaipa Canyon, cutting through the northern end of the Galiuro Mountains, remains a classic example of desert riparian habitat. Arizona ash, sycamore, walnut, fremont cottonwood, willow, hackberry, oak, and box elder line the entire eleven-mile river corridor. The uplands above the river support saguaro cactus, barrel cactus, yucca, ocotillo and other plants typical of the Sonoran Desert. Sharp-eyed hikers frequently see desert bighorn sheep, which inhabit the upper reaches of the canyon, peering down from the rim. Other wildlife abounds. Troops of coatimundi are frequently encountered in the Aravaipa Wilderness region, as well as mule and white-tailed deer, mountain lion, black bear, ringtail, and coyote. The creek is habitat for minnows and suckers. Peregrine falcons nest on

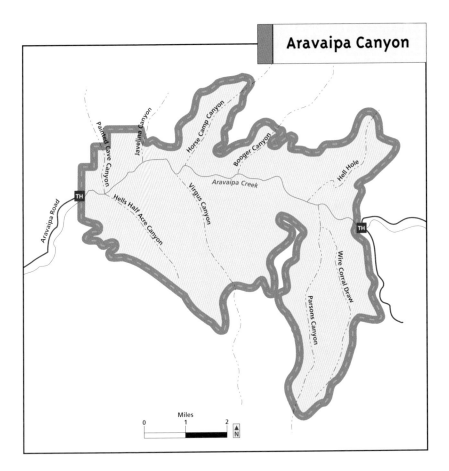

Aravaipa Canyon

Painted Cave Canyon

Javelina Canyon

Horse Camp Canyon

Booger Canyon

Hell Hole

Aravaipa Creek

Aravaipa Road

TH

Hells Half Acre Canyon

Virgus Canyon

Wire Corral Draw

TH

Parsons Canyon

Miles
0   1   2
N

the cliffs above the canyon, and, as is typical with desert riparian habitats, an enormous variety of birds congregate along the creek bottom.

The remains of dwellings show that paleo-Indians lived in Aravaipa Canyon region, and until the late nineteenth century, the wilderness area was inhabited by Apache people.

HIKING THE CANYON

Although I have backpacked the eleven-mile length of the Aravaipa Canyon Wilderness during June when the temperature registered 105 degrees Fahrenheit and in December when my water bottles froze, the best times of the year to be in the wilderness are spring and fall. The stream flows year-round, with water levels fluctuating from thigh-deep to ankle-deep, depending on the amount of precipitation. Most of the hiking is in the stream bottom, which means that your feet are always wet. In anticipation of stream-bed hiking, I usually put aside a pair of worn hiking shoes or boots for the job. Although I've encountered other hikers wearing river sandals, I don't recommend them as adequate protection against sharp rocks.

Adding to the adventure of hiking in the Aravaipa Canyon Wilderness is the exploration of such side canyons as Horse Camp and Booger where water sometimes collects in deep pools. On one such exploration, I discovered a small California fan palm, which I presumed to be wild. How it got there is a mystery.

A number of excellent camp sites are available along the canyon bottom and in side canyons. The only drinking water available in the wilderness is the creek itself, which should be treated before drinking, of course.

Aravaipa Canyon Wilderness can be entered from the east or west. To reach the western trailhead, drive 11 miles south from Winkelman on State Route 77 to the Aravaipa Canyon Road. Turn left to the trailhead at road's end. Although the road becomes rough as it nears the trailhead, it is passable in most vehicles.

To reach the eastern trailhead, drive 15 miles west from Safford on U.S. Highway 70 to the Klondyke Road and turn left. Continue 24 miles to the Aravaipa Canyon Road. Turn right and drive approximately 20 miles, passing the townsite of Klondyke along the way, to the trailhead. Flooding near the trailhead has made the last few miles virtually impassable to all but either high-clearance or four-wheel-drive vehicles. Check road conditions with the Bureau of Land Management (BLM).

To better preserve the canyon, the BLM limits the number of hikers and campers to 50 per day and limits duration of stay to three days and two nights. Permits are required. These can be obtained by writing or telephoning the Safford Field Office of the BLM which is listed in Appendix 2.

Sunrise from Centella Point

THE CHIRICAHUA WILDERNESS is one of Arizona's oldest. First established as an 18,000-acre preserve in 1933, the National Forest portion of the wilderness was expanded to 87,700 acres by the 1984 Arizona Wilderness Act. A 9,440-acre unit in the Chiricahua National Monument was set aside as wilderness in 1976, and another 850 acres in 1984. This section treats the National Forest and National Monument wilderness units as one.

Named for the Chiricahua Apaches— Geronimo, Cochise, and others—who once roamed the territory, the Chiricahua range is the largest and perhaps best known of southeastern Arizona's "sky island" mountain ranges. Lying close to the border with Mexico on the south and the continental divide on the east, the Chiricahuas

LOCATION: Approximately 35 miles southeast of Willcox

SIZE: 97,140 acres

ELEVATION RANGE: 5,200 to 9,797 feet

MILES OF TRAILS: More than 100

HABITATS: Grasslands, riparian gallery forests, piñon-juniper, oak woodland, boreal forests, alpine meadows

ADMINISTRATION: Coronado National Forest, Douglas Ranger District and National Park Service

TOPOGRAPHIC MAPS: Rustler Park, Chiricahua Peak, Portal, Portal Peak, Fife Peak, Stanford Canyon, Swede Peak, Cochise Head

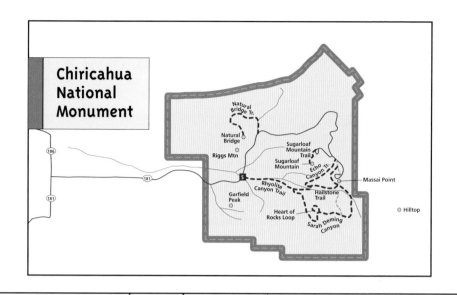

Chiricahua National Monument

- Natural Bridge Tr.
- Natural Bridge
- Riggs Mtn
- Sugarloaf Mountain Trail
- Sugarloaf Mountain
- Echo Canyon Tr.
- Massai Point
- Rhyolite Canyon Trail
- Garfield Peak
- Hailstone Trail
- Heart of Rocks Loop
- Sarah Deming Canyon
- Hilltop

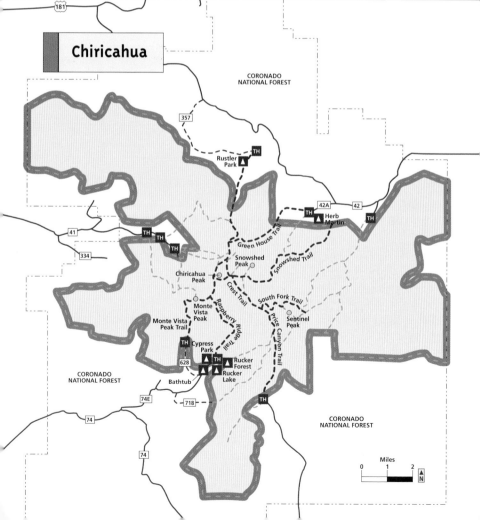

Chiricahua

181

CORONADO NATIONAL FOREST

357

Rustler Park **TH**

41

334

42A 42 **TH**

TH Herb Martin

Green House Trail

Snowshed Peak

Snowshed Trail

TH TH

TH

Chiricahua Peak

Crest Trail

South Fork Trail

Monte Vista Peak

Sentinel Peak

Raspberry Ridge Trail

Monte Vista Peak Trail

TH Cypress Park

628

Rucker Forest

Price Canyon Trail

Bathtub

Rucker Lake

CORONADO NATIONAL FOREST

74E

718

TH

74

74

CORONADO NATIONAL FOREST

Miles
0   1   2

N

provide habitat for Sierra Madrean, Rocky Mountain, eastern, and western species of plants, animals, and birds. Troops of coatimundi forage its slopes; elegant trogans and numerous species of hummingbirds nest along Cave Creek Canyon, one of the prime birding sites in the United States; all four species of skunks native to Arizona—the spotted, striped, hooded, and hog-nosed—occur here; and Chiricahua Peak supports the southernmost stand of Engelmann Spruce in the continental U.S.

The value of southeast Arizona's mountain ranges as wildlife corridors is illustrated by 1996 photographs of a rare Mexican jaguar taken by a mountain-lion hunter working near the Baker Canyon Wilderness Study Area in the Peloncillo Mountains just southeast of the Chiricahuas. In July, 1997 the Mexican jaguar was listed as endangered by the U.S. Fish and Wildlife Service. An attempt to reintroduce the thick-billed parrot, extirpated since the early 1900s in the wilderness, was abandoned in 1996. And, although no release is planned, the Chiricahua Wilderness has been discussed as a site for reintroduction of the Mexican gray wolf.

A hiker standing atop Sugarloaf Mountain in the Chiricahua National Monument portion of the wilderness can look across the famous Heart of Rocks to the Turkey Creek Caldera, an extinct volcano that 30 million years ago spewed hot volcanic gases over an area of 700 square miles. Subsequent fracturing of the earth's crust thrust up tilted layers of Rhyolite, a rock formed by the accumulation of volcanic ash. Then wind, frost, lichens, and rain worked their magic on the cracks. Softer materials eroded more rapidly, creating an amazing display of weathered spires and balanced rocks. The most fantastic of these forms can be seen in the Heart of Rocks, where such well-known rock formations as Totem Pole, Big Balanced Rock, and Punch and Judy are located.

In 1994 the Rattlesnake Fire raged through the Chiricahuas for one full month, devastating 27,500 acres of mixed-conifer and ponderosa pine forest. The firestorm, which cost more than $6 million to control, severely damaged wilderness trail systems and clogged mountain springs with fire ash. The blaze also sparked another in a series of battles between the Forest Service and the Southwest Center for Biological Diversity. The environmental organization sought to save burned trees from salvage logging, arguing that decaying burned trees return nutrients to forest soil and are more valuable as nesting and feeding sites or as sanctuaries for wildlife than as ceiling vigas for Santa Fe-style houses.

Richly carpeted with wildflowers in spring, alpine meadows strung along the Chiricahua's Crest Trail are among the favorite destinations of hikers and backpackers. The Crest Trail, which travels a north-south route along the central ridge of the range, is the best access route to the National Forest portion of the wilderness. Numerous trails branching east and west off the Crest Trail offer excellent hiking opportunities. Except during drought years, mountain springs are reliable sources of water.

DAY HIKE: SUGARLOAF MOUNTAIN TRAIL
One-way length: 1.0 mile
Low and high elevations: 6,853 to 7,307 feet
Difficulty: easy

An easy climb of some 500 feet leads to the summit of 7,307-foot Sugarloaf. A modest peak by regional standards, Sugarloaf is one of the high points in the Chiricahua National Monument, affording excellent views all around. There's a fire-lookout cabin at the summit, bolt-anchored to granite, where lightning strikes are monitored during the summer monsoon thunderstorms. In the southern foreground are the weathered spires and balanced rocks of Heart of Rocks, and a bit farther south is etched the outline of the Turkey Creek Caldera, an extinct volcano. Below and east of the summit are the Echo Canyon and Massai Point trailheads. And way off north is Cochise Head, shaped like the face of a man reclining—domed forehead, long curved nose, and a 100-foot pine for an eyelash.

DAY HIKE: NATURAL BRIDGE
One-way length: 2.5 miles
Low and high elevations: 5,500 to 6,000 feet
Difficulty: moderate

This hike up through oak-juniper woodlands into pine forest at Picket Park in Chiricahua National Monument features a natural bridge at the end of the trail. The trailhead is about 1.25 miles beyond the visitor center on the Bonita Canyon Road.

DAY HIKE: RASPBERRY RIDGE TRAIL
One-way length: 4.6 miles
Low and high elevations: 6,100 to 9,280 feet
Difficulty: strenuous

To reach the trailhead, drive about 30 miles south from Interstate 10 on U.S. Highway 191 to Rucker Canyon Road. Turn left (east) and drive 6.0 miles to Rucker Forest Camp. From the Forest Camp, hike about 50 yards up an abandoned logging road to where the trail leaves Rucker Creek and heads into Bear Canyon toward Raspberry Ridge. Wide at the beginning, the trail soon narrows and becomes difficult to follow. Washed out in places and crisscrossed by game trails and cattle paths, the route is marked by trail blazes and cairns. Watch closely for them.

The trail heads up into a side canyon coming in from the east and then, in less than a mile, gains 1,000 feet up a series of steep switchbacks to Raspberry Saddle. Gaining an additional 300 feet as it ascends to a second saddle, the trail now enters a forest of Douglas fir as it climbs more moderately to its junction with the Crest Trail at 9,280 feet. Closely heed Forest Service trail signs as you move above Raspberry Saddle.

DAY HIKE: MONTE VISTA PEAK
One-way length: 4.9 miles
Low and high elevations: 6,600 and 9,357 feet
Difficulty: moderate

The Monte Vista Trail begins on an old road near the Bathtub Campground in Rucker Canyon on the east slope of the Chiricahuas. Soon, the road becomes a footpath that climbs in a series of switchbacks to Buckskin Saddle. At the saddle, the trail begins to switchback 1.2 miles up the peak itself to Monte Vista Lookout. About 0.5 mile before the junction with the Crest Trail, a signed spur trail leads to Bear Spring, usually a reliable water source. The summit is a short walk west on the Crest Trail.

The hike starts in oak woodland and moves up through ponderosa pine and Apache pine, a tree that reaches its northernmost range here near the borders of Arizona and New Mexico. When the 1994 Rattlesnake fire swept through the Monte Vista Peak area, it destroyed many trees between Buckskin Saddle and the summit. The views from the fire tower are splendid in all directions. Remember, in season, fire observers occupy the Monte Vista Peak fire tower; request permission before ascending the stairs.

> ## DAY HIKE: SOUTH FORK TRAIL
> One-way length: 6.8 miles
> Low and high elevations: 5,360 to 8,800 feet
> Difficulty: moderate

To reach the trailhead, follow the directions to Portal (see Snowshed Trail below) and drive west on Forest Route 42 to the South Fork Day Use Area.

This lovely trail, a favorite among bird watchers, follows the South Fork of Cave Creek, crossing and recrossing the stream as it wanders through a forest of Arizona walnut, Arizona sycamore, Arizona cypress, Apache, Chiricahua, and ponderosa pine, Douglas fir, and Arizona madrone. You may see an elegant trogon along this route, or a red-faced warbler, or one of the many hummingbird species that frequent Cave Creek.

If you're lucky enough to hike the South Fork Trail in autumn, you may be treated to the vivid reds of bigtooth maples in the general area of Maple Camp, about 1.5 miles from the trailhead. Beyond Maple Camp, the trail continues up the drainage between high cliffs before turning up a side canyon to the Crest Trail. In its upper reaches, the trail passes through aspen and Douglas fir.

> ## DESTINATION HIKE: SNOWSHED TRAIL
> One-way length: 10.1 miles
> Low and high elevations: 5,300 to 9,665 feet
> Difficulty: strenuous

To reach the trailhead, drive 28 miles south from Interstate 10 on U.S. Highway 80 (in New Mexico) and turn right (west) 7.0 miles to Portal. Continue 4.0 miles westbound on Forest Route 42 to the trailhead.

One of the main features of this route is the views it provides of Cave Creek Canyon, one of southern Arizona's beauty spots and a favorite destination for bird watchers from all over the world. Unique in character, this steep-walled canyon, a kind of mini-Yosemite, features caves, pinnacles, and lofty cliffs.

Climbing toward the Chiricahua high country, the trail passes through oak, woodland, and Arizona madrone into ponderosa pine. About a half mile below Deer Spring, the Snowshed Trail intersects three other routes. A northeast turn switchbacks up to Snowshed Peak. Straight ahead climbs to the Crest Trail near Chiricahua Peak. And a left turn goes south toward Juniper Spring on the Crest Trail.

> **LOOP HIKE:** ECHO CANYON LOOP
> One-way length: 3.5 miles
> Low and high elevations: 6,200 and 6,900 feet
> Difficulty: moderate

From the trailhead at the Echo Canyon parking lot in the Chiricahua National Monument, the trail descends through towering rock formations to the cool pine-shade of Echo Park. This short loop, one of the most scenic in the park, returns to the parking area via the Hailstone Trail.

> **LOOP HIKE:** HEART OF ROCKS LOOP
> One-way length: 9.0 miles
> Low and high elevations: 5,400 to 6,870 feet
> Difficulty: strenuous

Totem Pole, Punch and Judy, and Big Balanced Rock are only a few of the famous rock formations that the Heart of Rocks Trail leads through. The trail begins at either the Echo Canyon or Massai Point parking area and descends through tall pine and fir. Just beyond Big Balanced Rock, the trail detours a short distance into the Heart of Rocks itself. The return trip is via the Sara Deming and Hailstone Trails. To cut two miles off the distance, simply return along the same route that brought you in.

> **SHUTTLE HIKE:** CREST – PRICE CANYON TRAILS
> One-way length: 13.2 miles
> Low and high elevations: 6,000 and 9,786 feet
> Difficulty: moderate

From Rustler Park, the trail climbs to Long Park where the Crest Trail begins. The trail travels along the central spine of the mountain through Round, Cima, and Anita parks, a series of alpine meadows. Anita Park, with good water at nearby Anita Spring, provides an excellent base camp for explorations of trails that spill from the Crest Trail down the east and west flanks of the mountain. The Greenhouse Trail, for example, descends nearly 3,000 feet in four miles from Cima Park to Cave Creek Canyon with an impressive view of Winn Falls along the way. Openings along the Crest Trail look out across the Sulphur Springs Valley to the west and to distant mountain ranges beyond. At its junction with Snowshed Peak Trail, Crest Trail descends 2.1 miles to the Price Canyon Trail. Here, Crest Trail branches east to the South Fork Trail, while the Price Canyon Trail descends due south toward your second vehicle parked at the end of Price Canyon Road (Forest Route 317) on the southeast side of the mountain. Except during drought years, water is usually available in springs and streams. Always treat it before drinking.

Dos Cabezas Mountains Wilderness

Indian grinding holes used to grind corn or other grains

A familiar landmark for those traveling in southern Arizona, the Dos Cabezas (two heads) Peaks are the most prominent feature of the mountain range that gives the Dos Cabezas Wilderness its name. Rugged and remote with no developed hiking trails, the Dos Cabezas is ideal for seekers of a true back-country experience.

Several springs, both natural and developed, provide water for the abundant wildlife of the wilderness. White-tailed and mule deer, mountain lion, golden and bald eagles, javelina, badger, and coyote inhabit the wilderness,

LOCATION: 40 miles south of Safford

SIZE: 11,998 acres

ELEVATION RANGE: 4,080 and 7,950 fee

MILES OF TRAILS: No marked or maintained trails

HABITATS: Desert riparian and mountains

ADMINISTRATION: BLM, Safford Field Office

TOPOGRAPHIC MAPS: Dos Cabezas, Bowie Mountain North, Luzena

and peregrine falcons have been known to migrate through here. The upper portions of Buckeye Canyon provide habitat for the beautiful collared lizard.

Vegetation varies with elevation from desert scrub in the lower reaches to oak, juniper, and mountain mahogany above 4,000 feet. Near springs, trees typical of a riparian association, such as ash, cottonwood, and Arizona sycamore, are found.

For hiking, spring and fall are the best seasons, and winter, although sometimes snowy and cold above 5,000 feet, can also provide some very pleasant recreation. Summer hiking is best avoided; the Dos Cabezas Wilderness becomes very hot during summer months.

HIKING THE WILDERNESS

There are no developed trails within the Dos Cabezas Wilderness. All hiking, therefore, is either cross-country bushwhacking or on unmaintained jeep roads.

Three routes, all approaching the Dos Cabezas from the east side, provide access to the wilderness. The main one is Happy Camp Canyon Road, 4.5 miles south of the town of Bowie on the Apache Pass Road. Drive west from the turnoff to the Indian Bread Rocks Picnic Area. At the picnic area, you may hike south cross-country into the wilderness area across a landscape of granite boulders.

Continuing west beyond the picnic area you will cross private land into Happy Camp Canyon. Here, the road becomes quite rough and may require a four-wheel-drive vehicle, or, at the very least, a high-clearance pickup. After about three miles, the road dead-ends at the wilderness boundary. From this point you can hike into Happy Camp Canyon.

In less than a mile, two canyons branch off Happy Camp: to the north is Howell Canyon; to the south Tar Box Canyon. Peak baggers may want to proceed straight ahead to the base of Cooper Peak, at 7,950 feet the highest point in the wilderness. On the other hand, Tar Box Canyon leads to a route up Government Peak (7,580 feet). Either high point opens onto long-distance views of the area's many mountain ranges and the Sulphur Springs and San Simon Valleys.

An unnamed four-wheel-drive route from Bowie approaches the Dos Cabezas Wilderness from the northeast. I found it by inquiring at the town's service station.

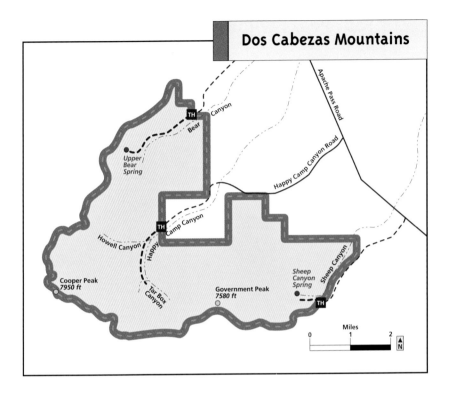

Dos Cabezas Mountains

About 4.5 miles out of Bowie, the road reaches the wilderness boundary where you must leave your vehicle and hike the now-closed jeep trail approximately 2.0 miles to Upper Bear Spring.

Finally, another four-wheel-drive road leaves Apache Pass Road and approaches Sheep Canyon Spring along the southeastern boundary of the Dos Cabezas Wilderness. At the wilderness boundary, you can hike a short distance on the closed portion of the road to Sheep Canyon Spring and into the wilderness beyond.

Use caution and carry plenty of water while backcountry bushwhacking. Although there are several springs in the Dos Cabezas Wilderness, their reliability, for both volume and potability, is questionable. Also, encounters with such hazards as poisonous snakes, insects, and poisonous plants are more likely while cross-country hiking.

34 Four Peaks Wilderness

Winter sunset

LOCATION: 25 miles northeast of Mesa

SIZE: 60,740 acres

ELEVATION RANGE: 1,600 and 7,657 feet

MILES OF TRAILS: 40

HABITATS: Sonoran Desert to oak woodland, pine and fir forest

ADMINISTRATION: Tonto National Forest, Mesa Ranger District

TOPOGRAPHIC MAPS: Four Peaks, Theodore Roosevelt Dam, Horse Mesa Dam, Mormon Flat Dam, Tonto Basin, Mine Mountain

VISIBLE FOR MANY MILES AROUND, the four impressively rugged peaks of the Four Peaks Wilderness are familiar landmarks in central Arizona. Elevations vary from 1,600 feet near Mormon Flat Dam to 7,657 feet at Brown's Peak, the highest of the four peaks. Impressive stands of saguaro cactus, along with other plants associated with the Sonoran Desert, are found at the lower elevations. At around 4,000 feet, arid grasslands, which blend with desert landscape features, begin to give way to chaparral, a mixture of piñon-juniper, Gambel oak, and thickets of manzanita. The ponderosa pine is the dominant tree of the highest reaches of the Four Peaks Wilderness. Some Douglas fir is also found there along with a few small groves of aspen on the north slope of Brown's Peak. Some of the narrow canyons of the wilderness are lined with cottonwood, willow, sycamore, and other vegetation typical of riparian zones.

Unusually sharp variations in topography mark the Four Peaks Wilderness. Below the rugged summits of the peaks themselves are a series of complex ridges and drainages. At lower elevations near the Apache and Canyon Reservoirs, steep bluffs and deep gorges mark the terrain.

Variations in elevation, terrain, and vegetation create diversity in wildlife. Although rare, sightings of desert bighorn sheep have been reported in the Four Peaks Wilderness, and data from the Arizona Game and Fish Department indicates that the wilderness contains one of the highest concentrations of black bears in Arizona. Ringtail, skunk, deer, javelina, mountain lion, and coyote are among the other mammals inhabiting the wilderness. A remnant herd of feral prospectors' burros also roams the wilderness. Numbering fewer than 20, they are tough, furtive, and seldom seen.

Few of us recall that the 1964 Wilderness Act permits "the grazing of livestock…subject to such reasonable regulations as are deemed necessary by the Secretary of Agriculture." And although the grazing permit for the area was once revoked, cattle still graze in the Three Bar, an area east of the peaks.

Soldiers from nearby Fort McDowell blazed many trails through the Four Peaks Wilderness during the Apache campaigns in the 1860s and early '70s. Some of the same trails are still used by hikers and backpackers today.

Lower elevation hiking is best done during the cooler months. Water may be available at springs and creeks within the wilderness but should be treated before drinking.

DAY HIKE: FOUR PEAKS TRAIL
One-way length: 10.0 miles
Low and high elevations: 3,800 to 6,600 feet
Difficulty: easy to moderate

To reach the Four Peaks Trailhead located at Lone Pine Saddle, drive north from Mesa on State Route 87 to Forest Route 143 (Four Peaks Road), which is about 11.5 miles north of the Verde River bridge and just past the Desert Vista Rest Stop. Turn east and follow Forest Route 143 18.8 miles to the El Oso Divide. Take a sharp right (south) onto Forest Route 648 and continue 1.3 miles to the trailhead. Steep and winding, Forest Route 143 requires a high-clearance vehicle and is considered unsuitable for horse trailers.

Easy to follow, the Four Peaks Trail moves south from the trailhead, traversing the north and east flanks of its namesake peaks before continuing southwest along Buckhorn Ridge toward its terminus at Forest Route 429, a four-wheel-drive road. There are steep, vaguely defined sections on the eastern and southern portions of the trail. A popular trail, the Four Peaks is heavily traveled.

DAY HIKE: CANE SPRING TRAIL
One-way length: 2.3 miles
Low and high elevations: 2,900 to 4,200 feet
Difficulty: moderate

Reaching the trailhead for this hike is difficult and requires a four-wheel-drive vehicle. From Mesa drive north on State Route 87 (the Beeline Highway) to Forest Route 143 (Four Peaks Road), which is about 11.5 miles north of the Verde River bridge and just past the Desert Vista Rest Stop. Turn east approximately 2.5 miles to Forest Route 401. Turn south 4.4 miles to Cottonwood Camp. At Cottonwood Camp, Forest Route 401 becomes four-wheel-drive-only for 5.8 miles to Cane Spring. The trail begins about one-quarter mile west of the Cane Spring Trailhead.

Seldom used, the Cane Spring Trail is poorly defined and somewhat difficult to follow. Over its 2.3 mile length to where it intersects the Soldier Camp Trail, it gains 1,300 feet.

> **DAY HIKE: CHILLICUT TRAIL**
> One-way length: 7.0 miles
> Low and high elevations: 2,840 to 6,440 feet
> Difficulty: strenuous

To reach the trailhead for the Chillicut Trail at Rock Creek, drive south approximately 10 miles from Punkin Center on State Route 188 to Forest Route 445 (Three Bar Road). Turn right (southwest) and drive approximately 3.0 miles to Forest Route 445A. Turn left for about one-quarter mile to a short spur road (Forest Route 153). Turn right to the trailhead. A high-clearance vehicle is recommended. Park near the creek, but avoid leaving your vehicle where flash floods could damage it.

The first 1.5 miles or so of the Chillicut Trail follows an old jeep road. This lightly used trail features steep up and down sections with quite a steep ascent to Buckhorn Mountain. The Chillicut Trail gains 3,600 feet in elevation as it travels from upper Sonoran Desert to ponderosa pine at the intersection with the Four Peaks Trail, the turn-around point.

> **LOOP HIKE: BROWNS – AMETHYST – FOUR PEAKS TRAILS**
> One-way length: 4.0 miles
> Low and high elevations: 5,700 to 6,760 feet
> Difficulty: moderate

The trailhead for Browns Trail is in Lone Pine Saddle and can be reached via directions for the Four Peaks Trail description. Constructed in the late 1980s, the trail is well maintained. It joins the Amethyst Trail just below Browns Saddle. Turn north on the Amethyst Trail and descend the steep grade to its junction with the Four Peaks Trail, which returns you to the trailhead at Lone Pine Saddle. Turning south onto the Amethyst Trail at Browns Saddle would take you to the Amethyst Mine, where the purple-violet gemstone for which the trail is named was quarried. The mine is private property; permission is required for entry.

> **LOOP HIKE: SOLDIER CAMP – CANE SPRING – ALDER CREEK – FOUR PEAKS TRAILS**
> One-way length: 25.5 miles
> Low and high elevations: 2,280 to 6,600 feet
> Difficulty: strenuous

This backpacker's loop begins at the Mud Spring Trailhead, which can be reached by driving north from Mesa on State Route 87 to Forest Route 143 (Four Peaks

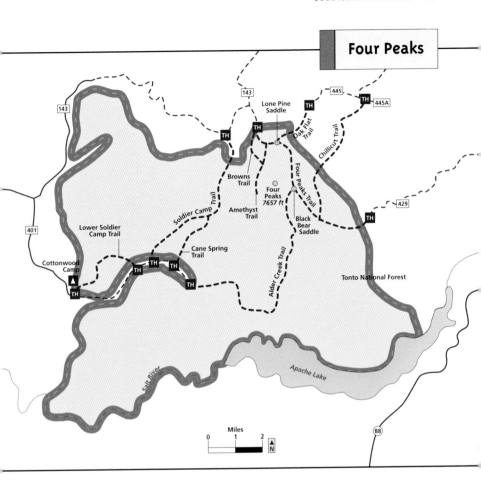

Road), approximately 11.5 miles north of the Verde River bridge and just past the Desert Vista Rest Stop. Turn east on Forest Route 143 and follow it for 16 miles to the trailhead on the south side of the road. Forest Route 143 is rough and winding and requires a high-clearance vehicle.

The first portion of the loop is on the Soldier Camp Trail, which travels along the open western ridges below Four Peaks. Hikers will enjoy good views of the Four Peaks and lower desert terrain. After about 6.0 miles, the Soldier Camp Trail joins the Cane Spring Trail, a little-used route that is unmaintained and difficult to follow. The Cane Spring Trail descends 1,300 feet to the Cane Spring Trailhead where it intersects the Alder Creek Trail, which curves around the southern slopes of Four Peaks to follow Alder Creek to near its headwaters. After about 12.0 miles it intersects the Four Peaks Trail. From this point it is approximately 5.0 miles to the trailhead at Lone Pine Saddle. A short hike of approximately one mile along Forest Route 143 will return you to the Mud Spring Trailhead.

36 Galiuro Wilderness

Prickly Pear cactus and eastern slopes

ORIGINALLY SET ASIDE BY CONGRESS as 52,717 acres in 1932 and enlarged to 76,317 acres by the Arizona Wilderness Act of 1984, the Galiuro Wilderness is remote, rough, and one of the least-visited backcountry regions in southeastern Arizona. Solitude awaits those who venture across miles of gravel roads to explore its rugged canyons.

Although quite low when compared to some neighboring mountain ranges, the Galiuros support a surprising diversity of plant life. Grasslands, scrub oak, and piñon-juniper dominate its lower slopes. Ponderosa pine covers the

LOCATION: 35 miles northwest of Willcox

SIZE: 76,317 acres

ELEVATION RANGE: 4,000 and 7,663 feet

MILES OF TRAILS: 75

HABITATS: Riparian, desert grassland, piñon-juniper, mixed conifer, aspen

ADMINISTRATION: Coronado National Forest, Safford Ranger District

TOPOGRAPHIC MAPS: Bassett Peak, Cherry Spring, Harrison Canyon, Kennedy Peak, Rhodes Peak, Winchester Mountains, Kielberg Canyon

higher elevations, and Douglas fir, alligator juniper, cottonwood, Arizona walnut, sycamore, and bigtooth maple grow in its cool, deep canyons. A few aspens grow in canyon bottoms, and a small grove of these trees clings to the north side of 7,663-foot Bassett Peak, the wilderness area's high point.

Hikers in the wilderness sometimes encounter troops of coatimundi foraging in the canyon bottoms or spot herds of desert bighorn sheep patrolling its rocky promontories. Birds inhabiting the wilderness include peregrine falcon, bald eagle, Scott's oriole, black-tailed gnatcatcher, Gila woodpecker, wild turkey, black phoebe, canyon towhee, Gambel's quail, scrub jay, Western tanager, cactus wren, and brown-crested flycatcher. Although a lone wolf was chased into and killed in nearby Aravaipa Canyon in the mid-1970s, Mexican gray wolves were extirpated in the Galiuros in the 1950s. Pronghorn, mountain lion, black bear, ringtail, mule deer, spotted skunk, rock squirrel, and several species of bats are at home in the wilderness. Reptiles and amphibians include Arizona black rattlesnake, Gila monster, gopher snake, treefrog, and collared lizard.

Cliff dwellings scattered throughout the wilderness indicate the presence of paleo-Indian cultures. Until the end of the nineteenth century when they were driven out and confined to reservations, Apache Indians foraged and hunted throughout the Galiuro Wilderness.

Along a trail that travels through the wilderness area's Rattlesnake Canyon, there's a cabin in a grassy meadow. Sunlit corrals, a shed with a horseshoe tacked above the door, and a surrounding grove of ponderosa pines lend an air of serenity to the place.

But the ground is blood-soaked. One wintry morning eighty years ago a furious shoot-out erupted there. When it ended three men were dead, and another lay dying.

It was Sunday, February 10, 1918, before dawn. The Graham County Sheriff, two deputies, and a deputized U.S. Marshall rode into Rattlesnake Canyon and approached the cabin. They called for its occupants, Jeff Power, his sons Tom and John, and their hired hand Tom Sisson, to come out with their hands raised. Some accounts say the law officers had come to arrest the Power brothers for World-War-I draft evasion. Others suggest bad blood between the brothers and one of the deputies.

A fierce gun battle ensued. When it ended, the sheriff and his two deputies lay dead and old man Power was mortally wounded. Tom and John Power each had an eye shot out.

The Power boys and Sisson fled, but were captured, tried, and sentenced to life in prison. Sisson died in prison, but the Power brothers were paroled in 1960 and granted a full pardon on January 25, 1969. For a time, the older of the two, John Power, lived in the tunneled entrance of a gold mine the family hoped would bring them wealth.

Back in the mid-1960s, backpackers described meeting an old man, supporting himself with a cane, walking about in Powers Meadow. His greeting was friendly and cheerful, they said. Later, looking at old news photos, they identified the old man as John Power. The old homestead, Powers Cabin, is now on the National Register of Historic Places.

October through March are the best seasons for hiking the Galiuro Wilderness. Winters are often cold and snowy, and, at low elevations, summers can be very hot.

DAY HIKE: POWERS GARDEN TRAIL
One-way length: 8.9 miles
Low and high elevations: 4,660 to 5,330 feet
Difficulty: moderate

To reach the trailhead, travel northwest 13.5 miles on U.S. Highway 70 to Klondyke Road. Turn left on Klondyke and drive 32 miles west to Aravaipa Road. Turn right and drive 3.5 miles northwest to the four-wheel-drive Powers Garden Road (Forest Route 96). Turn left (south) on Forest Route 96 and drive 11 miles to the trailhead at Powers Hill. This route to the trailhead should be attempted only by experienced four-wheel drivers.

Following an old road built by the pioneering Powers family in the early part of the twentieth century, the Powers Garden Trail travels along the bottom of Rattlesnake Canyon. The original wilderness boundaries did not include the road into the Power family's cabin and mine, but the 1984 Wilderness Act redrew the boundaries to include them.

Dry much of the year, Rattlesnake Canyon is nevertheless shaded by a dense canopy of riparian vegetation, and, in the fall, the bigtooth maples there turn vivid red. After about 4.0 miles the trail comes to Powers Garden, a portion of the canyon that was ranched and farmed by the Power family. About 5.0 miles farther along stands the cabin, corrals, junked equipment, and outbuildings of the Power family homestead, now occasionally used by Forest Service personnel. About midway between Powers Garden and Powers Cabin, the Powers Garden Trail intersects the scenic but difficult 4.2-mile Corral Canyon Trail, which climbs 2,000 feet to intersect the East Divide Trail near Kennedy Peak.

> **DAY HIKE: TORTILLA TRAIL**
> One-way length: 8.2 miles
> Low and high elevations: 5,000 to 6,000 feet
> Difficulty: moderate

The Tortilla Trail is a good way to get into the Galiuro Wilderness and to access other trails. It starts at the Deer Creek Trailhead, which can be reached by driving 17 miles south from Safford on U.S. Highway 191 to State Route 266. Turn right (west) on State Route 266 for 19 miles to the town of Bonita. Turn right (north) onto Aravaipa Road and drive about 19 miles to Deer Creek Ranch Road (Forest Route 253). Turn left (west) 8.4 miles to the trailhead.

From the trailhead, the Tortilla Trail heads across the grasslands of the eastern foothills of the Galiuros to Rattlesnake Canyon in the very heart of the wilderness. Crosshatched by a number of cattle trails, the route can be somewhat difficult to follow. At Mud Spring, the Sycamore Trail branches off, heading north. The Tortilla Trail drops into Sycamore Canyon, climbs to a saddle, drops steeply into Horse Canyon and, finally, into Rattlesnake Canyon to intersect the Powers Garden Trail.

> **DESTINATION HIKE: WEST DIVIDE TRAIL**
> One-way length: 23.7 miles
> Low and high elevations: 4,266 to 6,800 feet
> Difficulty: strenuous

The trailhead for the West Divide Trail actually begins at the end of a four-wheel-drive cherry-stemmed road through the Redfield Canyon Wilderness in the southern portion of the Galiuro Mountains. To reach the trailhead, drive east on Interstate 10 to exit 340 at Willcox, then head west-northwest for 32 miles via the Cascabel and Muleshoe roads to the headquarters of The Nature Conservancy's Muleshoe Ranch. From The Nature Conservancy's Registration Station, follow the four-wheel-drive Jackson Cabin Road (Forest Route 691) 13.5 miles to the trailhead situated in a side drainage of Redfield Canyon.

The West Divide Trail proceeds up this drainage into the main canyon, then continues upstream through steep walls and pinnacles before leaving Redfield Canyon near Powers Cabin to climb to high, undulating Grassy Ridge. From Grassy Ridge, the major peaks of the Galiuro range—Kennedy, Kielberg, Bassett, and Biscuit—are all visible, as are the peaks and ridges of the Santa Catalina Mountains, west across the San Pedro Valley. The trail ends at 7,000-foot Maverick Peak, where it intersects the 4.4-mile Pipestem Trail that heads east to meet the Powers Garden Trail about 1.0 mile west of Powers Hill.

Side trails along the route of the West Divide Trail offer loop or tangent hikes for multi-day stays in the Wilderness. One such trail is the 2.0-mile Field Canyon Trail that drops east from Grassy Ridge into Rattlesnake Canyon at Powers Garden.

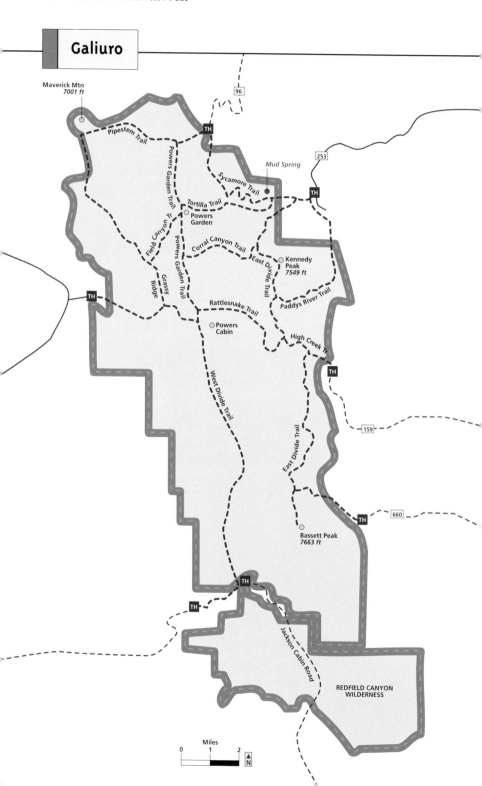

Galiuro

Maverick Mtn
7001 ft

Pipestem Trail

96

TH

Sycamore Trail

Mud Spring

253

TH

Powers Garden Trail

Tortilla Trail

Powers Garden

Field Canyon Tr

Corral Canyon Trail

East Divide Trail

Kennedy Peak
7549 ft

Powers Garden Trail

Grassy Ridge

Paddys River Trail

TH

Rattlesnake Trail

Powers Cabin

High Creek Tr

TH

West Divide Trail

159

East Divide Trail

TH

660

Bassett Peak
7663 ft

TH

TH

Jackson Cabin Road

REDFIELD CANYON
WILDERNESS

Miles
0   1   2

N

DESTINATION HIKE: EAST DIVIDE TRAIL
One-way length: 22.2 miles
Low and high elevations: 4,900 to 7,200 feet
Difficulty: strenuous

The East Divide Trail can be accessed from the Deer Creek Trail (see directions for Tortilla Trail on page 189).

A 22-mile ridgetop trail, the East Divide travels past some of the highest peaks and traverses the upper portions of some of the major canyons in the Galiuro Wilderness. From the trailhead, the East Divide travels along grassy uplands to the upper reaches of Oak Creek. It then climbs out of Oak Creek to the East Divide itself, one of the two major ridges that split the wilderness north to south. A short spur trail along this section leads to the summit of 7,549-foot Kennedy Peak.

The trail then drops from the ridgeline into Douglas Canyon, one of the cool niches of the wilderness that supports Douglas fir, ponderosa, and aspen. The route passes a junction with the 1.7-mile High Creek Trail, which offers a route east out of the wilderness to Forest Route 159. Before the trail drops into Ash Creek Canyon and proceeds to trail's end at Forest Route 660, another spur trail comes in from the south that offers a short hike to 7,663-foot Bassett Peak.

To reach the southern trailhead for the East Divide Trail, drive south from Bonita on the Fort Grant Road to Forest Route 651, then west to Forest Route 660. Forest Route 660 continues west to the trailhead. A four-wheel-drive vehicle is required.

Trails that branch off of the East Divide Trail to offer additional hiking opportunities for multi-day wilderness stays are the Paddys Trail that travels north-east to the Deer Creek Trailhead, and the 5.0-mile Rattlesnake Trail that heads west into Rattlesnake Canyon near Powers Cabin.

LOOP HIKE: SYCAMORE – POWERS GARDEN – TORTILLA TRAILS
One-way length: 17.7 miles
Low and high elevations: 4,800 to 6,000 feet
Difficulty: strenuous

For trailhead directions see Tortilla Trail description on page 189. From the Deer Creek Trailhead, head west for 1.0 mile on the Tortilla Trail to the Sycamore Trail junction at Mud Spring.

Strenuous, the Sycamore Trail winds along the slopes of Sycamore Canyon, descending into and out of riparian corridors lined with sycamore and oak. Along the trail there are good views of the rugged eastern escarpment of the Galiuro Range.

At Powers Hill, the Sycamore Trail meets the Powers Garden Trail which travels south along Rattlesnake Canyon to its intersection with the Tortilla Trail at Powers Garden. From this intersection, it's an 8.2-mile return hike via the Tortilla Trail to the Deer Creek Trailhead.

37 Miller Peak Wilderness

Golden hillsides under gossamer skies

LOCATION: Ten miles south of Sierra Vista

SIZE: 20,190 acres

ELEVATION RANGE: 5,200 to 9,466 feet

MILES OF TRAILS: 44

HABITATS: Desert Grassland to ponderosa pine, Douglas Fir, and aspen

ADMINISTRATION: Coronado National Forest, Sierra Vista Ranger District

TOPOGRAPHIC MAPS: Miller Peak, Huachuca Peak, Montezuma Pass

THE MILLER PEAK WILDERNESS, although small, is a gem of a place for hikers, backpackers, bird watchers, and nature lovers in general. The Chiricahua Apache Indian name for the mountain range in which the Miller Peak Wilderness is situated is Huachuca, meaning "thunder," quite likely referring to the great volumes of thunder and lightning accompanying summer monsoon thunderstorms that annually sweep through southeastern Arizona during July and August.

Established in 1984, the wilderness itself takes its name from 9,466-foot Miller Peak, the highest point in the Huachuca Mountains, a range that butts up against the Arizona-Mexico border. This proximity to Mexico brings to the wilderness area an astounding variety of wildlife. Seventy-eight species of mammals, including coatimundi, mountain lion, black bear, ringtail, white-tailed and mule deer, javelina, and Mexican oppossum, have been found in the wilderness.

New species of butterflies and moths are still being identified in some of the remote canyons; more than sixty species of reptiles have been found here; and the number of bird species identified exceeds 170, including fourteen species of hummingbirds and the Mexican spotted owl, a relative of the endangered Northern spotted owl. Adjacent to the Miller Peak Wilderness, the Nature Conservancy's Ramsey Canyon Preserve is perhaps the best known of southeastern Arizona's many famous birding sites. More than 165 species of birds have been identified there. Recently identified in Ramsey Canyon is a species of leopard frog that croaks underwater. And among the many plants and wildflowers found there is the rare lemon lily.

Hiking and backpacking are the principal recreational activities within the Miller Peak Wilderness and the trails that crisscross its slopes afford stunning views of the region's terrain, both in Arizona and across the international border into Mexico. To the east in the San Pedro River Valley lies the San Pedro Riparian National Conservation Area, which protects the perennially flowing San Pedro River. On clear days, Mexico's Sierra Madre Occidental range is visible to the southeast.

The Fort Huachuca Military Reservation, which comprises the western portion of the Huachuca Mountains, was established in 1877 to help fight during the Apache Wars. Black cavalrymen, known by the Indians as "Buffalo Soldiers," both for their dark visages and fierceness in battle, were stationed at the fort during the Indian campaigns. And during World War II, Fort Huachuca was used as a training base for black infantrymen. Presently, the fort is home for the U.S. Army Intelligence Center and School, and the Army's Information Systems Command.

DAY HIKE: CREST TRAIL TO MILLER PEAK
One-way length: 5.0 miles
Low and high elevations: 6,650 to 9,466 feet
Difficulty: moderate

The Crest Trail trailhead is across the road from the parking area at the Coronado National Memorial in Montezuma Pass along Forest Route 61, approximately twenty miles south of Sierra Vista. Well-maintained, the Crest Trail is the main route across the Miller Peak Wilderness, intersecting many trails as it moves twenty-four miles to its terminus in Blacktail Canyon near the west gate of Fort Huachuca Military Reservation outside the wilderness boundary. From the trailhead, the route climbs very quickly, gaining about 1,500 feet in the first 2.5 miles. As it climbs, the route offers spectacular views southeast into Montezuma Canyon before leveling off to follow the central ridge north. After about 4.5 miles, a spur trail climbs northeast 0.5 mile to Miller Peak. Miller Peak is the payoff. Once the site of a fire lookout tower, the summit offers stunning views in all directions.

DAY HIKE: CARR PEAK TRAIL
One-way length: 2.5 miles
Low and high elevations: 7,420 to 9,230 feet
Difficulty: moderate

To reach the Carr Peak Trail, drive south from Sierra Vista on State Route 92 about 8.0 miles to the Carr Canyon Road, then drive west 6.0 miles to a deadend at the

Ramsey Vista Campground. From the trailhead, the route proceeds southwest up a gentle slope until it reaches a trail fork. Stay right, or southwest, at this point. From here the trail climbs somewhat more steeply toward Carr Peak. As it rounds the peak on the north side, the trail passes through groves of aspen. At a signed trail junction, the trail to the peak itself turns right for 0.2 mile to the summit.

DAY HIKE: BEAR SADDLE – CARR PEAK LOOP
One-way length: 8.5 miles
Low and high elevations: 6,900 to 8,990 feet
Difficulty: moderate

From the trailhead at the Ramsey Vista Picnic Area, this pleasant loop hike around Carr Peak begins on the Carr Canyon Trail. The first leg drops in elevation to intersect the Wisconsin Canyon Trail after about 2.5 miles. From this point it climbs about 1,000 feet in a little more than a mile to Bear Saddle. From the saddle, the route climbs to its junction with the Carr Peak Trail before descending to the trailhead at the picnic area.

DAY HIKE: SUNNYSIDE CANYON TO PAT SCOTT PEAK
One-way length: 5.5 miles
Low and high elevations: 5,850 to 8,525 feet
Difficulty: moderate

In 1887, Samuel Donnelly established the town of Sunnyside as a religious colony. A nearby mine, the Copper Glance, was operated by members of the community. A sawmill prospered at the site, as did a one-room schoolhouse. Between 1914 and 1934, a post office served the town. Long after the religious colony ceased to exist, surviving members stayed on as caretakers, living at the town of Sunnyside until the late-1980s.

The trailhead into Sunnyside begins near the ghost town of Sunnyside off Forest Route 228 on the southwest side of the Miller Peak Wilderness. Traveling along an old jeep road which becomes a foot trail, the Sunnyside Canyon Trail climbs 2,600 feet in roughly five miles to join the Crest Trail. At the Crest Trail, jog a short distance north to the Pat Scott Canyon Trail. From there it's a short climb to Pat Scott Peak.

LOOP HIKES

A brief perusal of trail maps for the Miller Peak Wilderness shows spurs and connectors in the main trail system which will suggest any number of loop hikes to the experienced hiker.

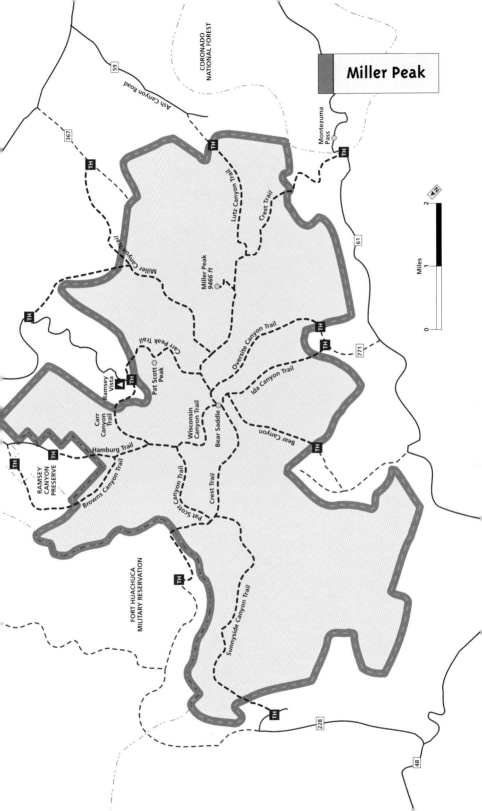

Miller Peak

CORONADO NATIONAL FOREST

Ash Canyon Road

59

367

Montezuma Pass

61

771

Miller Canyon Trail

Lutz Canyon Trail

Crest Trail

Miller Peak
9466 ft

Overside Canyon Trail

Ida Canyon Trail

Carr Peak Trail

Ramsey Vista

Pat Scott Peak

Carr Canyon Trail

Wisconsin Canyon Trail

Bear Saddle

Bear Canyon

Hamburg Trail

RAMSEY CANYON PRESERVE

Browns Canyon Trail

Pat Scott Canyon Trail

Crest Trail

FORT HUACHUCA MILITARY RESERVATION

Sunnyside Canyon Trail

228

48

Miles
0   1   2

N

38 Mount Graham Wilderness Study Area

View from the "Swift Trail" in the Pinaleño Mountains

LOCATION: 20 miles south of Safford

SIZE: 62,000 acres

ELEVATION RANGE: 3,500 to 9,900 feet

MILES OF TRAILS: 77

HABITATS: Lower Sonoran, oak wood and ponderosa pine, mixed conifer and aspen

ADMINISTRATION: Coronado National Forest, Safford Ranger District

TOPOGRAPHIC MAPS: Mt. Graham, Webb Peak, Shingle Mill Mountain, Stockton Pass, Gillespie Mountain, Fort Grant

SOARING TO NEARLY 11,000 FEET, Mount Graham in the Pinaleño Mountains is the loftiest of Southeastern Arizona's "sky islands." Surrounded by desert, the broad mountaintop, *dzil nchaa sí án,* "Big Seated Mountain" to the San Carlos Apaches for whom it is sacred, preserves a Pleistocene-relict spruce-fir forest, fourteen perennial streams, three high-elevation cienegas or wet meadows, and eighteen endemic plants and animals. A black bear foraging the mountain may in one day travel through six distinct life zones. Up in the spruce-fir forest near the summit, biologists have found bear scat containing seeds from prickly pear fruits consumed in the lower-Sonoran desert scrub down around 3,500 feet.

Cherished by biologists as an inland Galapagos, a rare cradle of evolution isolated when glaciers receded 11,000 years ago, Mount Graham is equally prized by University of Arizona astronomers as prime habitat for telescopes. According to astronomers, clear nights, minimal light pollution from nearby cities and towns, low humidity, and the absence of troublesome wind turbulence on the Pinaleño's high peaks make for ideal telescope viewing.

Biologists wanted the mountaintop, which they called a Pleistocene museum, set aside as wilderness, preserved for all time. Astronomers fought wilderness designation, fearing that peaks they considered ideal for astrophysical observation would be forever out of reach if assigned wilderness status.

Enter a small mammal, the now famous Mount Graham red squirrel, *Tamiasciurus hudsonicus grahamensis,* an eight-ounce, foot-long cousin of red squirrels of northern conifer forests. Its numbers fluctuate between 100 and 350, depending on the cone crop and who's doing the counting, but independent biologists agree that a population of less than 500 puts the squirrel in great jeopardy. It was federally listed as endangered in June, 1987.

In the press, the fight between wilderness advocates and astronomers was reduced to reductionist "scopes vs. squirrels" headlines like "jobs vs. owls" and other such slogans that obscure real issues. Nor was the fight about biology versus astronomy, or good science versus bad. What was really at stake was the University of Arizona's preeminence in the astronomy industry, a very serious business in southern Arizona that pumps millions of dollars annually into the Arizona economy.

The web of controversy regarding Mount Graham is a tangled one, and the conflict between environmental and astronomy interests became increasingly acrimonious. Then in October, 1988, a "rider" was attached to the Arizona-Idaho Conservation Act, one of those late-in-the-session omnibus bills that tied up some loose ends on land transfers. Backed by the entire Arizona congressional delegation, it established a Mount Graham International Observatory and ordered the Forest Service to issue a special-use permit for immediate construction of three of the proposed seven telescopes. Additionally, it proclaimed all environmental laws satisfied, specifically the National Environmental Policy Act and the Endangered Species Act. Finally, it exempted the telescope project from further administrative or judicial review.

Ten years later, two telescope installations are up and a third is under construction. Will the Mount Graham Wilderness Study Area (WSA), created in 1986, ever be assigned actual wilderness status? When I posed this question to a Forest Service employee, she answered, "It will take an act of Congress." Will Congress act? Nobody familiar with Mount Graham's recent history is optimistic.

Like all of southeastern Arizona's "sky island" mountain ranges, the Pinaleño Mountains support great biological diversity. In the lower elevations there are plants and animals characteristic of Sonoran Desert scrub habitats, while the upper reaches harbor species common to northern boreal forests. A one-hour drive on the Swift Trail from the base of the mountain to one of the alpine meadows at 9,000 feet is akin to driving from Mexico to Canada in the same day. The many riparian zones support rocky mountain maple, alder, Gambel oak, red-osier dogwood, thimbleberry, and skunk cabbage. American robin, summer tanager, yellow-eyed junco, spotted owl, hermit thrush, mountain chickadee, Townsend's solitaire, raven, black-headed grosbeak, flicker, white-throated swifts, red-faced warbler, hairy woodpecker, Steller's jay, pygmy nuthatch, and a variety of hummingbirds are seen in the wilderness study area.

The Pinaleños are prime habitat for black bear, mountain lion, bobcat, badger, ringtail, spotted skunk, gray fox, pocket gopher, the Mount Graham red squirrel, a great variety of other rodents, and both white-tail and mule deer.

In fact, the name Pinaleño itself is a Spanish variant of the Apache word for deer, pinal.

The lower elevations of the Mount Graham Wilderness Study Area can become exceedingly hot during summer with temperatures above 100 degrees Fahrenheit. Winter at the higher elevations produces heavy snow, closing the Swift Trail in the uppermost reaches of the mountain. Access is possible, however, and cross-country skiers can enjoy miles of good trails. For all-around hiking, the higher trailheads are best in summer.

DAY HIKE: WEBB PEAK TRAIL
One-way length: 2.8 miles
Low and high elevations: 9,120 to 9,960 feet
Difficulty: easy

The trailhead for this short scenic hike is across from the Columbine Visitor Information Station. Drive 9.0 miles south from Safford on U.S. Highway 191 to State Route 366 (Swift Trail), turn right (west), and drive 29 miles up the mountain to the Columbine Visitor Center. From the trailhead, proceed down the Ash Creek Trail for 0.5 mile to the intersection of the Webb Peak Trail. From this junction, the Webb Peak Trail climbs to the Webb Peak Lookout, which is staffed only when fire danger warrants it. The views from this high-elevation peak are splendid.

DAY HIKE: DEADMAN TRAIL
One-way length: 3.4 miles
Low and high elevations: 4,560 to 6,280 feet
Difficulty: moderate

To reach the trailhead from Safford, drive south on 20th Avenue to Golf Course Road and on to Pipeline Road around the golf course. Pipeline Road is rough and narrow and passes through several gates before reaching the trailhead.

Following Deadman Creek through an Upper Sonoran habitat, the trail heads for Deadman Peak, a rugged escarpment that from a distance appears to stand separately from the main ridges and peaks of the mountain. The stream, tumbling down the north side of the mountain through a steep canyon, features picturesque waterfalls during periods of peak streamflow. For the final quarter mile, the trail stays in the canyon bottom before intersecting the Round the Mountain Trail.

DAY HIKE: FRYE CANYON TRAIL
One-way length: 2.8 miles
Low and high elevations: 5,350 to 7,120 feet
Difficulty: easy

To reach the trailhead from Safford, drive northwest on U.S. Highway 70 to Stadium Street in Thatcher. Turn left (south) to Forest Route 103 and continue to Frye Mesa Reservoir. The trailhead is 32 miles beyond the reservoir at the end of Forest Route 103. A four-wheel-drive vehicle or high-clearance pickup is recommended for the section of Forest Route 103 above the reservoir.

Winding through a pleasant riparian zone along a gradually rising old road bed for much of its length, the Frye Canyon Trail is easy to follow except where it travels through rocky terrain. If you keep in mind that the trail follows the streambed, you should be able to pick it up again.

Riparian growth includes willow, Arizona sycamore, and Fremont cottonwood. In the uplands away from the stream, the vegetation is Upper Sonoran Desert. In the first mile, the Frye Canyon Trail is intersected by the Ash Ridge Trail, which travels to the end of Forest Route 508. The Frye Canyon Trail ends at its junction with the Round the Mountain Trail. This junction, called Inception, is the site of an old ranger station.

DAY HIKE: BEAR CANYON TRAIL
One-way length: 6.0 miles
Low and high elevations: 4,840 to 8,780 feet
Difficulty: moderate

To reach the trailhead, drive 9.0 miles south from Safford on U.S. Highway 191 to State Route 366 (Swift Trail) and turn right (west) 17 miles to Ladybug Saddle.

The Bear Canyon Trail is an important connector to two other trails that descend from Ladybug Saddle: Ladybug Trail and Dutch Henry Trail. From its upper reaches, you can see the Dos Cabezas Mountain Wilderness east of Willcox, the Greasewood Mountains, and the Sulphur Springs Valley. Descending from heavily forested terrain through oak and piñon-juniper, the Bear Canyon Trail ends among Upper Sonoran vegetation at its junction with State Route 266. Aptly named, the Bear Canyon Trail moves through prime black bear habitat.

DAY HIKE: LADYBUG TRAIL
One-way length: 5.9 miles
Low and high elevations: 5,200 to 8,780 feet
Difficulty: strenuous

To reach the trailhead follow directions for the Bear Canyon Trail (above).

From the trailhead parking area, take the Bear Canyon Trail for 0.5 mile to the Ladybug Trail junction. Beginning in mixed conifer, the trail travels along

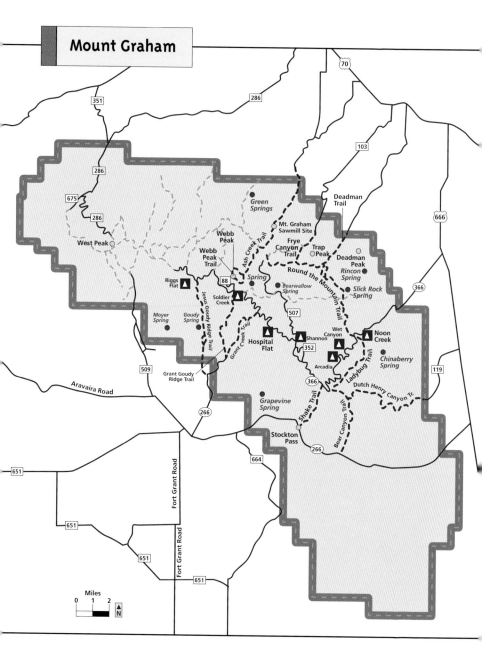

the Wilderness Study Area boundary, crossing Jacobson Ridge and ending at Angle Orchard. As you descend, you will enjoy good views of Jacobson Canyon, the Swift Trail, the Gila Valley, and Gila Mountains. The very steep trail moves from mixed conifer through various life zones to the desert scrub vegetation at the orchard. There is no water available along this trail. Ladybug Peak derives its name from the vast numbers of ladybug beetles that swarm to the peak in the warmer months.

Most people use the upper trailhead for this hike, but if you prefer to climb you can locate the lower trailhead at milepost 128 along State Route 366, the Swift Trail. A short, unsigned 0.5-mile spur trail on the left side of the road leads to the Ladybug Trail.

DAY HIKE: DUTCH HENRY CANYON TRAIL
One-way length: 7.2 miles
Low and high elevations: 3,838 to 8,120 feet
Difficulty: strenuous

To reach the trailhead follow the directions for the Bear Canyon Trail (page 199).

From the trailhead, take the Bear Canyon Trail 0.9 mile to its junction with the Dutch Henry Canyon Trail. One of the few trails that heads east off the mountain, the little-used Dutch Henry Canyon Trail heads into some of the most remote country of the Wilderness Study Area. Beginning among mixed conifers, it descends a steep grade through piñon-juniper, oak, and, finally, sotol, cholla, beargrass and other plants characteristic of the Upper Sonoran life zone. In its lower reaches, the trail winds in and out of Dutch Henry Canyon, an ephemeral stream that flows only in spring. Trail's end is at Forest Route 119 outside the Wilderness Study Area at the site of a corral and windmill.

DAY HIKE: GRANT CREEK TRAIL
One-way length: 5.5 miles
Low and high elevations: 5,520 to 8,895 feet
Difficulty: moderate

To reach the trailhead, drive 9.0 miles south from Safford on U.S. 191 to State Route 366 (Swift Trail), turn right (west) and drive 26 miles to the Cunningham Camp and corral on the left side of the road. The trailhead is at the back of the campground.

From the campground, the trail drops very steeply down a series of switchbacks into Post Creek Canyon. Views to the west across the Sulphur Springs Valley include the Galiuro Mountains and the Winchester Mountains. On very clear days, the Rincon and Santa Catalina Mountains near Tucson are also visible.

Once in the canyon, the trail descends gradually beside Post Creek and then along Grant Creek. The trail ends at the end of Forest Route 157 near Fort Grant. To access the lower trailhead, it is necessary to obtain a key from the Fort Grant Arizona State Prison Administration Building.

DAY HIKE: GRANT–GOUDY RIDGE TRAIL
One-way length: 6.4 miles
Low and high elevations: 5,000 to 9,500 feet
Difficulty: strenuous

To reach the trailhead, drive 9.0 miles on U.S. Highway 191 to State Route 366 (Swift Trail), turn right (west) and drive 29 miles to the Soldier Creek Campground on the left.

The Grant-Goudy Ridge Trail is an old pack trail descending the southwest face of the Pinaleños to historic Fort Grant. A nineteenth-century outpost during the Apache Wars, the fort was abandoned in 1905 and later reopened as an Arizona State Prison. Soldiers stationed at the fort used to escape summer heat by using the trail to climb into the cooler mountain zones.

Winding down the ridge that separates Grant and Goudy Canyons, the trail passes through every life zone offered by the Wilderness Study Area, from cool mixed conifer forests down to the hot desert landscape on the floor of the Sulphur Springs Valley. Views to the west are of the Galiuro and Winchester Mountains.

DAY HIKE: JESUS GOUDY RIDGE TRAIL
One-way length: 8.5 miles
Low and high elevations: 4,840 to 9,140 feet
Difficulty: strenuous

To reach the trailhead, drive 9.0 miles south from Safford on U.S. Highway 191 and turn right (west) on State Route 366 (Swift Trail). The trailhead is at the top of the mountain, 0.5 mile east of the Riggs Lake turnoff.

This very steep trail descends more than 4,000 feet along Goudy Ridge on the southwest flank of the Pinaleños to reach a point a short distance south of the Fort Grant State Prison. Starting above 9,000 feet, the Jesus Goudy Ridge Trail descends from mixed conifer forests, through ponderosa pine, piñon-juniper woodland, oak woodland, desert grassland, and Upper Sonoran life zones. Its south-facing aspect is very hot in summer and there is no water available along the trail. Be sure to pack plenty. Access to the lower trailhead is somewhat difficult. Contact the Safford Ranger District for specific directions.

DAY HIKE: SHAKE TRAIL
One-way length: 5.1 miles
Low and high elevations: 5,500 to 8,500 feet
Difficulty: moderate

To reach the upper trailhead, drive 9.0 miles south from Safford on U.S. Highway 191 to State Route 366 (Swift Trail). Turn right (west) and drive 17.5 miles to the trailhead on the left side of the road. To reach the lower trailhead, drive 19 miles south from Safford on U.S. 191 to State Route 266, turn right (west) and drive 12 miles to the Stockton Pass Picnic Area. The trailhead is in the northwest corner of the picnic area, beyond the fence.

The lower Shake Trail begins in oak woodland and grassland, leading through piñon-juniper up to ponderosa pine forests. A somewhat challenging 3,000-foot climb, the trail winds along slopes that provide great views of the Greasewood Mountains and the Sulphur Springs Valley.

DESTINATION HIKE: ASH CREEK TRAIL
One-way length: 8.2 miles
Low and high elevations: 4,200 to 9,440 feet
Difficulty: strenuous

To reach the upper trailhead, drive to the Columbine Visitor Center (directions on page 198). The trailhead is across the road from the Visitor Center parking lot. The trail along Ash Creek is my favorite hike in the Pinaleño Mountains. Leaving the trailhead, the route drops steeply to follow the drainage, one of the larger streams in the WSA, for almost its entire length. Along the way the trail passes through all of the life zones representative of this spectacular mountain range.

Turn-of-the-century logging on the mountain was very active and in the canyon you will find old mill sites and long-abandoned equipment, including an old wooden flume. The canyon is rich with wildlife; bear, deer, and coatimundi sightings are quite common. In the deeper pools along the middle sections of Ash Creek, there are native Apache trout.

Although the trail is suitable for pack animals, a section of slickrock can be avoided by taking an alternate route. A sign just before the slickrock section warns of the danger and advises a detour. Just below that area, a spectacular waterfall is visible on the right side of the trail. Near the bottom of the trail, outside the Wilderness Study Area, you come to Oak Flat, where there are large Gambel oak, ponderosa pine, and alder—all extremely large. One very large ponderosa at Oak Flat, one of the biggest I've seen, was roughly 15 feet in circumference.

DESTINATION HIKE: ROUND THE MOUNTAIN TRAIL
One-way length: 15.0 miles
Low and high elevations: 5,200 to 9,240 feet
Difficulty: moderate

To reach the trailhead, drive 9.0 miles south from Safford on U.S. Highway 191 to State Route 366 (Swift Trail). Turn right (west) and drive 8.0 miles to the Round the Mountain Picnic Area and trailhead, which is about 1.0 mile beyond the Noon Creek Picnic Area.

Although it does not actually travel around the mountain, this trail is nevertheless an excellent introduction to the varied offerings of the Wilderness Study Area. Starting at 5,200 feet, the Round the Mountain Trail circles the northeast flank of the Pinaleños as it travels from oak woodland up to mixed conifers above 9,000 feet. Along its gradually ascending course, it offers panoramic views of the Gila River Valley, the Gila Mountains, Deadman Peak, Heliograph Peak, and Mount Graham. Water is available at stream crossings and springs, including Marijilda, Deadman, Gibson, and Frye Creeks, and Round the Mountain Spring.

39 Mount Wrightson Wilderness

Slopes of Mount Wrightson

LOCATION: 30 miles south of Tucson

SIZE: 25,260 acres

ELEVATION RANGE: 3,700 to 9,453 feet

MILES OF TRAILS: 52

HABITATS: Oak woodland, pine-fir forest, aspen, alpine meadow

ADMINISTRATION: Coronado National Forest, Nogales Ranger District

TOPOGRAPHIC MAPS: Mount Wrightson, Mount Hopkins, Helvetia

LOCATED IN THE SANTA RITA MOUNTAINS, one of the most popular backcountry regions in southern Arizona, the 25,260-acre Mount Wrightson Wilderness was set aside by the 1984 Arizona Wilderness Act. The centerpiece of the wilderness is its 9,453-foot namesake peak, Mount Wrightson. A visible landmark from Tucson and its surrounding communities, the peak, familiarly known as Mt. Baldy, rises 7,000 feet above the Santa Cruz Valley floor, towering above the arid hills and grasslands leading into the wilderness.

Continental Road, a paved road into the wilderness, travels through Madera Canyon, a bird-watcher's paradise. Mexico is just a short distance south, and with birds migrating with ease from all directions, the canyon attracts great varieties of both common and rare birds. Two hundred and thirty different species of birds have been counted in Madera

Canyon and more than one hundred species are known to breed there. The broad-billed hummingbird, sulphur-bellied flycatcher, elegant trogon, and flammulated owl are among the rare birds spotted in the canyon.

Although prime birding season in Madera Canyon is March through September, rare sightings are possible during any time of year. On a winter hike into Madera, I scoped an Aztec Thrush and a Rufous-backed Robin, both strays from Mexico. Other Mexican strays occasionally seen in Madera Canyon and other southeast Arizona sky islands, summer and winter, include the gray silky-flycatcher, golden-winged warbler, yellow grosbeak, varied thrush, and the Berylline hummingbird.

Other wildlife abounds. The Santa Rita Mountains are prime habitat for black bear, mountain lion, deer, coatimundi, fox, coyote, bobcat, and rare butterflies, moths, and reptiles.

Typical of mountains in Arizona's Basin and Range Province, the Santa Ritas are rugged and steep with vegetation ranging from ocotillo, mesquite, prickly pear, and other desert species at lower elevations up through oak and piñon-juniper to aspen, ponderosa pine, Chiricahua pine, Apache pine, Douglas fir, and aspen in the higher portions. Arizona walnut, cottonwood, ash, and Arizona sycamore are among the trees growing along streambanks.

Hiking is the principal recreational activity in the Mount Wrightson Wilderness Area, along with bird-watching and wildlife photography. Temperatures at lower elevations can be quite hot in summer, so its best to head for the high country. Occasionally, winter-sports enthusiasts snowshoe Wrightson's trails, but the steepness of the terrain is discouraging. Locals, who know how to find the deeper pools, bathe in wilderness streams.

DAY HIKE: OLD BALDY TRAIL
One-way length: 5.4 miles
Low and high elevations: 5,400 to 9,453 feet
Difficulty: strenuous

Two trails, the Old Baldy Trail and the Super Trail, climb to the summit of Mount Wrightson from the Roundup Picnic Area at the end of the paved Continental Road in Madera Canyon. The shorter, steeper Old Baldy Trail ascends 2.5 miles to Josephine Saddle before continuing 2.0 miles to Baldy Saddle, then another 0.9 mile to the summit. The hike begins in oak woodland and moves up through pine and aspen. Openings along the way afford splendid views of the Tucson Valley and the Santa Catalina Mountain Range to the south. Virtually treeless, Baldy Saddle is a favored campsite among backpackers, so the area is pretty well beaten down and littered with the remains of many camp fires.

At 9,453 feet, Mount Wrightson is the highest point in this part of southern Arizona. On a clear day, hikers can see south to the Sierra San José and the Sierra Mariquita in Mexico and, lying along various compass points north of the border, most of southeast Arizona's major wilderness mountain ranges: the Santa Catalinas, Rincons, Galiuros, Pinaleños, Chiricahuas, and Huachucas.

Southeastern Arizona is synonymous with astronomy. Tall mountains, wide open spaces, clear skies, little air turbulence, mild weather, and the relative absence of "light pollution" from big cities create what astronomers call "good seeing." Several peaks in southern Arizona are home to important telescope installations. One of these is the Smithsonian's Whipple Observatory on Mount Hopkins, just below and to the west of Mount Wrightson. On the western horizon is Kitt Peak, home of the world's largest collection of optical telescopes.

A fire lookout was maintained on Mount Wrightson until the 1950s. Now, all that remains of the original lookout cabin is a portion of its foundation. Many area residents still refer to Wrightson as Mount Baldy or Old Baldy, a reference to the bald dome of an Army captain serving at nearby Fort Buchanan. In 1930 the peak was officially named after William Wrightson, a prominent local citizen killed by Indians.

> **DAY HIKE: SUPER TRAIL**
> One-way length: 8.1 miles
> Low and high elevations: 5,400 to 9,453 feet
> Difficulty: moderate

The Super Trail, also beginning at the Roundup Picnic Area, is an easier alternate route to Mount Wrightson. Briefly, it merges with the Old Baldy Trail at Josephine Saddle, then loops gradually around the south side of Mount Wrightson to converge again with the Old Baldy Trail at Baldy Saddle before ascending the final 0.9 mile to the summit.

Many hikers approach the summit of Mt. Baldy by a combination of the two trails. After a short, steep 2.2-mile hike to the Josephine Saddle via the Old Baldy Trail, for example, a hiker may then complete the climb on the gentler Super Trail. Similar options are available coming down, of course.

> **DAY HIKE: JOSEPHINE CANYON**
> One-way length: 5.0 miles
> Low and high elevations: 5,200 to 7,100 feet
> Difficulty: moderate

Hike to Josephine Saddle on the Old Baldy or the Super Trail (see above). At the saddle, the Josephine Canyon Trail drops into the canyon in a southwesterly direction. When it reaches the canyon bottom, the trail becomes somewhat indistinct, but old blaze marks, visible on some trees, are helpful. Hikers should pause occasionally to take their bearings. Josephine Creek carries water most of the year, and, in season, red and yellow monkeyflower and yellow columbine are abundant. Extremely large alligator junipers and ponderosa pines also grow in the canyon bottom and some pools are deep enough for bathing. High ground near the ruins of an old miner's cabin about two miles into the canyon provide an excellent campsite. Mount Hopkins, to the west, is the site of the Smithsonian Institution's Whipple Observatory, which is occasionally visible through breaks in the forest.

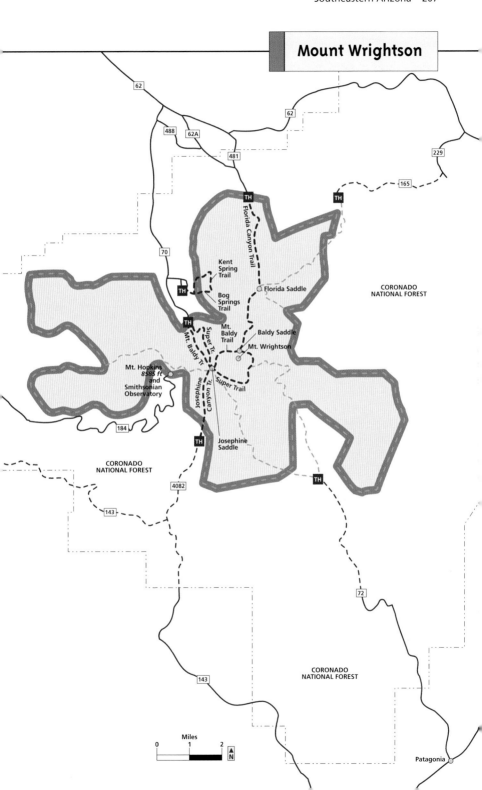

Mount Wrightson

LOOP HIKE: BOG SPRINGS – KENT SPRING
One-way length: 5.0 miles
Low and high elevations: 5,900 to 6,600 feet
Difficulty: moderate

The trailhead for this pleasant hike that passes three springs along its route is at the Bog Springs Campground in Madera Canyon. Less than a mile from the trailhead, the trail enters Bog Springs which is lined with large Arizona sycamore, one of the more striking trees of the Southwest's riparian zones. The trail climbs out of Bog Springs about 1.2 miles south to Kent Spring, a permanent source of water, which like all wilderness water sources should be treated before drinking. From Kent Spring, the highest point of the hike, the trail descends steeply 2.3 miles to the trailhead.

SHUTTLE HIKE: FLORIDA TRAIL – OLD BALDY TRAIL
One-way length: 12.1 miles
Low and high elevations: 4,340 to 9,453 feet
Difficulty: strenuous

The Florida Canyon trailhead begins at the parking area for the University of Arizona's Santa Rita Experimental Work Station on the north side of the range and climbs 3,600 feet to Florida Saddle where four trails, the Florida, Cave Canyon, Sawmill Canyon, and Crest, converge. From the saddle the Crest Trail climbs two miles south to Baldy Saddle. Springs along the way are usually reliable. From Baldy Saddle you may choose either to proceed less than a mile to Mount Wrightson's summit or descend directly to the Roundup Picnic area on either the Old Baldy Trail or the Super Trail, keeping in mind that, although less steep, the Super Trail adds almost three miles to the overall distance to the picnic area.

Florida means "pretty flowers" in Spanish and, in season, wildflowers, including dwarf lupine, monkeyflower, and columbine are abundant along the trail which climbs through oak, piñon-juniper, and a small stand of Arizona madrone before entering ponderosa pine and Douglas fir. Robinson Spring, along the way, is overarched by a canopy of Arizona sycamore, oak, and walnut. Most of the hikes in the Mount Wrightson Wilderness provide wonderful views of the surrounding terrain.

Pajarita Wilderness

Evening reflection in Sycamore Canyon

NO LURE IS MORE POWERFUL than running water to a desert dweller, and Sycamore Canyon in the Pajarita Wilderness, snugged up against the Arizona-Mexico border, is one among a handful of perennial streams in Southern Arizona. Located in the Atascosa Mountains, a range wild enough to make the short list as a Mexican gray wolf reintroduction site, the Pajarita Wilderness, although small, is a magical place.

The creek bubbles to the surface at the trailhead near historic Hank and Yank Springs, which in the 1880s was the site of a ranch owned by John

LOCATION: 15 miles west of Nogales

SIZE: 7,420 acres

ELEVATION RANGE: 3,800 to 4,800 feet

MILES OF TRAILS: 9.5

HABITATS: Desert Riparian

ADMINISTRATION: Coronado National Forest, Nogales Ranger District

TOPOGRAPHIC MAPS: Ruby

"Yank" Bartlett and Henry "Hank" Hewitt, famous mule skinners and Army scouts. In 1886 the ranch was attacked by Indians who killed a neighbor, Phil Shanahan, and wounded Yank. Yank's son, Johnny, made a daring escape and brought help from nearby Oro Blanco.

From the spring, verdant with clumps of watercress, the creek flows 5.3 miles south into Mexico. The first couple of miles are part of the Goodding Research Natural Area, named for botanist Leslie N. Goodding. Several Southwestern plant species bear Goodding's name, including the Goodding willow and the rare Goodding ash.

Typical of natural environments along the border with Mexico, more than 600 species of plants, including a number that are rare or endangered, are found in the Pajarita Wilderness. Growing here, for example, is a species of fern found only in two other places in the world.

With water flowing year-round in Sycamore Canyon, the Pajarita Wilderness is a haven for wildlife. The rare Tarahumara frog, now believed to be extirpated in southern Arizona, was formerly found in the creek, and the elegant trogon is among the rare birds identified here. And, of course, the creek bottom is not only a corridor of movement but also a lifeline for the many mammals that inhabit the wilderness. The terrain in the uplands away from the creek bottom is woodland consisting of several varieties of oak.

DAY HIKE: SYCAMORE CANYON
One-way length: 5.3 miles
Low and high elevations: not available
Difficulty: easy

To reach the Sycamore Canyon Trailhead, drive south from Tucson on Interstate 19 to Peña Blanca Road (State Route 289). Turn west for 9 miles to Peña Blanca Lake where State Route 289 joins Forest Road 39. Continue west on Forest Route 39 for approximately 9 miles to the turnoff to Sycamore Canyon.

For the first few miles, the trail along the creekbed meanders between soaring cliffs, quite narrow in places. Following periods of heavy rain, some of the pools in Sycamore Canyon can become quite deep. After three miles the canyon chokes to a narrows where water drops over a small waterfall and runs a narrow

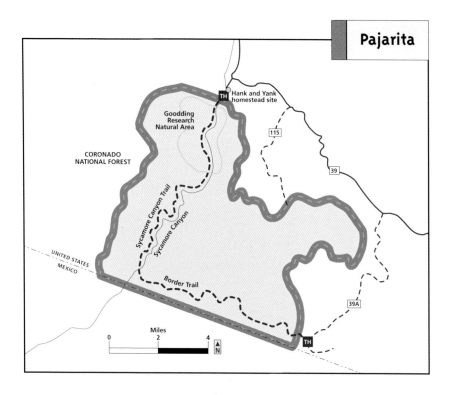

chute to fill a large pool, one of my favorite swimming holes. About a mile beyond the pool the creek is lined with tall and beautiful Arizona sycamore, the canyon's namesake tree.

The best times to hike the canyon are spring and fall. I've hiked it in summer, but on one occasion I was driven out by biting insects. Winter hikes are possible, but the narrow canyon can become extremely cold in winter.

The hike ends at the international border, which is clearly marked by a barbed wire fence. Another trail parallels the border fence, but I don't recommend it.

41 Peloncillo Mountains Wilderness

Massive rock formations

LOCATION: 9 miles northeast of San Simon

SIZE: 9,440 acres

ELEVATION RANGE: 4,100 and 6,400 feet

MILES OF TRAILS: No marked or maintained trails

HABITATS: Desert scrub, semidesert grassland, oak-juniper woodland

ADMINISTRATION: BLM, Safford Field Office

TOPOGRAPHIC MAPS: Doubtful Canyon, San Simon, Engine Mountain, Orange Butte

IT'S NEITHER ONE OF THE MOST EXPANSIVE nor among the highest of southeast Arizona's numerous mountain ranges, but from the standpoint of biodiversity, the Peloncillo ("bald hills" in Spanish) Mountains along the Arizona-New Mexico border are no less important. Peregrine falcons nest on its sheer cliff faces, and Gould's turkey, scaled quail, white-tailed deer, badger, porcupine, harvest mouse, white-throated wood rat, mule deer, gray fox, desert bighorn, mountain lion, pallid bat, Western kingbird, black-tailed gnatcatcher, burrowing owl, horned lark, red-tailed hawk, rock wren, mountain lion, bobcat, cactus wren, Say's phoebe, ash-throated flycatcher, white-winged dove, desert cottontail, and a host of reptiles and amphibians inhabit the wilderness. In 1986 the Arizona Game and Fish Department released 31 desert bighorn sheep in the Peloncillo Wilderness. By 1994, when

15 additional bighorns were released, the original herd had increased to approximately 55 animals.

In March 1996, rancher Warner Glenn encountered a Mexican jaguar, believed to be extirpated in Arizona, in a southern portion of the Peloncillo Mountains, outside the wilderness, down along the Mexican border. The amazingly powerful jaguar, which can weigh up to 250 pounds, kills and eats large mammals such as deer, javelina, and bighorn sheep. The U.S. Fish and Wildlife Service has since put the jaguar on the endangered list for Arizona, New Mexico, and Texas, opening up the possibility that the jaguar may eventually extend its range throughout its historical habitat in southeast Arizona's mountain wildlands.

Located in a region where the Chihuahuan Desert fingers its way west into Arizona, the Peloncillo Mountains Wilderness features both Sonoran and Chihuahuan plants and animals. Spring finds Mexican poppy, spectacle pod, desert marigold, and wild heliotrope blooming on the hillsides. Creosote bush, honey mesquite, desert holly, feather dalea, banana yucca, lechuguilla, century plant, ocotillo, sotol, bear grass, Mexican palo verde, soaptree yucca, and four-wing saltbush are among the trees, shrubs, and grasses found in the Peloncillos, along with a variety of cacti.

The Peloncillo Mountains marked the eastern boundary of a former large reservation in southeastern Arizona that Chiricahua Apache leader, Cochise, successfully negotiated in a settlement with U.S. Army General O.O. Howard. And it was in Skeleton Canyon in the southern portion of the Peloncillos where Geronimo surrendered for the fourth and final time on September 4, 1886.

The historic Butterfield Stage Line, originating near St. Louis and running all the way to San Francisco, traveled through a pass near the southern end of the present wilderness on its leg between El Paso and Tucson. Passengers aboard the stage, which took almost a month to make the trip, were expected to assist the crew in fighting off Apache marauders.

October through mid-May are the best times to enter the Peloncillo Wilderness. Winters are quite cold and often snowy; summers can be extremely hot.

WILDERNESS ACCESS

Primitive roads leading into the wilderness generally require a four-wheel-drive vehicle, although in good weather it is possible to enter the west side of the wilderness in a high-clearance two-wheel-drive. Check your topo maps carefully before venturing out on these roads.

To reach the west side of the wilderness from the small community of San Simon, north of Interstate 10, drive north from town on Kennedy Road. Approximately 10 miles from town, a road heading into Ward Canyon comes in from the east. Explorations into Ward Canyon and cross-country hiking into the wilderness are possible from this access point. If you continue driving north along Kennedy Road, you will find routes into the wilderness at Indian Springs Canyon and at Tule Canyon near Tule Well.

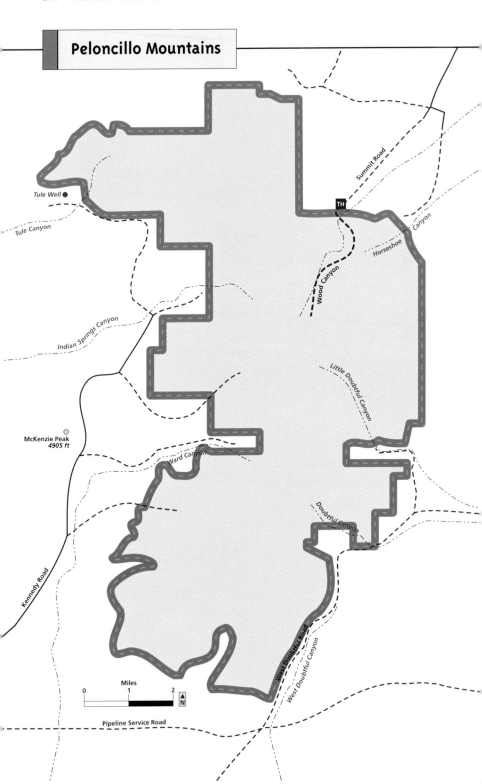

Peloncillo Mountains

Summit Road

TH

Tule Well ●

Tule Canyon

Horseshoe Canyon

Wood Canyon

Indian Springs Canyon

Little Doubtful Canyon

McKenzie Peak
4905 ft

Ward Canyon

Doubtful Canyon

Kennedy Road

West Doubtful Road

West Doubtful Canyon

Miles
0   1   2

N

Pipeline Service Road

A natural gas pipeline road provides access to the southeastern portion of the wilderness. To reach this road, drive about 4.0 miles north from San Simon on Kennedy Road. Turn east on the pipeline road for about 5.0 miles to West Doubtful Road and turn north a short distance to the wilderness boundary. The road continues about 3.0 miles north along the wilderness boundary to West Doubtful Canyon and Little Doubtful Canyon. Cross-country hiking into the wilderness is possible from these access points.

To reach the northeastern portion of the wilderness, drive about 17 miles east from Duncan on State Route 70 to Summit Road. Turn south on Summit Road and proceed about 5.0 miles to Wood Canyon. From this point you can follow Wood Canyon into the wilderness. Horseshoe Canyon can also be accessed via the Summit Road.

42 Pusch Ridge Wilderness

Sunset along the Arizona Trail

LOCATION: Santa Catalina Mountains, north of Tucson

SIZE: 56,933 acres

ELEVATION RANGE: 2,800 and 9,000 feet

MILES OF TRAILS: More than 100

HABITATS: Sonoran desert to Canadian Life Zone

ADMINISTRATION: Coronado National Forest, Safford and Santa Catalina Ranger Districts

TOPOGRAPHIC MAPS: Mt. Lemmon, Oro Valley, Tucson North, Sabino Canyon

THE SANTA CATALINA MOUNTAINS, the northern rampart of the Tucson Valley, along with the Rincon Mountains, which define the valley's eastern perimeter, are what earn Tucson, Arizona its reputation as one of the West's top cities for quick access to the backcountry. Several trails heading into the Pusch Ridge Wilderness can be reached from the Santa Catalina foothills on the city's north side. Others are easily accessible, either along the paved Catalina Highway, which travels twenty-six miles from the base of the range to the village of Summerhaven near its summit, or from Catalina State Park on the range's west flank.

The path of Pusch Ridge toward wilderness status began in 1927 when the U.S. Secretary of Agriculture established the Santa Catalina Research Natural Area, the first such classification in the United States. When population growth and development began to encroach on the Santa Catalina foothills, Congress enacted the Endangered American Wilderness Act of 1978, which set aside several areas across the nation, including the 56,933-acre Pusch Ridge Wilderness.

The succession of names for the Santa Catalina range and its peaks reflects the cultural heritage of the Tucson basin. To the Tohono O'odham, the native people of this region, it was and is *Babat Duag,* Frog Mountain. In 1697, Jesuit missionary Padre Eusebio Francisco Kino arrived and named the range Santa Catarina, reportedly after his sister. That spelling held for about 150 years when it was changed to Catalina. The range's principal peak, Mount Lemmon (9,157 feet), was named for Sara Lemmon, a botanist who, with her husband, John, identified many new species while working near the summit.

Typical of block-faulted mountain ranges in southeast Arizona, the Santa Catalinas feature steep, vertical rock faces creased by deep canyons on the south flank and rounded, gentle slopes on the north. The Pusch Ridge Wilderness lies, for the most part, within the rugged terrain of the south-facing slopes. Like all of the area's "sky islands," the Santa Catalinas contain great biological diversity. Ecosystems range from lower Sonoran desert scrub at around 3,000 feet to spruce-fir at 9,000 feet. The major canyons throughout the range are rich with riparian vegetation including Arizona sycamore, cottonwood, ash, willow, walnut, and box elder. Climate in the wilderness varies with elevation. Precipitation rates range from approximately twelve inches annually at lower elevations to more than thirty inches, mostly snow, at the highest reaches.

With trail systems interlacing mile after mile throughout the wilderness, hiking and backpacking are the main recreational activities in the Pusch Ridge Wilderness, but rock climbing, snowshoeing, cross-country skiing, and horseback riding are also popular. Rock climbing is especially popular in Sabino Canyon, the Wilderness of Rocks area, and at Windy Point, about halfway up the mountain on the Catalina Highway.

Desert bighorn sheep occupy the wilderness centerpiece, the rugged escarpment known as Pusch Ridge. Be aware that the Forest Service limits activities within the bighorn sheep management area. Dogs are NOT allowed within the management area, ever. During the lambing period, January 1 through April 30, hiking and camping are limited and group-size restrictions are imposed. For additional information contact the Santa Catalina Ranger District (see Appendix 2).

DAY HIKE: SEVEN FALLS
One-way length: 2.3 miles
Low and high elevations: 2,750 and 3,250 feet
Difficulty: easy

The trailhead into the Bear Canyon Trail, which leads to Seven Falls, is located at the Lower Bear Canyon Picnic Area 1.7 miles from the Sabino Canyon Visitor Center. Several times in the first two miles the trail crisscrosses Bear Creek, which, during periods of heavy rain, can run swift and deep. Use caution. The hike up the creek bottom is an excellent introduction to the Sonoran Desert riparian habitat, passing through magnificent stands of Arizona sycamore. The uplands away from the creek are vegetated with saguaro cactus, mesquite, and palo verde.

After the final crossing, the trail climbs out of the creek and travels about 0.5 mile to the falls which are clearly visible on the left. One of the more popular areas in Tucson's backcountry, Seven Falls is spectacular after periods of heavy runoff. Then, pools at the base of most falls are deep enough for swimming. The rocks can be very slippery when wet, however, so climb carefully.

DAY HIKE: SABINO – BEAR CANYON LOOP
One-way length: 11.1 miles
Low and high elevations: 3,300 and 4,800 feet
Difficulty: moderate

The Sabino Canyon Trail begins at the end of a paid shuttle ride four miles up the paved road in the Upper Sabino Canyon Recreation Area. The trail climbs about 200 feet out of the shuttle parking area to intersect the Phone Line Trail. From the intersection, the Sabino Canyon Trail continues for 2.0 miles along a ridge above Sabino Creek to Sabino Basin, where several trails join. The East Fork Trail climbs out of the basin for 2.0 miles to the junction of the East Fork, Sycamore Canyon, and Bear Canyon Trails. From there the trail drops south into Bear Canyon and 4.3 miles to Seven Falls, then 2.3 miles to the Lower Bear Canyon picnic area where hikers may either walk 1.7 miles to the visitor center parking lot or catch another shuttle-bus ride.

A longer version of this hike can be had by abandoning the shuttle bus ride at the beginning and hiking instead along the Phone Line Trail, which traces the wilderness boundary for 3.2 miles along the east ridge of Sabino Canyon to its intersection with the Sabino Canyon Trail. From there, proceed as outlined above.

With Arizona sycamore, ash, cottonwood, walnut, hackberry, alder, alligator juniper, and Arizona cypress, Sabino and Bear Canyons are classic riparian habitats. Excellent campsites with good swimming holes are located in the vicinity of Sabino Basin and along Bear Creek. Oak, manzanita, and piñon are found in the upper sections of this loop hike.

DAY HIKE: PIMA CANYON TRAIL
One-way length: 8.6 miles
Low and high elevations: 2,900 to 7,255 feet
Difficulty: moderate

To reach the trailhead, drive north on Oracle Road to Magee Road and turn right (east) to the parking area and trailhead. It looks like the suburbs at the beginning, but the trail soon leaves the residential areas behind as it climbs a v-shaped notch carved into the south face of Pusch Ridge. Although dry for much of the year, Pima Canyon is a good example of a desert riparian area, where plenty of vegetation

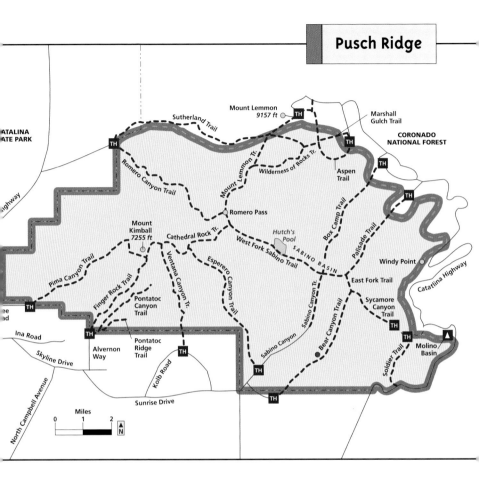

Pusch Ridge

attracts many birds and mammals. As the trail climbs, views of Tucson, the Santa Cruz River Valley, and distant mountain ranges become better and better. Beyond Pima Spring the trail becomes steeper and more difficult as it climbs to the junction with the Finger Rock Trail, the turnaround point. Good views of Cathedral and Window rocks are the bonus for climbing to trail's end.

DAY HIKE: ROMERO TRAIL
One-way length: 6.6 miles
Low and high elevations: 2,800 to 6,000 feet
Difficulty: moderate

The trailhead is in Catalina State Park, nine miles north of Tucson on State Route 77 (Oracle Road). Because it is hatchworked by a number of crossing trails in its lower elevations, the Romero Trail is initially somewhat difficult to follow. From its lower reaches, the trail offers good views of Pusch Ridge and Cathedral Rock. As the trail climbs to Romero Pass, vistas to the south and west open up. Along the route you will pass Montrose Pools and Romero Pools, which usually carry water year-round. At Romero Pass, which is your turnaround, connecting trails provide access to the summit of Mount Lemmon, to the Wilderness of Rocks area, and to Sabino Basin and beyond to Sabino Canyon.

DAY HIKE: SOLDIER TRAIL
One-way length: 2.6 miles
Low and high elevations: 3,200 to 4,900 feet
Difficulty: easy

To reach the trailhead, drive up the Catalina Highway to the Old Prison Camp Road at milepost 7. Turn left and follow the road to the trailhead. This easy trail follows the route of an old road to the site of a former prison camp. As the trail climbs, it offers good views of Tucson before descending into Soldier Canyon. After periods of snowmelt or heavy rain, there are some impressive waterfalls in Soldier Canyon. Spur paths leading to overlooks can be somewhat confusing, so keep an alert eye on the trail.

LOOP HIKE: WILDERNESS OF ROCKS – LEMMON TRAIL LOOP
One-way length: 13.6 miles
Low and high elevations: 7,300 and 8,800 feet
Difficulty: strenuous

The trail begins at the Marshall Gulch Picnic Area about a mile south of the village of Summerhaven. From Marshall Gulch, the route proceeds up the lush canyon bottom for 1.2 miles to Marshall Saddle where it intersects the Aspen and Carter Ridge Trails. The trail is graced by large pine and fir trees and, in wetter seasons, a plethora of wildflowers. At Marshall Saddle, the Wilderness of Rocks Trail descends gradually into an area of enormous weathered boulders that give the area its name. After about 1.7 miles, the Lemmon Rock Trail comes in from the north and the Wilderness of Rocks Trail proceeds west through the fantastically eroded outcroppings another 2.3 miles to the intersection of the Mt. Lemmon Trail. At this point the Mt. Lemmon Trail turns north and climbs steeply for 3.5 miles to the Lemmon Rock Lookout, which is just inside the northern edge of the wilderness. The Lookout is a great rest stop with wonderful views into the surrounding canyons.

From the Lemmon Rock Lookout the Lemmon Rock Trail descends 2.0 miles to its intersection with the Wilderness of Rocks Trail. From this point, it is 2.9 miles east to the trailhead at Marshall Gulch.

SHUTTLE HIKE: ESPERERO – VENTANA CANYON LOOP
One-way length: 14.8 miles
Low and high elevations: 2,850 and 7,000 feet
Difficulty: moderate

The Esperero Canyon trailhead begins at the Cactus Picnic Area less than one mile north of the Sabino Canyon Visitor Center. After climbing over a low ridge the trail drops into Rattlesnake Canyon, rises several hundred feet to a mesa, and then descends to Bird Canyon. At this point, the trail briefly crosses private land and hikers should avoid camping or picnicking until reentering the wilderness area. From here the trail climbs in a series of switchbacks to a saddle overlooking Esperero Canyon. Straight ahead is the magnificent spire of Cathedral Rock. Now the trail descends into Esperero Canyon and proceeds through the canyon bottom among stands of impressive oak trees. Camping is good in this portion of the canyon, although water is scarce. Bridal Veil Falls, to the left of the trail approximately 0.5 mile above Esperero Canyon, provides an excellent campsite and reliable water except during the driest seasons. The falls are about 5.5 miles and approximately 2,500 feet above the trailhead.

From the falls, the trail climbs about 1.0 mile to its intersection with the West Fork Trail which branches east into the West Fork of Sabino Canyon. The Esperero Trail turns west at this point and climbs to a saddle at the head of the canyon where it continues to switchback across the ridge into Ventana Canyon.

Here the downward portion of your hike begins as the trail descends steeply into Ventana Canyon for approximately 2.0 miles to a natural feature called The Window. At this point you are about 6.4 miles from the Ventana Canyon trailhead.

43 Redfield Canyon Wilderness

Evening light beyond Redfield Canyon with Rincon Mountains in distance

LOCATION: 32 miles north of Benson

SIZE: 6,600 acres

ELEVATION RANGE: 3,400 to 4,000 feet

MILES OF TRAILS: No marked or maintained trails

HABITATS: Desert Riparian

ADMINISTRATION: BLM, Safford Field Office

TOPOGRAPHIC MAPS: The Mesas, Cherry Spring Peak

IF WHAT IS PROTECTED AS WILDERNESS is a measure of value, the Redfield Canyon Wilderness is among the most treasured. The reason is water. Redfield contains running water year-round. In terrain where average annual precipitation is less than twelve inches, the presence of running water, live water, perennial water (the variety of ways we express the idea indicates the degree to which it is cherished) is magical.

Another of the smaller wilderness areas managed by the Bureau of Land Management (BLM), Redfield Canyon, located at the southern terminus of the Galiuro Mountains, is a narrow, beautiful canyon, strewn with boulders. The terrain away from the river is typical of desert uplands vegetated with saguaro cactus, mesquite, sotol, prickly pear, deer grass, ocotillo, shin dagger, and catclaw acacia. The creek bottom is vegetated by a more or less typical assemblage of riparian

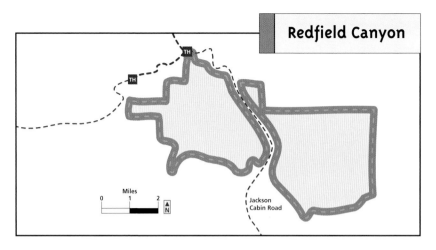

vegetation: Arizona walnut, sycamore, bigtooth maple, ash, alder, willow, hackberry, cottonwood, canyon grape, and Arizona cypress.

The Gila chub, an endangered fish, survives in the creek. A species of long-nosed bat and the common black hawk are two other threatened or endangered species found in Redfield Canyon.

The canyon wren, signature bird of Southwestern canyons, rings the steep red walls of Redfield with its descending trill. Other birds commonly identified here include red-tailed and Swainson's hawks, ravens, kestrels, and the phainopepla, or silky flycatcher.

HIKING THE CANYON

Access to the Redfield Canyon Wilderness can be a problem. There are two ways in. The most direct route is achieved by driving 40 miles north on the Pomerene Road from Benson to an unmarked turnoff at the small townsite of Redington. A rutted jeep trail that parallels Redfield Canyon travels east about 10 miles to the trailhead. Since the road crosses both private and State Trust Land, permission must be obtained from the State Land Department (see Appendix 2) and, at least theoretically, from private landowners, although in the past most landowners have not objected.

About 9.0 miles east of Pomerene Road, the jeep road turns sharply north. Here, fire rings dot a broad flat favored by hunters and campers. Park here and hike. A rough jeep road drops away sharply to the south, heading down into the canyon itself. After about 1.0 mile the old jeep road becomes a trail. Once in Redfield you can hike upstream or downstream in the roughly 10-mile long canyon, exploring side canyons along the way.

The other route into Redfield Canyon Wilderness can be accessed by driving east on Interstate 10 to exit 340 at Willcox, then heading west-northwest for 32 miles via the Cascabel Road and the Muleshoe Road to the headquarters of The Nature Conservancy's Muleshoe Ranch. From The Nature Conservancy's Registration Station, follow the four-wheel-drive Jackson Cabin Road (Forest Route 691), which is cherry stemmed out of the wilderness, for 13.5 miles into Redfield Canyon.

44 Saguaro Wilderness East

Blue sky and tall Saguaro cacti

LOCATION: 10 miles east of Tucson

SIZE: 98,520 acres

ELEVATION RANGE: 3,000 to 8,666 feet

MILES OF TRAILS: 77

HABITATS: Sonoran Desert to ponderosa pine, spruce-fir forest

ADMINISTRATION: National Park Service and Coronado National Forest, Santa Catalina Ranger District

TOPOGRAPHIC MAPS: Tanque Verde Peak, Mica Mountain, Rincon Peak, Soza Canyon, Piety Hill, Happy Valley, Galleta Flat West

ALTHOUGH ADMINISTRATIVELY SEPARATE, the Rincon Mountain Wilderness and Saguaro National Park East encompass the same terrain in the Rincon Mountains rising above the Tucson Valley's eastern margin. Treating each independently would be repetitive and confusing. To avoid that, I have decided in this book to combine them into a single unit, here referred to as Saguaro Wilderness East.

The first wilderness designation for this desert and mountain terrain came in 1976 when 59,390 acres of Saguaro National Monument (now Saguaro National Park) was set aside as Saguaro Wilderness East. Then in 1984, a 38,590-acre allocation of adjacent forest land created the Rincon Mountain Wilderness. Together these two units, which share common boundaries, preserve nearly 100,000 acres of back-country wildlands.

The change in lifezones as you hike upward along one of the longer ridges of Saguaro Wilderness East is quite marked, if not dramatic. Cactus forests of saguaro, barrel, cholla, and prickly pear mix with mesquite, palo verde, and ocotillo in the lower elevations. Higher up, grasses appear along with bear grass, sotol, and century plant. Oak, manzanita, and piñon-juniper begin to come in at about the 5,000-foot level and, as you approach 7,000 feet, the first ponderosa pines mingle with Gambel oak. Finally, in the highest reaches of the wilderness, Douglas fir and occasional groves of aspen can be found.

In spring and early summer, particularly after periods of ample fall and winter rainfall, wildflowers—including Mexican poppy, tackstem, fairy duster, wild hyacinth, lupine and others—bloom abundantly in the canyons and hillsides of Saguaro Wilderness East.

Black bear, deer, ringtail, fox, javelina, bobcat, mountain lion, badger, raccoon, and coyote are at home in the wilderness, as are a variety of birds, including cactus wren, Scott's oriole, phainopepla, curve-billed thrasher, common flicker, red-tailed hawk, great horned owl, poorwill, scrub and pinyon jay, and yellow-eyed junco.

Not as vast nor as rugged as the nearby Santa Catalina Mountains, their sister range to the north, the lesser-traveled Rincon Mountains nevertheless provide even greater opportunities for wilderness solitude. Most trails leading into the wilderness are long and steep, discouraging all but the hardiest of hikers. On the domed summit, a network of trails offers a number of day-hiking routes from Manning Camp, a high-elevation base camp. Camping within Saguaro Wilderness East requires a permit from the National Park Service and is limited to six primitive campgrounds within the wilderness.

In winter, the upper elevations of Saguaro Wilderness East are cold and snow-covered. In summer, daytime temperatures at the lower elevations routinely exceed 100 degrees Fahrenheit. Hikers are well-advised to choose their seasons wisely and to carry plenty of water. A number of very short but scenic hiking trails criss-cross lower portions of the wilderness. Maps for these may be obtained at the Park Service visitor center.

Some trails are closed to pack stock; off-trail hiking is forbidden in some portions of the wilderness; and camping is limited to one of six designated wilderness campsites. Inquire at the Visitor Center about these and other regulations.

> **DAY HIKE: ITALIAN SPRING TRAIL**
> One-way length: 4.8 miles
> Low and high elevations: 4,300 to 6,800 feet
> Difficulty: moderate

Although the Italian Spring Trail is the shortest route to the high country of Saguaro Wilderness East, its trailhead is the toughest to reach and requires a four-wheel-drive vehicle. To reach it drive east from Tucson on the paved Tanque Verde Road, the name of which changes to Redington Pass Road before it turns into gravel. From the beginning of the gravel section continue for 9.6 miles on the Redington Pass Road to the Italian Spring turnoff, Forest Route 37, where a sign with an Arizona

Trail logo is erected. From here it is approximately five miles south to the Italian Spring Trailhead.

The Italian Spring Trail begins outside the wilderness boundary, and is quite steep. The trail climbs more than 3,000 feet in about five miles to reach the North Slope Trail near Italian Spring. This is the turnaround point for day hikers.

DAY HIKE: MILLER CREEK TRAIL TO RINCON PEAK
One-way length: 8.1 miles
Low and high elevations: 4,200 to 8,482 feet
Difficulty: strenuous

To reach the Miller Creek Trailhead drive east from Tucson on Interstate 10 to the Mescal Road-J-Six Ranch turnoff (exit #297). Travel north on Mescal Road to Forest Route 35. Continue north on Forest Route 35 for 16 miles to a sign for the Miller Creek Trail. Turn left (west) for 0.2 mile to the trailhead.

Beginning outside the wilderness boundary, the Miller Creek Trail climbs about 2,000 feet in 4.5 miles to Happy Valley Saddle and the intersection of the Heartbreak Ridge Trail, which heads north and south from the intersection. Turn left (south) on the Heartbreak Ridge Trail for 0.5 mile to where it connects with the Rincon Peak Trail near the Happy Valley Campground. From this point the Rincon Peak Trail travels south 3.2 miles to the 8,482-foot summit of Rincon Peak.

The Rincon Creek Trail proceeds from the Happy Valley campsite to the Madrona Ranger Station, 8.0 miles south. There is no trailhead access at the ranger station. After about 4.0 miles, the north-heading portion of the Heartbreak Ridge Trail intersects the crosshatch of trails in the vicinity of Manning Camp.

DAY HIKE: TURKEY CREEK TO DEARHEAD SPRING
One-way length: 6.2 miles
Low and high elevations: 4,600 to 6,600 feet
Difficulty: moderate

To reach the Turkey Creek Trailhead follow the directions for accessing the Miller Creek Trailhead but continue on Forest Route 35, 0.4 mile beyond the Miller Creek Trail turnoff to Forest Route 4408 and go another 0.4 mile to a gate. The trail starts up a grassy ridge on the opposite side of the creek.

The chief advantage of the Turkey Creek Trail over the Miller Creek Trail is that it's a shorter route to the network of trails at the top of the mountain. The Turkey Creek Trail, which begins outside the wilderness, climbs about 2,000 feet in approximately 6.2 miles to reach the Deer Spring Trail. From this junction, it is only 0.6 mile north to Spud Rock Spring where the Deer Spring Trail connects with the Devil's Bathtub Trail, linking with the Fire Loop Trail, leading to the Bonita Trail, and so forth.

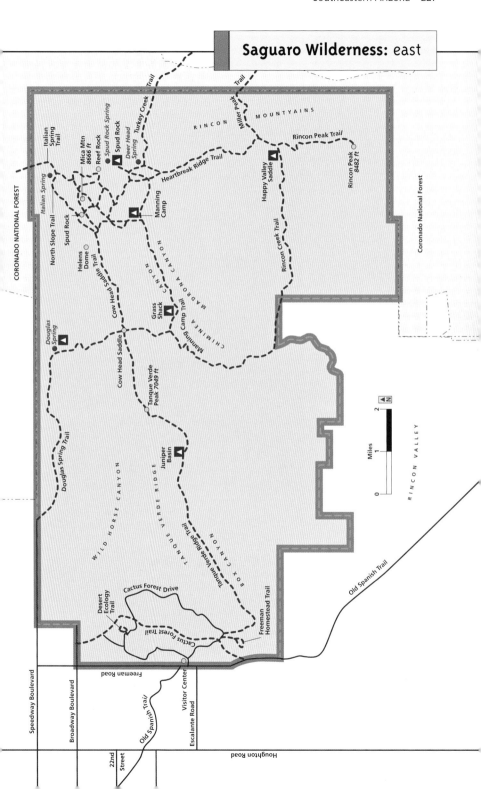

Saguaro Wilderness: east

DESTINATION HIKE: DOUGLAS SPRING –
COW HEAD SADDLE TRAIL

One-way length: 12.5 miles
Low and high elevations: 2,700 to 8,000 feet
Difficulty: moderate

To reach the trailhead for the Douglas Spring Trail, drive west from the Tucson city limits on Speedway Boulevard until it deadends. There are two trailheads at this point, one for packstock, the other for hikers.

The Douglas Spring Trail crosses a number of drainages and winds for more than a mile through classic giant Saguaro forest before it begins to ascend a long ridge toward Douglas Spring. During the summer of 1994 a wildfire raged in the Rincons, closing many trails, Douglas Spring among them. Although the charred remains of the fire are still visible, the vegetation has come back stronger and healthier than before the fire. Climbing steadily, the trail offers splendid views of the Tucson Valley below, of distant mountain ranges, and of the sprawling City of Tucson itself.

After 6.2 miles the trail reaches Douglas Spring, one of the six primitive campsites within the wilderness. Stream-flow at Douglas Spring is erratic, occurring only after periods of heavy snowmelt or steady rainfall. It is not a reliable source of water. Many hikers stop here for the night before going on to Manning Camp.

From Douglas Spring the trail climbs 2.5 miles to Cow Head Saddle to connect with the Cow Head Saddle Trail heading north some 2,500 feet in elevation to Manning Camp. From the trail junction it is approximately four miles to Manning Camp. During summer months the old log cabin at Manning Camp is staffed by the Forest Service and fire crews are quartered nearby. It is also a back-country campsite. Water is available at Manning Camp.

On a web of trails that spreads from Manning Camp across the mountain's broad, forested dome, some interesting day hikes are possible. The Bonita, Devil's Bathtub, East Slope, Mica Mountain, and Mica Meadow trails are all accessible from Manning Camp. The aforementioned Mica Mountain Trail travels to the summit of its namesake peak, the 8,666-foot Mica Mountain, the highest point in the Rincons.

DESTINATION HIKE: TANQUE VERDE RIDGE TO MANNING CAMP

One-way length: 19.4 miles
Low and high elevations: 2,700 to 8,000 feet
Difficulty: moderate

The Tanque Verde Ridge Trail begins at the Javelina Picnic Area within Saguaro National Park. For the first mile it travels across lower-Sonoran Desert terrain before beginning its ascent of Tanque Verde Ridge, a long, prominent spine ascending the southeastern flank of the Rincon Mountains. The trail follows the ridge line to Juniper Basin, a primitive campsite some seven miles and 3,000 feet in elevation from the trailhead.

From Juniper Basin, the route climbs for 2.0 miles to reach Tanque Verde Peak, a 7,049-foot summit. From the peak, the Tanque Verde Trail drops to Cow Head Saddle, some 1,000 feet and 2.5 miles down the trail.

Three other trails connect with the Tanque Verde Trail at Cow Head Saddle: the Douglas Spring Trail, the Cow Head Saddle Trail, and an unnamed trail heading south. Take the south-heading trail for approximately 1.5 miles to its junction with the Manning Camp Trail and turn east approximately 4.0 miles to where the Devil's Bathtub Trail comes in from the east. Turn north about 1.0 mile to Manning Camp.

If you prefer an overnight stop before proceeding to Manning Camp, try the Grass Shack campsite, which lies approximately one-half mile east of the junction of the unnamed trail and the Manning Camp Trail.

45 Saguaro Wilderness West

Evening color at Saguaro National Monument

LOCATION: 10 miles west of Tucson

SIZE: 13,470 acres

ELEVATION RANGE: 2,600 to 4,687 feet

MILES OF TRAILS: 15

HABITATS: Sonoran Desert

ADMINISTRATION: National Park Service

TOPOGRAPHIC MAPS: Avra Valley, Brown Mountain, Jaynes, Cat Mountain

UPGRADED IN 1994 from national monument status, two units of Saguaro National Park grace the eastern and western city limits of Tucson, Arizona. Created by congress in 1976, the 73,400-acre Saguaro Wilderness is divided between the eastern and western portions of the park, with the 13,470-acre western, or Tucson Mountain, portion (the subject of this section) being the smaller of the two.

Heavily forested by quite possibly the most beautiful stand of giant saguaro cactus in the world, the Saguaro Wilderness is quintessential Sonoran Desert Uplands, rich in a variety of desert plants and abundant with wildlife. Desert arroyos in the wilderness are lined with mesquite, palo verde, desert hackberry, and other trees. Ocotillo, jojoba, and creosote bush are common, and prickly pear, barrel, and varieties of cholla are among cacti found here.

Common birds include the cactus wren, Gila woodpecker, curve-billed thrasher, Gambel's quail, roadrunner, and canyon towhee. Many varieties of hawks and owls are at home in the Saguaro Wilderness as are mule deer, bobcat, javelina, mountain lion, kit and gray fox, ringtail, and an enormous variety of reptiles and amphibians. Stunning spring wildflower displays that carpet hillsides with Mexican poppy, desert lupine, wild hyacinth, parish larkspur, desert marigold, globe mallow, mariposa lily, and numerous other species, usually follow wet fall and winter seasons.

Summer, when daytime temperatures exceed 100 degrees Fahrenheit, is the only season when hiking in the Tucson Mountain Unit of the Saguaro Wilderness is unpleasant. Wasson Peak, at 4,687 feet the highest point in the wilderness, is a favorite destination among wilderness hikers. On clear days the Four Peaks and Superstition Wilderness areas, east of Phoenix, are visible from Wasson Peak.

DAY HIKE: HUGH NORRIS TRAIL
One-way length: 4.9 miles
Low and high elevations: 2,600 to 4,687 feet
Difficulty: moderate

The longest trail in the wilderness area, the Hugh Norris Trail to Wasson Peak begins at the Sus Picnic Area on the Bajada Loop Drive skirting the Saguaro National Park's western edge. The trail climbs steeply to the central ridge of the Tucson Mountain range and heads east to a junction with the Sendero Esperanza Trail, which comes in from the north. Views of the surrounding valleys are splendid along the trail. To the south lies the world-famous Arizona-Sonora Desert Museum and beyond it the broad plains of the Avra and Altar Valleys. The Hugh Norris Trail continues east to its junction with the Sweetwater Trail, which comes in from the south in a saddle near Amole Peak. From the junction, it's 0.3 mile to the summit of Wasson Peak, an excellent spot for trail lunch.

DAY HIKE: SWEETWATER TRAIL
One-way length: 4.4 miles
Low and high elevations: 3,000 to 4,687 feet
Difficulty: moderate

The Sweetwater Trail, accessed from the end of El Camino del Cerro Road on the northeast side of the wilderness, is one of the lesser traveled routes in the Saguaro Wilderness. The trail travels across classic desert terrain before climbing up through Sweetwater Canyon to a broad saddle where it joins the King Canyon Trail coming in from the south. From the saddle, the Sweetwater Trail turns right to climb approximately 1.0 mile to a shallow saddle where it meets the Hugh Norris Trail. From this junction, it's a short climb east to Wasson Peak.

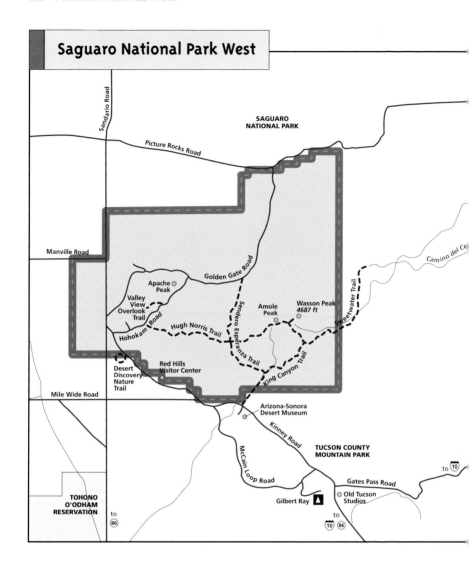

Saguaro National Park West

DAY HIKE: KING CANYON TRAIL
One-way length: 3.5 miles
Low and high elevations: 2,900 to 4,687 feet
Difficulty: moderate

The King Canyon Trail, which begins in a parking area north of the Arizona-Sonora Desert Museum, climbs up King Canyon 0.9 mile to the Mam-A-Gah Picnic Area where the trail forks. To the left is the Sendero Esperanza Trail; to the right the King Canyon Trail continues climbing to a prominent saddle where it joins the Sweetwater Trail to the summit of Wasson Peak. Because of its easy accessibility, the King Canyon Trail is the busiest route in the wilderness area.

DAY HIKE: SENDERO ESPERANZA
One-way length: 3.2 miles
Low and high elevations: 3,000 to 4,000 feet
Difficulty: easy

The Sendero Esperanza or "Trail of Hope" trailhead is located near the Ez-kim-in-zin Picnic Area off Golden Gate Road along the Saguaro Wilderness Area's northern boundary. For the first 1.2 miles the trail follows an old jeep road, sometimes tracing the path of a wash, before ascending 0.6 mile to a shallow saddle where it crosses the Hugh Norris Trail along the Tucson Mountain's central ridge. From this junction, the Sendero Esperanza Trail descends 1.4 miles to the Mam-A-Gah Picnic Area, passing the abandoned Gould Mine along the way. Many open mine shafts dot the landscape in the wilderness area. They are best avoided.

LOOP HIKES

As can be seen from the trail descriptions, any of the hikes in the Saguaro Wilderness can be lengthened by adding one or two loops. For example, after hiking up the Sweetwater Trail to its junction with the King Canyon Trail, then on to Wasson Peak, one could hike west via the Hugh Norris Trail to the Sendero Esperanza Trail, south to the Mam-A-Gah Picnic Area, northeast on the King Canyon Trail to the Sweetwater Trail junction, then back to the trailhead. Imaginative hikers, limited only by time and energy, can easily figure out other loop or shuttle hikes in this small wilderness area.

46 Superstition Wilderness

Massive display of Brittle Bush

LOCATION: 7 miles east of Apache Junction

SIZE: 160,200 acres

ELEVATION RANGE: 2,000 and 6,265 feet

MILES OF TRAILS: 180

HABITATS: Sonoran Desert, oak woodland, piñon-juniper, riparian-gallery

ADMINISTRATION: Tonto National Forest, Mesa Ranger District

TOPOGRAPHIC MAPS: Weavers Needle, Goldfield, Mormon Flat Dam, Horse Mesa Dam, Iron Mountain, Haunted Canyon, Pinyon Mountain, Two Bar Mountain

LOCATED JUST SOUTH of the Four Peaks Wilderness, the Superstition Wilderness may be Arizona's best known wilderness unit. Designated a Forest Reserve in 1908 and as the Superstition Primitive Area in 1939, its status was changed to wilderness designation by the 1964 Wilderness Act which set aside 124,000 acres. Already quite large at that size, the Superstition Wilderness became even bigger when the Arizona Wilderness Act of 1984 added 36,000 acres. The new acreage eliminated cherry-stem corridors and added picturesque boulder fields and peaks high enough to support the growth of conifers.

Native people, called the Hohokam, inhabited the area within the wilderness from about A.D. 800. Eventually, a blending of architectural styles and cultures produced what archaeologists have called the Salado Indians. Some of their ruined cliff dwellings can still be found in the wilderness. Other groups followed: the Yavapai and Pima, particularly.

Americans entered the region after it became a United States territory at the end of the Mexican-American War in 1848. The 1870s and '80s were boom times for mining in the region, but contrary to popular belief, no veins of rich gold were found and then lost.

The most widely circulated lost-mine legend in Arizona is the story of the Lost Dutchman. Jacob Walz, who was actually a German, not Dutch, claimed to have rediscovered mines developed by the Peralta family of Sonora, Mexico. Among them, Walz claimed, was a rich gold mine. When Walz died in 1891, newspaper accounts embellished the story, creating the stuff of legend. Subsequent accounts further embroidered these meager facts, until the legend of the Lost Dutchman Mine assumed a life of its own. Even now, reports periodically emerge claiming the Lost Dutchman has been rediscovered.

Desert vegetation—saguaro cactus, cholla, palo verde, and ocotillo— dominate the lower elevations of the Superstition Wilderness. After wet winters, spring wildflowers—wild hyacinth, anemone, Mexican poppy and desert lupine—carpet the slopes. Moving upslope the succession of plants includes piñon-juniper and several species of oak. Ash, desert hackberry, walnut, cottonwood, and sycamore grow in the riparian zones, and, at the highest elevations, a few ponderosa pine are found.

Birds in the wilderness include the cactus wren, curve-billed thrasher, Gambel's quail, Gila woodpecker, white-crowned sparrow, ash-throated flycatcher, great-horned owl, and red-tailed hawk. Among mammals are mule deer, bobcat, banner-tailed kangaroo rat, coyote, and mountain lion.

The main recreational activities within the Superstition Wilderness are hiking and backpacking, but rock climbing is also very popular, especially at Weavers Needle, a 4,553-foot monolith in the southeast corner of the wilderness. Climbers should be aware that the Tonto National Forest has banned the use of bolts and pitons.

Because of its proximity to Phoenix, the Superstition is one of the more heavily used wilderness areas in Arizona. It is interlaced with miles of trails, ranging in condition from poor to excellent. Hiking in summer when the wilderness becomes scorching hot is inadvisable. Winter hiking in the Superstitions is ideal. Water may be available at springs and creeks but should, of course, be treated.

The network of trails in the Superstition Wilderness is so vast that I have selected four longer hikes that cover major portions of the wilderness. These routes, combined with any number of connecting trails, provide inventive hikers with scores of combinations for hiking the Superstition Wilderness. Note that all these routes may be hiked in either direction.

SHUTTLE HIKE: DUTCHMAN'S TRAIL TO PERALTA TRAILHEAD
One-way length: 18.2 miles
Low and high elevations: 2,280 to 3,250 feet
Difficulty: moderate

This trail is accessed at the First Water Trailhead in the northwest corner of the wilderness. To reach the trailhead drive 5 miles north from Apache Junction on State Route 88 (the Apache Trail) to Forest Route 78. Turn right (east) on Forest Route 78 and drive about 3 miles to the trailhead.

The Dutchman's Trail is a long meandering trail across the drainages of the western portion of the wilderness. It ends at the Peralta Trailhead along the southwest border of the wilderness. A second vehicle may be parked at the Peralta Trailhead (described below).

SHUTTLE HIKE: PERALTA TRAIL TO CANYON LAKE TRAILHEAD
One-way length: 14.0 miles
Low and high elevations: 1,680 to 3,760 feet
Difficulty: moderate

To reach the Peralta Trailhead drive 8.5 miles southeast from Apache Junction on U.S. Highway 60 to Peralta Road (Forest Route 77). Turn left (northwest) and drive 8 miles to the trailhead.

Because the footing is bedrock in places, the 6.3-mile Peralta Trail is not recommended for horses. One of the more heavily used trails in Arizona, it climbs 1,300 feet in two miles to reach Fremont Saddle. The saddle offers a closeup view of Weaver's Needle, named for Paulino Weaver, famed mountain man, scout, trapper, and miner. The needle is a favorite destination for rock climbers, many of whom haul up camping gear to spend the night on the summit.

From the saddle, the Peralta Trail drops down East Boulder Canyon and ends at the Dutchman's Trail where you pick up the Boulder Canyon Trail. From this point it is 7.3 miles to the Canyon Lake Trailhead. The Boulder Canyon Trail is rough and subject to flooding where it crosses Boulder Creek.

To leave a second vehicle at the Canyon Lake Trailhead, drive 17 miles north from Apache Junction of State Route 88 to the Canyon Lake Marina. Trail access is on the south side of the highway.

SHUTTLE HIKE: DUTCHMAN'S TRAIL TO REAVIS TRAILHEAD
One-way length: 42.8 miles
Low and high elevations: 2,280 to 5,360 feet
Difficulty: strenuous

From the First Water Trailhead (see directions above) follow the Dutchman's Trail across Black Top Mesa Pass and up La Barge Canyon to Charlebois Spring to connect with the Peters Trail. Follow the Peters Trail, which may be somewhat vague,

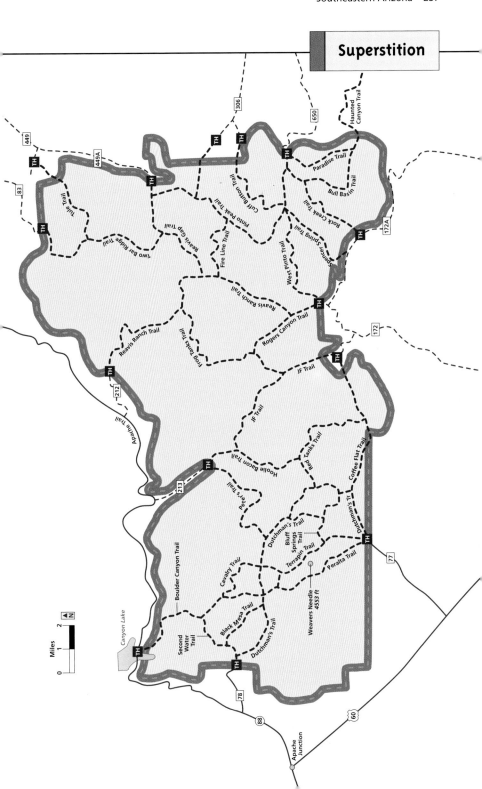

Superstition

to the Tortilla Trailhead and its connection with the JF Trail. Named for Jack Fraser, a pioneer cattleman, the JF Trail travels southeast to its junction with the Rogers Canyon Trail. The very scenic Rogers Canyon Trail, with many creek cross- ings, moves northeast, then southeast to join the Reavis Trail. Take the 15.3-mile Reavis Trail, which follows an old homestead roadway for much of its length, north to the trailhead.

To reach the Reavis Trailhead follow the driving directions for the First Water Trailhead but continue on State Route 88 for an additional 24.5 miles to the Forest Route 212 (Reavis Road) turnoff. Turn right (south) 3 miles to the trail- head. High-clearance vehicles are recommended.

SHUTTLE HIKE: JF TRAIL TO WOODBURY TRAILHEAD
One-way length: 9.4 miles
Low and high elevations: 3,250 to 4,560 feet
Difficulty: moderate

The JF Trail begins at the Tortilla Trailhead which can be reached by driving north 23.5 from Apache Junction on State Route 88 to the Forest Route 213 (Tortilla Road) turn-off. Four-wheel-drive vehicles can proceed to the trailhead at the dead-end. Others should park here and walk 2 miles to the trailhead.

The JF Trail moves from grassland up through mountain mahogany, juniper, mesquite, acacia and century plant into the central portion of the Superstition Wilderness. The trail crosses a number of saddles before descending into Goat Canyon, then crosses another saddle into the Tortilla Creek drainage. From this point it is a short climb to Tortilla Pass with a view of La Barge Mountain rising to 5,077 feet.

From the pass, the JF Trail descends south into Randolph Canyon and to the gate at the Woodbury Trailhead. The trail may be indistinct in places but is easily picked up if you continue on a southward bearing.

To leave a second vehicle at the Woodbury Trailhead drive east from Apache Junction on U.S. Highway 60 to Florence Junction. Continue U.S. 60 two miles east of Florence Junction to the Queen Valley Road turn-off. Turn left (north) on Queen Valley Road for about 2 miles to Forest Route 357 (Hewitt Station Road). Turn right and follow Forest Route 357, 3 miles to Forest Route 172 (JF Road). Turn left 11.2 miles to the end of the road. A high-clearance vehicle is required. Forest Route 357 crosses Queen Creek several times. High water after heavy rains may make this road impassable.

White Canyon Wilderness 47

Yellow poppies scattered through White Canyon Wilderness

THE SONORAN MUD TURTLE, many species of song-birds, deer, bobcat, willow, ash, Arizona walnut, desert hackberry, hawks and falcons, ephemerally flowing water, sheer cliffs soaring above the canyon bottom—these are the features of White Canyon, a small but special wilderness area. But its path to wilderness status was temporarily barred by the presence of nearby mining activity and its future may be uncertain. Put under wilderness protection in 1990, the White Canyon Wilderness is threatened by the potential development of a large open pit mine at Copper Butte, perhaps a mile south of the wilderness.

Caves in the canyon walls show evidence of Indian habitation. In 1980, Arizona State University archeologists excavated Hankat Cave within the wilderness where they found evidence of a pre-ceramic culture dating from about

LOCATION: 14 miles south of Superior

SIZE: 5,800 acres

ELEVATION RANGE: 2,200 to 4,053 feet

MILES OF TRAILS: No marked or maintained trails

HABITATS: Desert riparian and uplands

ADMINISTRATION: BLM, Tucson Field Office

TOPOGRAPHIC MAPS: Teapot Mountain, Mineral Mountain

1,500 B.C. Water was what attracted them to this lovely little canyon, and it is water that brings hikers and other recreational users to the White Canyon Wilderness today.

HIKING THE WILDERNESS

The way into the White Canyon Wilderness is on Battle Ax road, a dirt road that turns west toward White and Walnut canyons off of State Route 177 about one-half mile south of mile post 159. Road conditions, which are usually quite rough, can vary with weather. A high-clearance vehicle or four-wheel-drive are recommended. Approximately 4 miles from State Route 177 the road approaches Walnut Canyon where a developed spring is maintained. At this point the road has been damaged by periodic flooding and requires a four-wheel-drive vehicle. The route continues west for nearly one mile to a fork. Stay right to reach the White Canyon Trailhead.

You can hike along the stream bottom through boulder chokes, sand, pools of water, and slickrock for about 3.0 miles before White Canyon leaves the wilderness. Along the route there are side canyons that invite exploration. When water is flowing in White Canyon, which occurs in all but the driest seasons, it is a magical place.

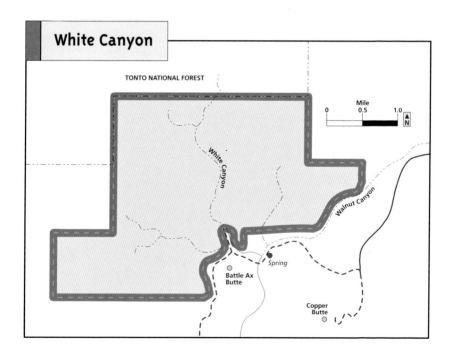

White Canyon

TONTO NATIONAL FOREST

Mile
0   0.5   1.0
N

White Canyon

Walnut Canyon

Spring

Battle Ax
Butte

Copper
Butte

Claret Cup cactus, Tonto National Forest

Western Arizona:
Sonoran and Mohave Deserts

Western Arizona's Basin and Range region divides into two sections—the Sonoran Desert section, which lies along the Colorado River Valley extending north to the Bill Williams River, and the Mohave section, a narrow band along the Colorado River extending north from the Bill Williams River to the state line.

Rivaling the heat and aridity of Death Valley, the Sonoran Desert region along the Colorado River is one of the hottest, driest places in North America. At ground level, summer temperatures sometimes register 180 degrees Fahrenheit, while the air just a few feet above the surface exceeds 120 degrees Fahrenheit. In places annual rainfall is less than three inches, and some locations have gone three years without rain. Super-aridity and intense solar radiation form the Sonoran Desert region into one of the harshest natural environments imaginable.

Broad, flat valleys between small, barren mountain ranges are covered by miles of drought-adapted creosote bush and white bursage. Except in areas that receive up to eight inches of rainfall annually, such as Organ Pipe Wilderness, trees and large columnar cacti survive only in the beds of washes. In fact, in the driest of regions, almost all plants are limited to xeroriparian communities, making dry washes virtual reefs amid vast desert seas. The low mountains support a greater variety of shrubs and cacti, but required to compete for scarce water, such plants are set widely apart. Annual plant species, which appear abundantly only in the wettest years, make up more than half the flora. One such wet year was the winter and spring of 1998, when the wildflower efflorescence was described by some as the bloom of the century. Rainfall increases as you move eastward toward the Arizona Upland subdivision of the Basin and Range region, and with it comes an increase of plant diversity and density.

Moving northward along the Colorado River Valley, the Sonoran Desert section of Arizona's Basin and Range province merges imperceptibly with the Mohave Section, a narrow corridor that parallels the Colorado River up to the Nevada-Utah border. Because its broad basins are drained internally, some biologists argue that the Mohave is just a southern extension of the Great Basin Desert. Like the Great Basin, hard freezes are not uncommon in the Mohave Desert, and it gets most of its annual two to four inches of rain in winter. The Mohave is lower and warmer than the Great Basin, however, and because it records more frost-free days, irrigated agriculture is possible.

Golden poppies and lupine in Grass Canyon, Organ Pipe Cactus National Monument

Low shrubs are the dominant perennial plants in the Mohave subdivision and in times of generous rainfall annual wildflowers may carpet the ground. The signature tree of the Mohave Desert is the Joshua Tree, an arborescent yucca that grows in extensive colonies above 3,000 feet.

48 Big Horn Mountains Wilderness

Craggy rock and morning sun

LOCATION: 60 miles west of Phoenix; 11 miles northwest of Tonopah

SIZE: 21,000 acres

ELEVATION RANGE: 1,400 to 3,480 feet

MILES OF TRAILS: No marked or maintained trails

HABITATS: Sonoran Desert

ADMINISTRATION: BLM, Phoenix Field Office

TOPOGRAPHIC MAPS: Big Horn Peak, Burnt Mountain, Little Horn Peak

TO TRAVEL EAST TO WEST IN ARIZONA is to move from regions that average ten to twelve inches of rain annually to areas that average two inches—and in some years, none at all. There is a point along Interstate 10, not quite halfway between Phoenix and Blythe, California, which has some of the driest terrain in the state. In summer, low mountain peaks north and south of the highway shimmer jaggedly in waves of heat. Big Horn Peak, in the Big Horn Mountains Wilderness is one such peak.

The terrain is Sonoran desert with saguaro cactus growing on broad alluvial fans called bajadas. Other desert plants include ironwood, mesquite, palo verde, prickly pear, brittlebush, cholla, bursage, creosote, and ocotillo. Desert bighorn sheep inhabit craggy peaks and ridges, and the wilderness also provides habitat for mountain lion, bobcat, gila monster, diamondback rattlesnake, bark scorpion, tarantula, gray fox, desert tortoise, and mule deer. Cactus wren and curve-billed thrasher nest among the branches of the spikiest cholla cacti. White-winged doves feast on saguaro fruits. Birds of prey include the red-tailed hawk, golden eagle, and Cooper's hawk.

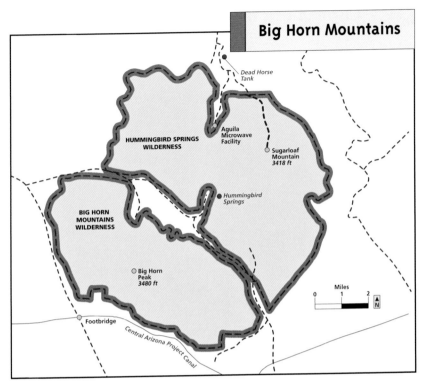

Big Horn Mountains

November through March are the best times to visit the Big Horn Mountains Wilderness. Winter camping and hiking are ideal.

WILDERNESS ACCESS

Although there are no established trails within the Big Horn Mountains Wilderness, the terrain is open and it is possible to hike for miles across the gentle bajadas. For peak-baggers, the 3,480-foot summit of Big Horn Peak is always a destination. Be forewarned: it's a tough bushwhack in rugged terrain.

Because no water is available in the wilderness, cross-country hiking is best done during the cooler months when your hydration requirements are less and you may lighten your load a bit.

The easiest access to the wilderness is along a well-maintained gravel road that runs between the Big Horn Mountains Wilderness and the Hummingbird Springs Wilderness to the north. To reach this road drive west from Tonopah on the gravelled Indian School Road parallel to Interstate 10. After 5.0 miles turn right (north) onto a dirt road that reaches an intersection just after passing beneath I-10. Turn left, then right to cross the Central Arizona Project canal. After a short distance you arrive at a gate. You are now approximately 11 miles from Tonopah and about to enter the wilderness, which is marked by signs on either side of the road.

The Big Horn Mountains Wilderness may also be accessed from the south and west. Check topo maps for these unnamed routes.

Road conditions may vary with weather, but most of the roads that provide access to the wilderness are suitable for high-clearance two-wheel-drive vehicles.

49 Cabeza Prieta Refuge Wilderness

Golden light of morning in the Cabeza Prieta Mountains

LOCATION: Five miles west of Ajo

SIZE: 803,418 acres

ELEVATION RANGE: 300 to 3,027 feet

MILES OF TRAILS: No marked or maintained trails

HABITATS: Sonoran Desert

ADMINISTRATION: U.S. Fish and Wildlife Service

TOPOGRAPHIC MAPS: Pozo Nuevo Well, Agua Dulce Mountains, North of Agua Dulce Mountains, O'Neill Hills, Las Playas, Monument Bluff, Palo Verde Camp, Antelope Hills, Pinta Playa, Paradise Canyon, Sierra Arida, Tule Mountains, Sierra de la Lechuguilla, Temporal Pass, Saguaro Gap Well, Granite Mountains South, Granite Mountains North, Bryan Mountains, Isla Pinta, North of Isla Pinta, Christmas Pass, Cabeza Prieta Peak, Coyote Water, Growler Peak, West of Growler Peak, Monreal Well, Point of the Pintas, Buck Peak, East of Buck Peak, Quitobaquito Springs

THE CABEZA PRIETA REFUGE WILDERNESS is the nation's largest intact ecosystem south of Alaska—nearly half the size of the State of Connecticut. It is a land of broad, flat valleys and *playas*, ringed by low mountains—the Gila, Agua Dulce, Growler, Sierra Pinta, and the lava-capped range that give the wilderness its name, *Cabeza Prieta*, "dark head." It is a land of little rain. In a good year only three inches fall on the western portions of the wilderness, but up to eight inches on the east side, a distance of only sixty miles. Coming in two seasons, summer and winter, the rains water desert arroyos where palo verde, mesquite, acacia, and giant saguaro trace ribbons of greenery across the parched landscape. It is an unpopulated land, untamed, what the Mexicans call *desplobado*—wilderness.

Lying along its southern edge is an old road, first used by Spanish explorer Melchior Diaz more than sixty-five years before the first English-speaking settlement was established at Jamestown. The intrepid "padre on horseback," Father Eusebio Francisco Kino, founder of many Southwestern mission churches, followed the route in 1699. During the Gold Rush years of the mid-1800s, miners flocked across the desert to California on this road. Unprepared for the harsh conditions, many died. The remains of a few of their graves are still visible. The road became known as *El Camino del Diablo*, "The Devil's Highway." It is the only route across this otherwise untracked wilderness.

Untracked, but not uninhabited. While the majestic desert bighorn and endangered Sonoran pronghorn get most of the attention, more than sixty species of mammals are present in the wilderness. More than eleven species of bats alone live in the Cabeza, along with the black-tailed and antelope jackrabbit, rock squirrel, pocket mouse, gopher, woodrat, kit and gray fox, ringtail, badger, spotted skunk, bobcat, mountain lion and mule deer.

Birds include the American kestrel, red-tailed hawk, Gambel's quail, prairie falcon, white-winged and mourning dove, elf owl, Costa's hummingbird, Gila wood-pecker, Northern flicker, Western wood peewee, Say's phoebe, Western kingbird, raven, verdin, cactus wren, rock wren, black-tailed gnatcatcher, mockingbird, phainopepla, loggerhead shrike, black-throated sparrow, Scott's oriole, and house finch.

The red-spotted toad, Colorado River toad, desert tortoise, desert banded gecko, chuckwalla, desert horned lizard, rosy boa, Sonoran whipsnake, gopher snake, Arizona coral snake, Western diamondback, Mojave rattler, and sidewinder are among the numerous reptiles and amphibians found in the Cabeza Prieta Refuge Wilderness.

The dominant plants include elephant tree, white thorn and catclaw acacia, blue and foothills palo verde, ironwood, mesquite, desert willow, saguaro, organ pipe cactus, cholla, barrel cactus, fishhook pincushion cactus, chuparosa, desert honey-suckle, fairy duster, agave, beargrass, bursage, burrobush, desert broom, brittlebush, turpentine bush, rabbit tobacco, barberry, mustard, peppergrass, jackass clover, desert morning glory, and Ajo lily.

Established in 1939, the 860,000-acre Cabeza Prieta National Wildlife Refuge shares a fifty-six-mile international border with Sonora, Mexico. Although most of the refuge's numerous mountains rise less than 3,000 feet above the valleys, they are extremely rugged. The 1990 Arizona Wilderness Act added 803,418 acres of the refuge to the nation's wilderness system.

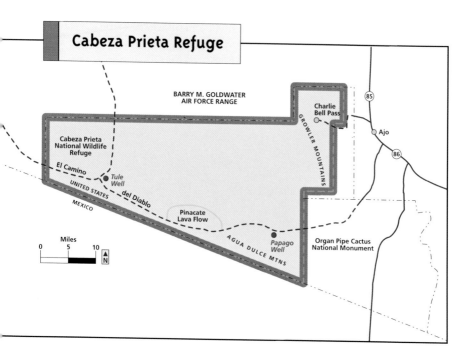

Winter, when daytime temperatures often warm into the 70s, is the ideal season to visit the Cabeza Prieta Refuge Wilderness. Outside that, the best times to be in the wilderness are between the months of November and March. I have been in the wilderness during July when daily temperatures exceeded 110 degrees Fahrenheit. Except for the most committed and experienced desert rats, summer is not the time to go in.

WILDERNESS ACCESS

The first thing to know about visiting the Cabeza Prieta Refuge Wilderness is that permits are required from the U.S. Fish and Wildlife Service (see Appendix 2) to venture out on either El Camino del Diablo or the Charlie Bell Pass Road, the two four-wheel-drive routes that access the wilderness. And since there are no maintained trails within the wilderness, cross-country hiking is the only way to cover ground on foot. Much of the terrain is open, however, making foot travel relatively easy.

El Camino del Diablo begins outside the wilderness south of Ajo, Arizona. Passing across the northwest section of Organ Pipe Wilderness and then into the Cabeza, it travels for some sixty miles across the wilderness. The total distance from entrance to the exit point near Yuma is approximately 110 miles.

If you plan to drive across El Camino del Diablo, prepare carefully. Carry spare tools, spare tires, gasoline, lots of water, a tow chain, and other necessities of wilderness travel. Highlights along the Devil's Highway include the Agua Dulce Mountains, Papago Well, the Pinacate Lava Flow, Cabeza Prieta Peak, and Tinajas Altas ("high tanks"), a last-chance water hole for travelers heading west across one of the meanest, driest stretches of desert in the wilderness.

The eighteen-mile route to Charlie Bell Pass in the Growler Mountains begins in Ajo and moves west into the northeast portion of the wilderness. Again, the open terrain presents a number of excellent possibilities for cross-country hiking.

Because the Barry M. Goldwater Air Force Range abuts the northern boundary of the Cabeza Prieta Refuge Wilderness, the solitude of the wilderness is often shattered by low-flying F-16s and other military aircraft. Occasionally you may also hear bombs exploding on the nearby practice range. Defenders of Wildlife has sued the Air Force, claiming the bombing violates the Endangered Species Act.

Both natural and manmade, scattered waterholes throughout the wilderness serve the needs of wildlife. They are not dependable sources of drinking water for humans.

50 Eagletail Mountains Wilderness

Sunset over the Eagletail Mountains

LOCATION: 65 miles west of Phoenix

SIZE: 100,600 acres

ELEVATION RANGE: 1,150 to 3,300 feet

MILES OF TRAILS: 24

HABITATS: Sonoran Desert

ADMINISTRATION: BLM, Yuma Field Office

TOPOGRAPHIC MAPS: Cortez Peak, Columbus Peak, Nottbusch Butte, Cortez Peak NW Eagletail Mountains East, Eagletail Mountains West, Little Horn Mountains NE, Lone Mountain SW

NAMED FOR THREE COLUMNAR STONE SHAFTS that resemble the tail feathers of an eagle, the feature attraction of the Eagletail Mountains Wilderness is rock. There are trees, to be sure, and other types of vegetation; an interesting botanical phenomenon, in fact, is a relict, low-elevation population of juniper and oak on the north slope of Eagletail Peak. But rock—sawtooth ridges, natural arches, towering spires, buttes, monoliths—is what brings many backcountry enthusiasts, including technical rock climbers, to this wilderness.

The wilderness includes fifteen miles of the Eagletail Mountains ridgeline to the north and Cemetery Ridge to the south with a large desert plain in between. Rock climbers head for Courthouse Rock or Eagletail Peak. It's not great rock, climbers will tell you, but the faces are huge and offer numerous routes.

Eagletail Mountains

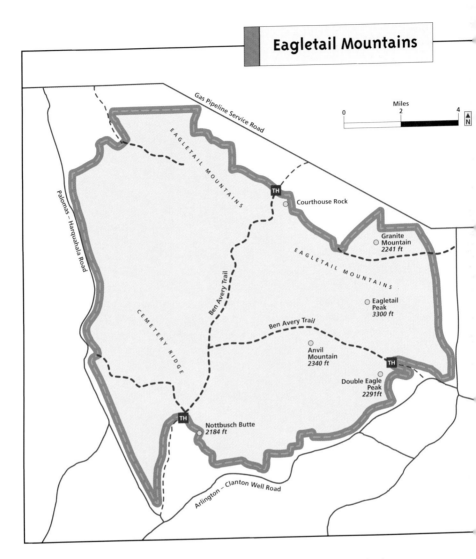

Except for that unusual and unexpected stand of juniper and oak, the vegetation in the Eagletail Mountains Wilderness is typically Sonoran Desert. Palo verde, mesquite, saguaro cactus, creosote bush, barrel cactus, cholla, ocotillo, desert hackberry, tomatillo, and range ratany are the principal plants. Mule deer, cactus wren, desert tortoise, red-tailed hawk, peregrine falcon, king snake, great horned owl, American kestrel, coyote, bobcat, mountain lion, kangaroo rat, cottontail, Sonoran shovelnose snake, and ash-throated flycatcher are among the many animals that inhabit the wilderness.

The warmer months, which in the low deserts run from May through October, are less than ideal for visiting the Eagletail Mountains Wilderness. For ideal temperatures and wonderful light for photography, you cannot beat the dead of winter or early spring. Spring comes to the desert early, of course, and you may begin to see wildflowers as early as February.

> ## DAY HIKE: BEN AVERY TRAIL
> One-way length: 10.2 miles
> Low and high elevations: 1,200 to 1,750 feet
> Difficulty: moderate

To reach the trailhead, drive west from Phoenix on Interstate 10 to Exit 81, the Harquahala Road. Travel south on the Harquahala Road about 5.0 miles to the Courthouse Rock Road. Drive west on Courthouse Rock Road which merges with the Pipeline Road that parallels the northern boundary of the wilderness. After about 11 miles look for a road heading south from the Pipeline Road. Drive 1.5 miles south on this road to the trailhead. Road surfaces will vary with weather conditions, but this route is usually passable in a high-clearance two-wheel-drive vehicle.

The trail is named for the late Ben Avery, an *Arizona Republic* political and outdoor writer who successfully pushed for the formation of Arizona's State Park system, the youngest in the nation. The trail, an old road turned footpath, travels south across the wilderness for 12 miles to a southern trailhead near Nottbusch Butte. About two-thirds of the way across, a spur of the Ben Avery Trail branches east for approximately 8.0 miles to a trailhead near Double Eagle Peak.

In addition to the Ben Avery Trail, cross-country hiking is also available in the Eagletail Mountains Wilderness. Other wilderness access points are available along the Arlington-Clanton Well Road that skirts the southern boundary. Cemetery Ridge, in the southwest corner of the wilderness, may be approached from the Palomas-Harquahala Road.

Harquahala Mountains Wilderness

Sunset in Harquahala Mountains from Browns Canyon Area

HARQUAHALA is derived from a Mohave Indian word meaning "always water," but, although there are some springs and riparian areas in the Harquahala Wilderness, I would not stake my life on finding any potable water there. Lying just outside the wilderness boundary, the 5,691-foot summit of Harquahala Mountain provides a stunning panorama of desert and mountain terrain. The highest point in southwestern Arizona, the peak is the former site of an astronomy observatory erected and operated by the Smithsonian Institution between 1920 and 1925. Today, it is listed on the National Registry of Historic Places.

A distinctive feature of the Harquahala Wilderness is a screened interior canyon system in which relict ecosystems, such as chaparral and desert grassland, are preserved. These

LOCATION: 34 miles west of Wickenburg

SIZE: 22,880 acres

ELEVATION RANGE: 2,200 to 5,691 feet

MILES OF TRAILS: 6

HABITATS: Sonoran Desert

ADMINISTRATION: BLM, Phoenix Field Office

TOPOGRAPHIC MAPS: Harquahala Mountain, Socorro Peak, Tiger Well

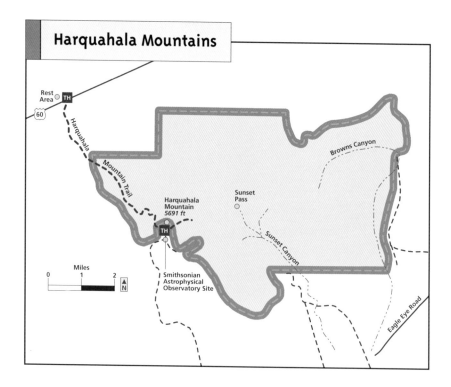

are leftovers from a time when the region was cooler and wetter. Rare cacti are also found within the wilderness.

Barrel cactus, saguaro, ocotillo, cholla, creosote bush, bursage, mesquite and palo verde are among the Sonoran Desert plants that thrive in the wilderness. Animals include desert bighorn sheep, desert tortoise, mule deer, Gila monster, red-tailed hawk, great horned owl, cactus wren, curve-billed thrasher, Gila woodpecker, coyote, bobcat, mountain lion, and a great variety of reptiles, insects, and spiders.

Winters are ideal for hiking and camping in the Harquahala Wilderness. Summer heat is prohibitive. The best months for visits are November through March.

DAY HIKE: HARQUAHALA MOUNTAIN TRAIL
One-way length: 6.0 miles
Low and high elevations: 2,400 to 5,691 feet
Difficulty: strenuous

To reach the trailhead for this route that climbs to Harquahala Mountain from the northwestern corner of the wilderness, drive southwest on U.S. Route 60 to a rest area about 13.5 miles southwest of Aguila. Turn south and drive approximately 2.0 miles on a rutted four-wheel-drive road to the trailhead. From this point it is approximately 6.0 miles to the summit. The terrain is rough and steep. Use caution, and carry plenty of water.

ADDITIONAL WILDERNESS ACCESS

Roads leading to the boundary of the Harquahala Wilderness are rutted and steep, requiring, for the most part, a four-wheel-drive vehicle. To reach Browns Canyon drive south from Aguila on Eagle Eye Road for 9.8 miles and make a right turn (west) onto a four-wheel-drive road. Browns Canyon lies about 10 miles west-northwest of this point. Use topo maps to determine the route.

Browns Canyon itself travels about three miles along a corridor lined with cottonwood and other trees associated with riparian ecosystems.

Another access point along Eagle Eye Road is Sunset Canyon in the southern portion of the wilderness. This is perhaps the only way into the wilderness that does not require a four-wheel-drive vehicle. From Aguila drive about 15.6 miles south on Eagle Eye Road, then turn right (north) for 3.0 miles. From this point, you may have to park and walk across fairly open terrain. Sunset Canyon itself is somewhat brushy and tangled, so you will have to pick your way up.

52 Hassayampa River Canyon Wilderness

Looking toward the Hassayampa River Canyon Wilderness

LOCATION: 20 miles north of Wickenburg

SIZE: 11,840 acres

ELEVATION RANGE: 2,600 to 4,500 feet

MILES OF TRAILS: No marked or maintained trails

HABITATS: Sonoran Desert, riparian canyon

ADMINISTRATION: BLM, Phoenix Field Office

TOPOGRAPHIC MAPS: Morgan Butte, Sam Powell Peak, Wagoner, Yarnell

PROBABLY NO ONE WILL EVER REALLY KNOW how the Hassayampa River got its name. Early mining notices list it variously as "Assamp," "Hassamp" or "Hasiamp." A secretary of the mining district, it is said, revamped the spelling to "Hassayamp," which he believed to be more authentically Spanish. One account asserts that the river was named by legendary mountain man and guide Pauline Weaver who declared it meant "beautiful waters." Probably not, but we do know that the Weaver Mountains, the range in which the wilderness is located, were named for Weaver. Another story, crediting the Yuma Indians with the name, says it means "water that is hidden" or "dry bed." Just as interesting as the uncertainty about the Hassayampa's etymology is the legend warning travelers that to drink from the river's waters was to risk becoming a perpetual liar, which inspired a versifier named Orick Jackson to write:

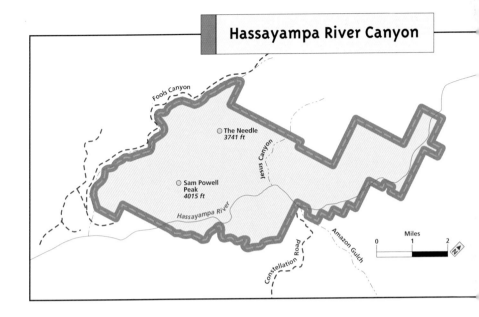

Hassayampa River Canyon

You've heard about the wondrous stream
    They call the Hassayamp.
They say it turns a truthful guy
    into a lying scamp.
And if you quaff its water once
    It's sure to prove your bane
You'll ne'er forsake the blasted stream
    or tell the truth again.

In the late 19th century, the general region of the Hassayampa River
Canyon was one of the most mineral rich in the state, and miners swarmed to the
area like locusts. One of them, a prospector named Henry Wickenburg, discovered
an enormously rich gold vein in the nearby Vulture Mountains, and by 1870 the
Vulture Mine, no longer owned by Wickenburg, was producing half the gold in
Arizona. But most prospectors returned empty handed from expeditions up and down
the Hassayampa, their heads full of tall tales about the rich veins of ore they were ever
so close to striking. Perhaps therein lies the origin of stories about the effects of the
river's waters on truth-telling.

The centerpiece of the Hassayampa River Canyon Wilderness is its fifteen-
mile riparian corridor. There are sections of the Hassayampa that carry year-round
water, but the stretch through the wilderness area flows only intermittently. Trees in
the riparian canopy are typical of desert streams; they include Arizona walnut, ash,
cottonwood, willow, box elder, and Arizona cypress. Upland, away from the streambed,
the plants are those associated with a Lower Sonoran Desert environment: saguaro,
mesquite, barrel cactus, prickly pear, palo verde, acacia, and others. The Hassayampa
River Canyon Wilderness is on the cusp where the Sonoran and Mohave Deserts meet,

so as you move northwest away from the wilderness—perhaps thirty miles as the crow flies—you begin to see Joshua trees, a Mohave species.

Wildlife abounds in desert riparian zones, whether intermittently flowing or not. Mule deer, javelina, diamondback rattlesnake, gopher snake, desert tortoise, black-tailed jackrabbit, mountain lion, Gila monster, and many other animals inhabit the wilderness. Birdwatching is especially good in the Hassayampa River Canyon wilderness. Among the many bird species are cardinal, cactus wren, mourning dove, red-tailed hawk, white-crowned sparrow, ash-throated flycatcher, and peregrine falcon.

The best months to visit the Hassayampa River Canyon Wilderness are between October and April. Summers are too hot, as a rule.

WILDERNESS ACCESS

Two routes provide wilderness access, both requiring a four-wheel-drive vehicle. The first of these—a roadway along the bottom of Fools Canyon—parallels the wilderness boundary on its west side. From this side of the wilderness it is possible to hike cross-country to 4,015-foot Sam Powell Peak or to the 3,741-foot Needle.

The second route, which crosses private land just before reaching the wilderness boundary, begins in Wickenburg. So far, landowners have not prohibited access to the wilderness across their land, but as a matter of courtesy, it's a good idea to ask their permission. To reach the wilderness boundary and a signed trailhead, drive north from Wickenburg for about 15 miles on the Constellation Road to Amazon Gulch. From this point you may hike the river in either direction. If you choose to walk downstream about 2.0 miles you will come to Jesus Canyon, another possible hiking route. Other side canyons also invite exploration. Hiking along the streambed is relatively easy, but plan on getting your feet wet if the river is flowing. Flash-flooding is a potential danger during times of heavy rain.

Usually I only recommend treating all wilderness sources of water before drinking. But whether you believe it or not, the wisdom of folklore regarding the Hassayampa's power to make liars of us all suggests that I should perhaps caution instead: "Don't drink the water!"

Dramatic saguaro cactus against a multi-colored sky

JUDGING FROM THE MANY INSTANCES of the word "hell" in its place names, work and travel during Arizona's settlement days must have been hellaciously difficult at times. So when you come across a deep basin with sides so formidably steep that stockmen rounding up cattle called it Hell Hole, or see a deep chasm called Hell Hole Canyon standing athwart a stagecoach route, you understand why.

In the vicinity of the Hells Canyon Wilderness alone there are four such places. There is Hells Canyon itself, Hellgate Mountain, Big Hells Gate, and Little Hells Gate. I know nothing of the background of these names, although the spectacular narrows of Big and Little Hells Gates along Bitter Creek are strongly suggestive. On the other hand, "hellish" is not an adjective that readily comes to mind. I do know, however, that the Hieroglyphic Mountains, in which

LOCATION: 25 miles northwest of Phoenix

SIZE: 9,900 acres

ELEVATION RANGE: 1,850 to 3,381 feet

MILES OF TRAILS: No marked or maintained trails

HABITATS: Sonoran Desert

ADMINISTRATION: BLM, Phoenix Field Office

TOPOGRAPHIC MAPS: Garfias Mountain, Governors Peak

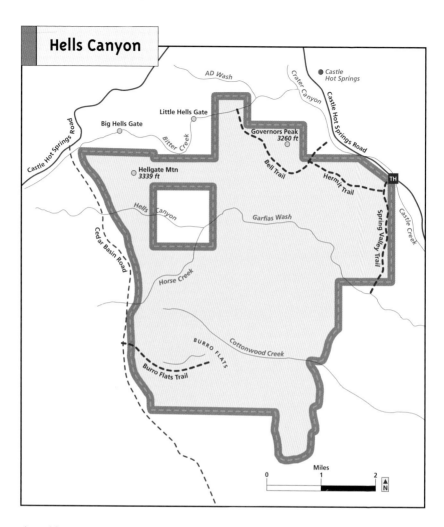

the wilderness is situated, derives its name from the Indian rock art—petroglyphs and pictographs—scattered throughout the range.

Although the Hells Canyon Wilderness is small, it is fairly heavily used, owing to the ease of travel along its lengthy arroyos, the beauty of its eroded rock forms and desert landscape, and its closeness to Phoenix. The natural environment of the wilderness is characteristically Sonoran Desert, featuring saguaro, barrel cactus, palo verde, prickly pear, range ratany, acacia, mesquite, cholla, creosote bush, brittle-bush, and triangle-leaf bursage. The animals, too, are those you would expect to find in any Lower Sonoran Desert setting: black-tailed jackrabbit, red-tailed hawk, desert tortoise, Scott's oriole, red-spotted toad, Gila monster, javelina, white-winged dove, cactus wren, black-throated sparrow, mule deer, and mountain lion. And, as you might expect in an area of former mining activity, some feral prospectors' burros still roam the wilderness.

When adequate fall and winter rainfall stimulate an abundant desert wildflower bloom, spring in the Hells Canyon Wilderness can be magical. Warm winter days are also ideal for excursions into the wilderness. The hottest months—May through September—are generally to be avoided.

WILDERNESS ACCESS

Although no regularly maintained trails enter the Hells Canyon Wilderness, the area is crisscrossed by any number of "wildcat" trails, originating perhaps as game trails and later used by livestock, ranchers, miners, hunters, and, finally, hikers. Some of these trails are indistinct and may be difficult to follow. Add two major east-west washes, used as wildlife corridors for hundreds of years, and you have miles of good hiking routes.

To reach the wilderness, drive north from Phoenix on Interstate 17 to the Carefree Highway (Exit 223) and turn west to State Route 74. Continue west on State Route 74 to the Lake Pleasant Regional Park turnoff and turn north. Drive approximately 5.5 miles north on the Lake Pleasant Road to the Castle Hot Springs Road and turn left. Drive about five miles to a narrow wash on the left side of the road.

Two unmarked trails begin at this point. The first, the difficult-to-follow Hermit Trial, proceeds west before turning north to leave the wilderness. The Bell Trail, an offshoot of the Hermit Trail, travels northwest to Bitter Creek.

A second trail, the easy-to-follow Spring Valley Trail, travels south for about 2.0 miles to reach Garfias Wash. Garfias wash moves west across the wilderness for about seven miles to the four-wheel-drive Cedar Basin Road, passing through Hells Canyon, a lovely riparian corridor, along the way. Be aware that approximately one mile of Garfias Wash crosses private land. Respect the rights of land owners; if you encounter a no-trespassing sign, turn back. A route branching off the Garfias Wash is Horse Creek which travels a few miles south to Cedar Basin Road. Note that Horse Creek also crosses a small portion of private land.

Access to the western boundary of the Hells Canyon Wilderness is possible along the four-wheel-drive Cedar Basin Road, which can be reached by driving approximately 7.0 miles west from Castle Hot Springs on the Castle Hot Springs Road and then turning south. Garfias Wash, Horse Creek, Burro Creek, and an old roadway now known as the Burro Flats Trail can be accessed via the Cedar Basin Road.

54 Hummingbird Springs Wilderness

Barrel cactus in Hummingbird Springs Wilderness

LOCATED IN THE BIG HORN MOUNTAINS, the character of the Hummingbird Springs Wilderness is only slightly different from its sister wilderness to the south. It has the same Sonoran Desert vegetation — saguaro cactus, ocotillo, palo verde, ironwood, mesquite, jojoba, creosote, and prickly pear. And the same animals — gila monster, golden eagle, kit fox, cactus wren, canyon towhee, mountain lion, desert tortoise, and prairie falcon. The only difference, and it's slight, is that the terrain is slightly less rugged than in the Big Horn Mountains Wilderness.

LOCATION: 60 miles west of Phoenix; 11 miles northwest of Tonopah

SIZE: 31,200 acres

ELEVATION RANGE: 1,550 to 3,418 feet

MILES OF TRAILS: No marked or maintained trails

HABITATS: Sonoran Desert

ADMINISTRATION: BLM, Phoenix Field Office

TOPOGRAPHIC MAPS: Big Horn Peak, Burnt Mountain, Hummingbird Springs, Little Horn Peak

Hummingbird Springs

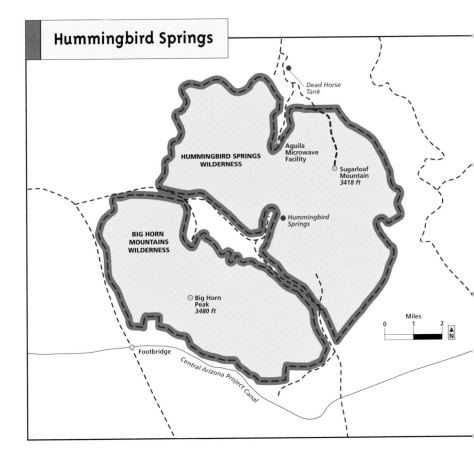

As with its sister wilderness, summer visits to the Hummingbird Springs Wilderness are to be avoided. The best times are between November and March, with winter being ideal for camping and hiking.

The wilderness can be accessed from the north or south on high-clearance two-wheel-drive gravel roads. To reach the gravel road that separates the Hummingbird

Springs Wilderness from the Big Horn Mountains Wilderness, follow the directions detailed on p. 244 for the Big Horn Mountains Wilderness.

About 5.0 miles beyond the wire gate in the above-mentioned description, a cherry-stem road heads north toward Hummingbird Springs, which lie beyond the end of the road about 0.5 mile inside the wilderness. From Hummingbird Springs you can climb about 2.0 miles via a now-closed jeep road to the Aguila microwave towers.

The best access into the wilderness from the north is via a high-clearance, two-wheel-drive gravel road that services the Aguila Microwave facility. The road starts along Eagle Eye Road south of the settlement of Aguila. Approximately 3.0 miles before the service road reaches the microwave installation, a four-wheel-drive spur road leads east—an old jeep road, this is the best route to the 3,418-foot summit of Sugarloaf Mountain.

Cross-country hiking excursions are possible throughout the wilderness. Although fairly easy on the slopes of the bajadas at lower elevations, the going can be rough and risky on the more rugged ridges and peaks of the wilderness area's heights.

Carry plenty of water. None is available in the wilderness.

Imperial Refuge Wilderness 55

Colorado River flowing through the Imperial Refuge Wilderness

THIRTY MILES LONG and encompassing 25,625 acres, the Imperial National Wildlife Refuge was established in 1941 to protect and preserve all forms of plant and animal life found in the lower Colorado River region. Originally consisting of 46,793 acres, the refuge was reduced to its present size by boundary changes and land swaps. Situated in both Arizona and California, the refuge protects desert and lower Colorado River environments. In 1990, the Arizona Desert Wilderness Act set aside 9,220 acres of the refuge as the Imperial Refuge Wilderness.

The Colorado River, the boundary between California and Arizona, is the feature attraction of the refuge. The wilderness area is a skinny corridor of some 10,000 riparian and upland acres running parallel to the refuge. Receiving an average of only 3.2 inches of rain annually and extremely hot in

LOCATION: 40 miles north of Yuma

SIZE: 9,220 acres

ELEVATION RANGE: 200 to 1,085 feet

MILES OF TRAILS: No marked or maintained trails

HABITATS: Sonoran Desert, riparian marshes

ADMINISTRATION: U.S. Fish and Wildlife Service

TOPOGRAPHIC MAPS: Red Hill SW, Picacho, Picacho SW, Picacho NW

summer, the arid, low-elevation Sonoran Desert upland in southwestern Arizona is in sharp contrast to the lush river system. Between the river and the desert is a transition zone of shallow sloughs and lakes that supports diverse plants and animals. With plenty of vegetative cover, these areas provide food, escape, thermal protection, and nesting sites for wildlife.

Nineteenth century travelers along the lower Colorado marveled at the large cottonwoods, varieties of willow, and mesquite bosques that lined the river's channel. Now tamarisk, an exotic from the Middle East introduced to control bank erosion, dominates the main channel. The native trees were long-ago clear-cut to feed the boilers of steam-powered sternwheel paddleboats that supplied mining camps or sawed into timbers to shore up mine shafts. Big cottonwoods survive only in secluded backwaters. Other plants along the banks of the Colorado and in the backwaters include cattail, carrizo, pencil tule, arrow weed, and willow. The desert uplands contain palo verde, ironwood, ocotillo, mesquite, smoke tree, and various cacti, including a few straggling saguaros.

Desert bighorn sheep, mule deer, black-tailed jackrabbit, cottontail, coyote, mountain lion and beaver are among the native mammals found on Imperial. And feral burros and mustangs are frequently seen coming to the river to drink.

Birds are the big attraction in the wilderness. A few of the bird species found there include Gambel's quail, great blue heron, cinnamon teal, Northern harrier, American white pelican, double-crested cormorant, ruddy duck, cinnamon teal, red-winged blackbird, osprey, bald eagle, Harris's hawk, peregrine falcon, great egret, Western screech owl, blue grosbeak, long-billed dowitcher, and Anna's hummingbird. Rattlesnake, zebra-tailed lizard, chuckwalla, and desert iguana are examples of reptile species that may be seen in the wilderness.

To observe migrating waterfowl and shore birds, winter is the best month to visit Imperial Refuge Wilderness. Spring is a good time to observe nesting songbirds. Spring wildflowers begin to bloom in February and continue into April and May. Around mid-May temperatures often nail the 100-degree mark for the first time. Summers in the wilderness are very hot.

WILDERNESS RECREATION

To reach the Imperial Wildlife Refuge headquarters from Yuma, drive north on Highway 95 for 25 miles. Turn west on Martinez Lake Road for 13 miles and follow signs to the visitor center. An observation tower near the headquarters provides a good view of the refuge and surrounding wilderness terrain. During winter months, waterfowl and marsh birds may be seen from the tower.

Hiking is available everywhere in the wilderness (except refuge areas closed to the public). A short distance from refuge headquarters, four lookout points provide excellent observation across marshes where waterfowl, marsh, and shorebirds are usually present in winter. These lookout points are also good starting points for cross-country hiking, and they provide limited access to several backwater lakes. To reach these lookouts, drive north from refuge headquarters along the Red Cloud Mine Road. The names of the lookouts and their distances from refuge headquar-

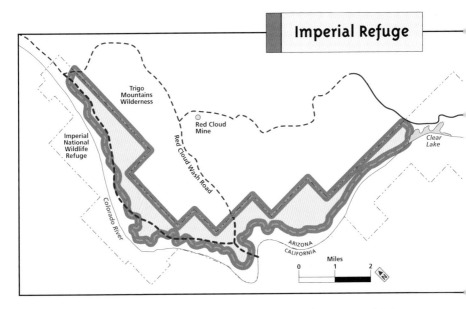

ters follow: Palo Verde Point, 1.3 miles; Mesquite Point, 2.2 miles; Ironwood Point, 3.1 miles; and Smoke Tree Point, 4.2 miles.

The Painted Desert Trail is a one-mile, self-guided trail that offers a close-up of desert plants, geological features, and great views of the river valley. Trail brochures are available at the trailhead, 2.8 miles north of refuge headquarters on Red Cloud Mine Road.

WATER SPORTS

Although not in the wilderness itself, the Colorado River offers recreational opportunities. Water skiing is permitted in only two areas of the refuge: the lower portion, upstream from Martinez Lake for four miles; and an eight-mile section parallel to Picacho State Recreation Area on the California side. Water skiing in backwater lakes, the upper part of Ferguson Lake, or the west half of Martinez Lake is strictly forbidden.

A seventy-mile canoe float from Blythe, California downstream to Martinez Lake is one of the best ways to observe the wonders of the wildlife refuge and adjacent wilderness. A booklet titled, *A Boating Guide to the Colorado River* is available free from refuge headquarters or from the Bureau of Land Management. Camping is *not* permitted anywhere within the refuge, so canoeists must camp in California's Picacho State Recreation Area. Other restrictions on camping also apply, so be sure to check regulations before you launch.

During the warmer months, an excess of powerboats on the river spoils the fun for self-propelled boats. Late fall, winter, and early spring are the best times to do a river float. I floated the lower Colorado in a sea kayak in mid-December one year and saw only one other boat (a small outboard-powered fishing boat) in four days. The water was very cold and nighttime temperatures dropped below freezing, but the solitude made it worthwhile.

56 Kofa Refuge Wilderness

Rock formations towering over cholla cactus

LOCATION: 50 miles north of Yuma

SIZE: 516,300 acres

ELEVATION RANGE: 700 to 4,877 feet

MILES OF TRAILS: 0.5

HABITATS: Sonoran Desert

ADMINISTRATION: U.S. Fish & Wildlife Service

TOPOGRAPHIC MAPS: Crystal Hill, Palm Canyon, Salton Tanks, Red Bluff Mountains, NW Engesser Pass SW, Stone Cabin, Kofa Butte, Hoodoo Well, Arch Tank, Kofa Deep Well, Charlie Died Tank, Engesser Pass, Castle Dome Peak, Slumgullion Pass, Neversweat Ridge, Livingston Hills, Livingston Hills NW, Owls Head, Cholla Tank

ESTABLISHED IN 1939, the Kofa National Wildlife Refuge encompasses 665,400 acres of desert and mountain terrain that is home to numerous desert bighorn sheep and the California fan palm, the only native palm in Arizona. In 1990 the Arizona Desert Wilderness Act dedicated 516,300 acres of the refuge as the Kofa Refuge Wilderness.

In the late 19th century, a number of mines were established in the mountainous areas of the refuge. One of the most notable was the King of Arizona, a gold mine. One story alleges that the owner of the mine, Colonel Eugene Ives, stamped mine property with a brand that read "KofA." Another account says that Ives simply coined the term Kofa as an acronym for King of Arizona. Whatever the truth, the name stuck for the mountain range. Other mines dotted the landscape. The North Star, another gold mine, was just north of the Kofa Mine, and the Castle Dome Mountains in the southern portion of the wilderness was the site of a lead mine called the Castle Dome Mine.

Although rather low, the Kofa and the Castle Dome mountains are extremely rugged and rise sharply from the surrounding desert plains, ideal habitat for the estimated 1,000 bighorn sheep in the wilderness, a healthy enough population to provide animals for transplanting throughout Arizona and neighboring states.

Palm Canyon, in the west end on the Kofa Mountains, is well known for its native California fan palms, *Washingtonia filifera*, relics of the late Pleistocene, some 10,000 years ago. Some botanists think that as the climate became hotter and drier these palms retreated into canyon niches, unique microhabitats, where they are watered by run-off and sheltered from the direct rays of the fierce mid-day sun. Numbering fewer than one hundred and among the few native palms in Arizona, these wild palms are smaller and more slender than their domesticated cousins that line our urban desert boulevards. Another rare plant in the wilderness, one found only in southwest Arizona, is the Kofa Mountain barberry.

Wildlife is abundant in the Kofa Refuge Wilderness. Notable mammal species include more than a dozen species of bats, desert kit fox, black-tailed jackrabbit, Harris's antelope squirrel, pocket mice, deer mice, porcupine, mule deer, bobcat, mountain lion, gray fox, and ringtail.

Among the 185 bird species in the Kofa are the American kestrel, Northern flicker, Say's phoebe, cactus wren, phainopepla, orange-crowned warbler, sharp-shinned hawk, turkey vulture, raven, Western screech owl, common poorwill, Costa's hummingbird, white-throated swift, Western wood peewee, ash-throated flycatcher, Say's phoebe, canyon wren, loggerhead shrike, dark-eyed junco, and white-winged dove.

Reptiles and amphibians include desert tortoise, spadefoot toad, Colorado River toad, red-spotted toad, band gecko, zebra-tailed lizard, desert horned lizard, chuckwalla, fringe-toed lizard, Gila monster, rosy boa, glossy snake, sidewinder, Western diamondback rattlesnake, Mojave rattlesnake, and black-tailed rattlesnake.

Extremely hot, bone-dry summer weather, when temperatures routinely rocket beyond 110 degrees Fahrenheit, make visits to the Kofa Refuge Wilderness between June and September inadvisable. Although night-time temperatures can drop to freezing in mid-winter, the best months to enter the wilderness are between October and April. After periods of sufficient fall and winter rain, wildflower displays can be quite strong in the Kofa.

Numerous vertical shafts, drift tunnels, and open pits—remnants of past mining activity—pockmark the wilderness. The potential for collapse or cave-in is extremely high in these places. Avoid them.

DAY HIKE: PALM CANYON
One-way length: 0.5 miles
Low and high elevations: 2,100 to 2,500 feet
Difficulty: easy

To reach Palm Canyon, drive 62 miles north from Yuma on U.S. Highway 95 and turn right (east) on Palm Canyon Road. Drive about 9.0 miles east on the well-maintained two-wheel-drive route to the end of the road and the trailhead.

A short, 0.5 mile walk up the wash will bring you to the mouth of a rincon, or side canyon, where the palms grow. The canyon is south-facing, so in summer it is in shade for most of the day, except when the sun reaches its meridian. Rainwater washes over the rim of the canyon to water the palms.

For a closer look at the palms you will have to climb loose rock up this steep side canyon. But when you finally crawl through a keyhole up where the palms grow, it's worth the effort. Some of the palm trunks are still blackened from a fire that swept through sixty years ago. White-throated Swifts fly high against the cliff face. Chuparosa, a tube-shaped hummingbird flower, and other flowers blossom beneath the palms. It's a true oasis.

ADDITIONAL WILDERNESS ACCESS

Although the Palm Canyon Trail is the only established route into the Kofa, the wilderness is wide-open for cross-country explorations. The easiest two-wheel-drive access roads to wilderness boundaries are on the west side, off of U.S. Highway 95. These routes include the Castle Dome Road, King Road, and the aforementioned Palm Canyon Road.

It is possible to enter the Kofa Refuge Wilderness from the east via a few four-wheel-drive routes. The condition of these roads varies greatly, so it is best to check with refuge management before heading in.

Directly north of the Kofa Refuge Wilderness lies the 24,600-acre, BLM administered New Water Mountains Wilderness, also prime desert bighorn sheep habitat. This wilderness area, which I view as kind of an adjunct to the Kofa, can be accessed via Blevens Road along its southern border or by the Gold Nugget Road, east of Quartzite, along Interstate 10.

To support wildlife, waterholes in the Kofa Refuge Wilderness have been enlarged and shaded. No surface water is available for human consumption. Carry plenty.

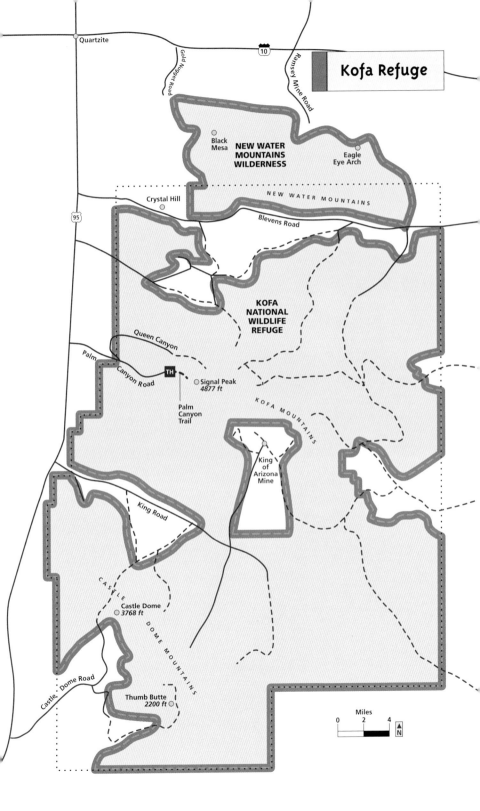

57 Mount Tipton Wilderness

Moonrise and Venus with Joshua trees

LOCATION: 25 miles north of Kingman

SIZE: 30,760 acres

ELEVATION RANGE: 3,440 to 7,148 feet

MILES OF TRAILS: No marked or maintained trails

HABITATS: Mohave Desert

ADMINISTRATION: BLM, Kingman Field Office

TOPOGRAPHIC MAPS: Chloride, Mount Tipton 3SE, Grasshopper Junction

NOTHING SPEAKS MORE EMPHATICALLY for the ruggedness of the Mount Tipton Wilderness in Arizona's Cerbat Mountain Range than the herds of mustangs—feral horses—that survive there despite continuing efforts to eliminate them. Periodically, the Bureau of Land Management (BLM) enlists the services of mounted cowboys, assisted by an airborne drover in a helicopter, to roundup the horses and offer them for adoption. The roundup reduces their numbers but it doesn't get rid of them. The deep canyons of the wilderness provide too many hiding places, places where cowboys and helicopters cannot follow. Horses escape to breed again, and, after a few years, the roundup starts over.

Somehow the wild horses have adapted to this hot, dry, nearly waterless Mohave Desert region of yucca, beargrass, and Joshua tree. The 7,148-foot summit of Mount Tipton gave the wilderness its name, but the Cerbat Pinnacles are the main scenic attraction. Below and north of the peak, the maroon spires of the pinnacles contrast sharply with the dun-colored terrain of the encircling desert. On the northeast

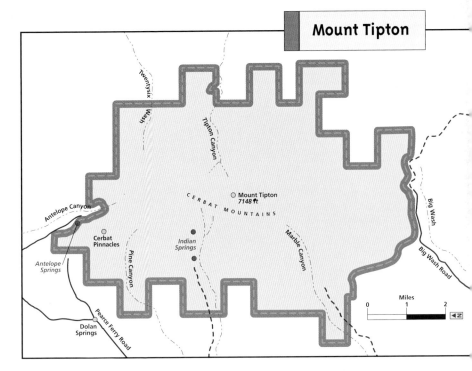

Mount Tipton

side of Mount Tipton, a small fugitive stand of ponderosa pine clings to existence, but the dominant trees and shrubs are piñon-juniper, scrub oak, and manzanita.

Peregrine falcons inhabit the sheer cliff faces of the Cerbat Pinnacles; other raptors in the wilderness include the red-tailed hawk, great horned owl, and golden eagle. Jackrabbit, mule deer, desert tortoise, side-blotched lizard, desert iguana, rosy boa, coyote, red-spotted toad, Western kingbird, and Northern flicker also inhabit the Mount Tipton Wilderness.

Silver, gold, lead, zinc, molybdenum and other metals were mined in the region. In nearby Chloride, a semi-ghost town south of the wilderness, seventy-five mines were in operation between 1900 and 1920 and the population of the town swelled to more than 2,000.

Winter is the ideal season for visits to the Mount Tipton Wilderness. Except in the highest elevations, summers become extremely hot.

WILDERNESS ACCESS

No developed trails traverse the Mount Tipton Wilderness, but it is possible to hike cross-country or to bushwhack routes in some of the washes and canyons. Big Wash Road parallels the southern boundary of the wilderness for approximately five miles. To reach the Big Wash Road turnoff, drive about 20 miles north from Kingman on U.S. Highway 93.

A few miles beyond the Big Wash Road, a road turns off of U.S. 93 and travels northeast into Marble Canyon. A four-wheel-drive vehicle is required for this four-mile approach to the wilderness.

58 Mount Wilson Wilderness

Evening light on creosote flats

LOCATION: 60 miles north of Kingman

SIZE: 23,900 acres

ELEVATION RANGE: 2,000 to 5,445 feet

MILES OF TRAILS: No marked or maintained trails

HABITATS: Mohave Desert

ADMINISTRATION: BLM, Kingman Field Office

TOPOGRAPHIC MAPS: Mount Wilson, Nelson 1 NE, Petroglyph Wash

LOOKS CAN BE DECEIVING. Driving across miles of creosote flats, you approach the Mount Wilson Wilderness in Arizona's Black Mountains, snugged up against the Lake Mead National Recreation Area along the Arizona-Nevada border. In the distance you see a long dun-colored ridge, and your mind free associates a kind of verbal desert roll-call: hot, dry, waterless, hostile to life. When you arrive at the wilderness boundary, your impressions are confirmed. Typical of the Mohave Desert, vegetation is sparse—yucca, cholla, creosote, catclaw acacia, mesquite, snakeweed, blackbrush, bursage, various cacti—plants programmed for survival in the harshest deserts.

But hiking across the bajadas you encounter abundant wildlife: the horned lark, ash-throated flycatcher, raven, verdin, gopher snake, coyote, horned lizard, desert tortoise, mockingbird, red-speckled rattlesnake, harvest mouse, jackrabbit, bobcat, mountain lion, desert bighorn sheep, mule deer, and turkey vulture.

It is spring, and annual wildflowers have burst into bloom—chia, phacelia, lupine, desert anemone, verbena,

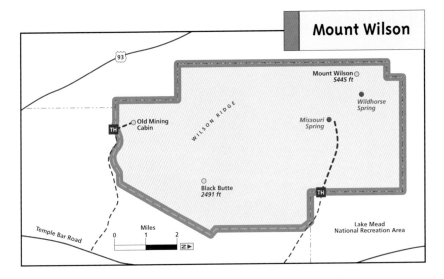

primrose, and desert marigold. Then, hiking along an old road, you discover a spring, and, in the soft earth around it, a filigree of imprints—bird, mammal, and reptile. A little water but lots of life—the epitome of desert survival.

In the Mount Wilson Wilderness, it is this small spring and several others that enable the survival of so much wildlife, including a bighorn sheep population of more than one hundred. For the sheep the 3,000-foot vertical relief of Wilson Ridge is a comfort zone. Hikers who cruise the ridge or reach the 5,445-foot summit of Mount Wilson itself will appreciate breathtaking views of Lake Mead and the cliffs and badlands of the surrounding terrain.

Animals know the locations of springs in the Mount Wilson Wilderness, but you may not find them. And during periods of prolonged drought, the springs may be dry. Carry plenty of water. Winter and spring are the best times to visit the wilderness—winter for the mild temperatures, spring for wildflowers.

WILDERNESS ACCESS

Two old roads travel west from the Temple Bar Road into the Mount Wilson Wilderness. To reach the Temple Bar Road, drive approximately 50 miles north from Kingman on U.S. Highway 93 and turn right (north). Drive a little more than 5.0 miles to a faint road that enters Temple Bar Road from the west. This road, which can be driven in a high-clearance two-wheel-drive vehicle, parallels a portion of the southern boundary of the wilderness. Turn left (west) and drive for approximately 4.0 miles to an old cabin just inside the wilderness boundary. Hikers with good map-reading and bushwhacking skills can ascend to Wilson Ridge from the vicinity of the cabin. Hiking the long ridgeline offers splendid views.

The second wilderness access road lies about 5.5 miles further along the Temple Bar Road. This road ends at the wilderness boundary after about 3.0 miles, but it is possible to proceed on foot from this point for another 2.0 miles to Missouri Spring. Hikers with good map-reading and bushwhacking skills can climb to the summit of Mount Wilson from this point.

59 North Maricopa Mountains Wilderness

Sundown showing rare Crested Saguaro Cactus

LOCATION: 12 miles northeast of Gila Bend

SIZE: 63,200 acres

ELEVATION RANGE: 840 to 2,813 feet

MILES OF TRAILS: 14

HABITATS: Sonoran Desert bajadas and mountains

ADMINISTRATION: BLM, Phoenix Field Office

TOPOGRAPHIC MAPS: Butterfield Pass, Cotton Center, Cotton Center SE, Cotton Center NW, Margies Peak, Mobile NW

AFTERNOONS, around the time of winter solstice, when pale light slants across the landscape and giant saguaros cast long shadows that hold forever, there's no more beautiful place on Earth than the Sonoran Desert. And the North Maricopa Mountains Wilderness is classic desert. Creosote, brittlebush, and bursage on the flats give way to saguaro forests upslope and along the bajadas. Chain-fruit and teddy bear cholla grow in impenetrable colonies. Ocotillo sprouts red floral banners after summer rains. Mesquite, palo verde, hackberry, and willow grow in or near wash channels where they contend with other plants for moisture in a place bereft of surface water. And there's the summer poppy, related to creosote, that sprouts only once in several seasons and then only after seasonal rains rinse germination-inhibiting chemicals from its seed coat.

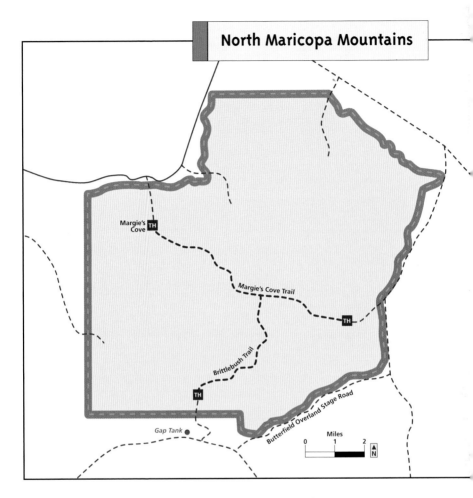

North Maricopa Mountains

Margie's Cove TH

Margie's Cove Trail

TH

Brittlebush Trail

TH

Gap Tank

Butterfield Overland Stage Road

Miles
0   1   2
N

Like desert plants, the animals that thrive in the North Maricopa Mountains Wilderness are adapted to drought. The cactus wren and white-winged dove, for instance, obtain most of their water from cactus fruits. The banner-tailed kangaroo rat never drinks, managing somehow to metabolize all its water from dry seeds. And another non-drinker is the kit fox, the kangaroo rat's chief predator. Bighorn sheep, mule deer, desert tortoise, Gambel's quail, curve-billed thrasher, Gila woodpecker, bobcat, black-tailed jackrabbit, roadrunner, and mountain lion all inhabit the wilderness.

During the Mexican War, ten years before the first stagecoaches began running along what is now the south border of the wilderness, Colonel Stephen Watts Kearny marched 1,650 men and sixteen artillery pieces over this trail enroute to California to establish U.S. control over the Southwest Territories. About a year after Kearny's march, Captain Philip St. George Cooke led volunteers made up entirely of members of the Mormon Church over the same ground. Under orders from Colonel Kearny, Cooke's soldiers, known as the Mormon Battalion, built a wagon road as they went along.

The first stagecoach to travel the wagon road was the San Antonio and San Diego Mail Line, dismissed as the "Jackass Mail" by its critics, who described it as "running from nowhere, through nothing, to no place." It ran for less than a year starting in 1857.

Owned by John Butterfield, the Overland Mail Company operated a stagecoach on the route between 1858 and 1861, carrying passengers and U.S. Mail from St. Louis and Memphis to San Francisco. The Butterfield Company built a stone tank for water storage at a place now called Happy Camp, hauling water from the Gila River to fill it. Today, a remnant 6.5-mile four-wheel-drive strip of the Butterfield Stage Road, designated as the Butterfield Stage Memorial, traces the southern boundary of the North Maricopa Mountains Wilderness.

Just twenty to thirty miles on a crow-line from Phoenix, the North Maricopa Mountains Wilderness provides backcountry as unspoiled as any hiker, backpacker, equestrian, or wildlife enthusiast might wish for. There are few trails in the wilderness, but the open terrain of the wilderness invites cross-country hiking. Two words of caution: do not hike in the North Maricopa Mountains Wilderness during summer; carry plenty of water at any time of the year. No water is available in the wilderness.

DAY HIKE: MARGIE'S COVE TRAIL
One-way length: 8.0 miles
Low and high elevations: 900 to 1,400 feet
Difficulty: easy

Within the North Maricopa Wilderness are a number of old jeep roads that have evolved into hiking trails. One of these is Margie's Cove. The easiest access is to the Margie's Cove Trailhead in the northwest corner of the wilderness. Drive south on State Route 85 from Interstate 10 for 20 miles to a dirt road heading east. Turn left (east) and follow the well-graded dirt road for 3.8 miles to another road leading south. Turn south for 1.8 miles to the wilderness boundary.

The Margie's Cove Trail travels southeast across the wilderness to its terminus at a trailhead on the eastern boundary. About halfway across it connects with the Brittlebush Trail which goes south 6.0 miles to Gap Tank, a bighorn sheep water hole along the four-wheel-drive Butterfield Stage Road. The Butterfield Stage Road can be reached by turning north onto a dirt road approximately 10 miles west of the Mobile Elementary School on Maricopa Road (SR 238). From the turnoff, signs point the way.

Organ Pipe Wilderness

Tall-standing Organ Pipe cactus

IF I WERE ASKED to pinpoint a half-dozen places on the southern Arizona map that embody the quintessence of the Sonoran Desert, Organ Pipe Cactus National Monument, set aside as wilderness in 1978, would be at the top of the list. The columnar organ pipe cactus reaches its northernmost limit on the south-facing slopes of its namesake wilderness, but it is only one of many flowering cacti, which include the saguaro, senita, cholla, barrel, prickly pear, hedgehog, and pincushion. Mesquite, jojoba, ironwood, foothills and blue palo verde, desert hackberry, brittlebush, century plant, Mexican jumping bean, and creosote bush are the dominant shrubs. Organ Pipe is one of the few places in the United States where you will find elephant tree, a native of the central Gulf of California region.

LOCATION: 15 miles south of Ajo

SIZE: 312,000 acres

ELEVATION RANGE: 500 to 4,808 feet

MILES OF TRAILS: 10

HABITATS: Sonoran Desert

ADMINISTRATION: National Park Service

TOPOGRAPHIC MAPS: Mount Ajo, Blankenship Well, Menagers Lake, Sentinel NE, Lukeville, West of Lukeville, Pozo Nuevo Well, Palo Verde Camp, Tillotson Peak, Kino Peak, Gunsight, Armenta Well, Bates Well, Diaz Peak

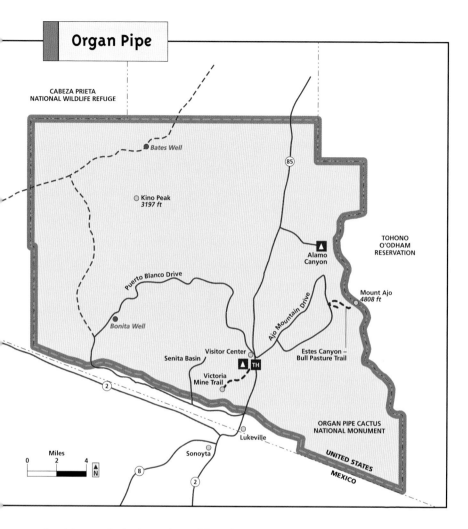

Surviving on the highest ridges of the wilderness area is a relict population of junipers, remnants of the wetter, cooler late Pleistocene. *Quercus ajoensis,* a species of oak found nowhere else in the world, mixes with other oak species in the riparian communities of canyon bottoms.

Spring bloom attracts many visitors to the Organ Pipe Wilderness, and in years of abundant fall and winter rain that promote seed germination, flowering plants in the wilderness burst into bloom. The spring of 1998 was such a time. Mexican poppy, desert lupine, owl's clover, desert chicory, globe mallow, Ajo lily, Parry's pensternon, globe mallow, mustard, larkspur, wild heliotrope, and wild hyacinth, blanketed the slopes. In turn, the cacti erupted in color, along with other perennially blooming plants, such as palo verde, ocotillo, creosote, ironwood, agave, brittle bush, and fairy duster. Old-timers said it had been more than twenty years since they had seen such an astounding efflorescence; others called it the bloom of the century.

The United Nations, recognizing the unique natural history of the entire region, has bestowed International Biosphere Reserve status on Organ Pipe Cactus National Monument along with the Sierra Pinacate and the Upper Gulf of California in northern Sonora, Mexico.

The Organ Pipe Wilderness is a dry and very hot place where summer temperatures routinely reach 110 degrees Fahrenheit. Rainfall averages only nine inches annually, with half falling in summer, half in winter. In drought years, that amount may decline to less than three inches, yet, the wilderness supports abundant wildlife.

On any spring morning birdsong fills the air. Cactus wren, curve-billed thrasher, white-winged dove, Gila woodpecker, Inca dove, Say's phoebe, ash-throated flycatcher, cardinal, flicker, Scott's oriole, and phainopepla are among the singers. Other birds of the more than 250 species living in the wilderness include raven, turkey vulture, burrowing owl, red-tailed hawk, Gambel's quail, and roadrunner. The Crested caracara is one of the rare birds occasionally spotted in Organ Pipe.

Mammals include a variety of desert rats, such as the banner-tailed kangaroo rat and the white-throated woodrat. Mule deer are here, as are mountain lion, javelina, coyote, bighorn sheep, pronghorn, jack rabbit, ringtail, kit fox, and badger. And, of course, no desert wilderness worth the name is without scorpions, kissing bugs, sidewinders, rattlesnakes, Gila monsters, and a great variety of insects, spiders, reptiles and amphibians.

An interesting geological feature of the Organ Pipe Wilderness is its watershed, which divides into two major drainage systems—one flowing north, the other south. Arroyos draining north eventually wind up in the Gila River; those draining south flow into the Rio Sonoyta in Sonora, Mexico.

In prehistoric times, the deserts in the region of Organ Pipe were inhabited by hunters and gatherers. The Hohokam came next and the Tohono O'odham moved into the region, following the disappearance of the Hohokam in the 1400s. Cattle ranching and mining both occurred within what is now Organ Pipe Wilderness. In fact, under special wartime legislation, mining continued until 1978, forty years after Organ Pipe became a unit of the national park system. Cattle grazing continued into the 1970s.

Although visitors arrive at Organ Pipe throughout the year, the best times are October through mid-May. Extreme heat in summer discourages hiking into the wilderness.

DAY HIKE: ESTES CANYON – BULL PASTURE LOOP
One-way length: 4.1 miles
Low and high elevations: 2,300 to 3,300 feet
Difficulty: easy

This trail begins at Estes Canyon about 8.0 miles along the Ajo Mountain Drive, a 21-mile loop through the eastern portion of the national monument. The route winds back and forth across the canyon bottom before switchbacking up a steep ridge to link with a short spur to Bull Pasture. The route then tops a ridge and begins a steep climb below a long cliff face to Bull Pasture. The pasture is an oval basin cupped between high ridges. Its luxuriant grasses inspired early ranchers to drive cattle up to pasture in this high-country meadow. Hiking back to the trailhead via the Bull Pasture portion of the loop is about 0.5-mile shorter.

Hardy hikers can reach the 4,808-foot summit of Mount Ajo by moving east along an indistinct route to the top. From the summit you can see the Gulf of California, more than seventy miles south.

DAY HIKE: VICTORIA MINE TRAIL
One-way length: 2.25 miles
Low and high elevations: 1,600 to 1,700 feet
Difficulty: easy

This very easy hike begins at the south end of the campground. Heading southwest across alluvial fans called bajadas to Victoria Mine, the oldest and richest gold and silver mine in the monument. Along the way the route passes some other old mines, machinery, and ruined buildings.

CROSS-COUNTRY HIKING

The best way to see the Organ Pipe Wilderness is to obtain a backcountry permit at the Visitor Center and explore cross-country. These hikes can begin from designated parking areas along the twenty-one-mile Ajo Mountain Drive or the fifty-three-mile Puerto Blanco Drive. The open terrain makes for easy orienteering, and a few old foot trails, jeep roads, and game trails can be followed for great distances into the wilderness.

Although there are a few springs and rock tanks, called *tinajas,* within the wilderness, there is no reliable water. Most backcountry expeditions are limited, therefore, to the amount of water you can haul. Discuss your route and time of return with a park ranger before heading out.

If you are fortunate enough to locate a tinaja, keep in mind that its chief function is to sustain wildlife. Don't bathe in it. Don't waste it. And make sure to treat it before drinking.

Sierra Estrella Wilderness 61

Elegant spires reach to the sky

AT NIGHT the city lights of Phoenix are clearly visible from the ridges of the Sierra Estrella, "star mountains," snugged up against the southwest corner of the Gila River Indian Reservation. So close do they seem that a hiker familiar with the layout of the sprawling metropolis can easily identify street grids in the light patterns. Yet, this small desert wilderness mountain, rising steeply above the desert floor, can seem as wild and remote as any patch of wilderness landscape in southern Arizona.

Saguaro cactus, teddy bear cholla, ocotillo, palo verde, creosote bush, mesquite, and even elephant tree dominate the vegetation in the lower elevations. Higher up a few oak and juniper cling to the rocky ridges. Gila monster, diamondback rattlesnake, bark scorpion, cactus wren, curve-billed thrasher, great horned owl, golden eagle, prairie falcon, mule deer, gray fox, red-tailed hawk, javelina, whip-tailed lizard, and desert tortoise are among the animals that thrive in the desert habitat.

LOCATION: 15 miles southwest of Phoenix

SIZE: 14,400 acres

ELEVATION RANGE: 1,400 to 4,119 feet

MILES OF TRAILS: 3

HABITATS: Sonoran Desert mountains

ADMINISTRATION: BLM, Phoenix Field Office

TOPOGRAPHIC MAPS: Montezuma Peak, Mobile NE

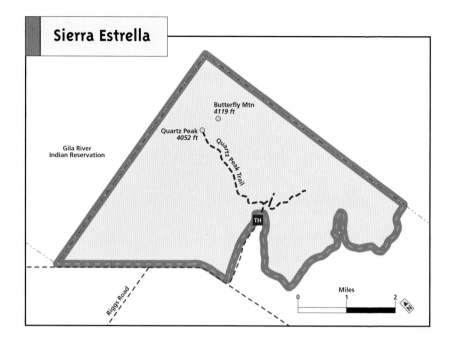

Avoid visiting the Sierra Estrella Wilderness in summer, which in southern Arizona extends from mid-May through September. No water is available in the wilderness, so hikers are required to carry in or cache water.

> **DAY HIKE:** QUARTZ PEAK TRAIL
> One-way length: 3.0 miles
> Low and high elevations: 2,100 to 4,052 feet
> Difficulty: easy

Access to the trailhead is from the Rainbow Valley to the west of the wilderness and requires a four-wheel-drive vehicle. From Phoenix drive west on Interstate 10 to exit 126, Jackrabbit Road. Drive south on Jackrabbit Road to Arlington Road and turn left (east), then right (south) onto Rainbow Valley Road. Continue south on Rainbow Valley Road to pavement's end, approximately 9.5 miles. Turn left (east) onto Riggs Road, a dirt road, and travel east to the power line road that parallels the Estrella Wilderness. Turn right (southeast) about 1.0 mile to a point where another road intersects from the left. Take this road about 2.0 miles until it dead-ends.

The Quartz Peak Trail travels across mostly open terrain to the summit of Quartz Peak. Near the beginning, the trail passes some old mica mines. Butterfly Mountain, a destination for peak-baggers, is just a short cross-country hike northeast of Quartz Peak. Because the terrain is reasonably open, cross-country jaunts are fairly easily accomplished in the Sierra Estrella Wilderness. Be advised, however, that this is rugged country in which you should never hike alone.

South Maricopa Mountains Wilderness

Valley of Saguaro cactus

CONSISTING OF THIRTEEN MILES of the Maricopa Mountain range amid extensive desert plains, the South Maricopa Mountains Wilderness is, like its sister wilderness to the north, classic Sonoran Desert. The eastern portion of the wilderness is mountainous with long ridges and isolated peaks, separated by plains and arroyos. The western section consists primarily of desert flats.

Triangle-leaf bursage, creosote, brittlebush, cholla, ocotillo, mesquite, palo verde, hackberry, willow, saguaro, prickly pear, and barrel cactus are the dominant plants. And the animals present are much the same as those found in the North Maricopa Mountains Wilderness: kit fox, gray fox, pocket mouse, desert tortoise, cactus wren, bobcat, roadrunner, mountain lion, mule deer, bighorn sheep, white-winged dove, great horned owl, red-tailed hawk, banner-tailed kangaroo, Gambel's quail, curve-billed thrasher, Gila woodpecker, bobcat, black-tailed jackrabbit, and roadrunner.

LOCATION: 16 miles east of Gila Bend

SIZE: 60,100 acres

ELEVATION RANGE: 1,250 to 3,183 feet

MILES OF TRAILS: No marked or maintained trails

HABITATS: Sonoran Desert

ADMINISTRATION: BLM, Phoenix Field Office

TOPOGRAPHIC MAPS: Big Horn, Estrella, Bosque, Lost Horse Peak, Conelly Well

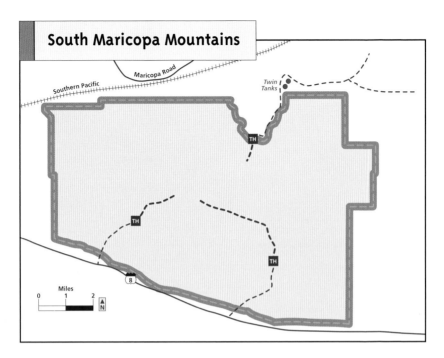

For me, a lasting impression of the South Maricopa Mountains Wilderness is the health and vigor of its saguaro forest. Living, as I do, in the backyard of Saguaro National Park near Tucson, I have seen many big saguaros, but on a winter visit to the South Maricopa Mountains Wilderness, I saw some of the largest, stateliest saguaros I had ever seen.

Winter is the best time to visit any low desert wilderness and that certainly holds true for the South Maricopa although the weather is tolerable just about any time between the months of November and March.

WILDERNESS ACCESS

Access into the South Maricopa Mountains Wilderness is difficult, so you may want to check with the BLM field office before going in. The principal difficulty is that you are required to enter off of Interstate 8, which parallels the southern wilderness boundary for a distance of approximately fourteen miles. Two unnamed roads travel north into the wilderness for a few miles before being closed to vehicles. No exit ramps mark these roads and their presence is indicated only by a couple of gates, so you must be very careful while exiting the interstate. Close the unlocked gates after you enter.

Access to the wilderness from the north is possible from the vicinity of Twin Tanks, but, again, it is difficult, mainly because the route in is convoluted. Follow the routes on your topo maps very carefully.

Cross-country hiking in the South Maricopa ranges from easy to difficult depending on terrain. The usual cautions about cross-country hiking apply: Carry plenty of water, let someone know your travel plans and times of entrance and exit, and always hike with a companion.

Tres Alamos Wilderness 63

Spindly Joshua trees

IT'S AN INTRIGUING NAME, *Tres Alamos*—in Spanish, "three cottonwoods." Trying to figure out how it fits this wilderness, you play a guessing game with whomever named it. Was there once a triplet of cottonwoods growing at the well-watered convergence of dry washes? Or is there something about the configuration of the wilderness area's central monolith, dubbed Tres Alamos, that reminded someone of a cottonwood grouping? That monolith, almost bumped up against the area's high point, 4,293-foot Sawyer Peak, is the most striking landscape feature of the wilderness.

The western portion of the Tres Alamos Wilderness is desert bajadas and plains, while the eastern section is comprised of the more scenic ridgelines, canyons, and washes of the southern reaches of the Black Mountains. The mix of vegetation in the wilderness is indicative of intermingling Sonoran and Mohave Desert biomes. Saguaro cacti, which have just about reached their northernmost range, grow cheek by jowl with large, arboreal Joshua trees. Palo verde

LOCATION:
30 miles northwest of Wickenburg

SIZE: 8,300 acres

ELEVATION RANGE:
2,300 to 4,293 feet

MILES OF TRAILS:
No marked or maintained trails

HABITATS: Sonoran and Mohave Desert

ADMINISTRATION:
BLM Kingman Field Office

TOPOGRAPHIC MAPS:
Date Creek Ranch NW, Ives Peak, Smith Peak NE, Malpais Mesa SW

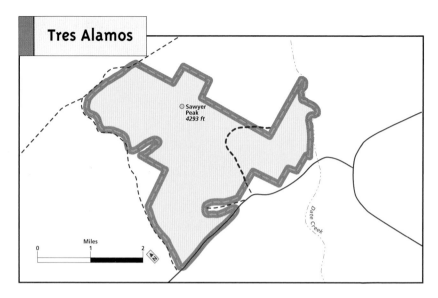

trees dot the upland bajadas; mesquite, acacia, hackberry and other xeroriparian species line the washes. Blooming annuals display spectacular wildflowers after rainy fall and winter seasons. Kit fox, desert tortoise, cactus wren, mule deer, prairie falcon, golden eagle, Gila monster, and Cooper's hawk are among the animals occupying these habitats.

Late fall, winter, and early spring are the best times to visit the Tres Alamos Wilderness. By mid-May, in most years, it has already become too hot. Extreme heat continues through September.

WILDERNESS ACCESS

There are no developed trails in the Tres Alamos Wilderness, but dry washes and open bajadas invite cross-country hiking. To reach the southern boundary of the wilderness, drive about 20 miles north from Wickenburg on U.S. Highway 93 to the Lake Alamo Road and turn left (west). Drive west approximately 6.5 miles on the Lake Alamo Road to a road fork and take the right fork. Continue for another 3.5 miles to a second road fork, and, again, stay right. The road then crosses the Date Creek Wash and passes some private homes. After approximately 3.0 miles an old road comes in from the north. Take this road a short distance to the wilderness boundary.

From the boundary line, the old roadway, now closed to vehicles, continues into the wilderness for perhaps 2.0 miles to reach a ridgeline overlooking the southern portion of the wilderness. Bajada hiking across adjacent portions of the wilderness is fairly easy beyond this point.

The road that parallels the southern boundary of the Tres Alamos Wilderness continues west to a four-wheel-drive road heading north. This route, which parallels the western boundary of the wilderness, offers a number of access points for hiking cross-country.

Another four-wheel-drive route, accessible from U.S. Highway 93, runs along the northern boundary of the wilderness. From this route it is possible to hike up washes that spill down the north flank of the high peaks.

Trigo Mountains Wilderness

Rust-red rocky vista

RUGGED, INHOSPITABLY HOT AND DRY, and hemmed in by a military weaponry proving ground on its eastern border and the Imperial National Wildlife Refuge to the south and west, the Trigo Mountains Wilderness area is not one of Arizona's most frequently visited outbacks. Characterized by sawtooth ridges, steep-walled canyons, and an interlacing system of arroyos, the wilderness consists of fourteen miles of the Trigo Mountain ridgeline bisected by the Clip Wash. Red Cloud Wash lies to the southeast and Hart Mine Wash to the north.

Trigo means wheat in Spanish and, according to local history, the Yuma Indians raised wheat in the river bottoms in the region. But mining, not wheat, brought boom times to the camps that dotted the banks of the nearby Colorado River. In its heyday, the now defunct gold-mining town of Picacho

LOCATION: 50 miles north of Yuma

SIZE: 30,300 acres

ELEVATION RANGE: 280 to 1,920 feet

MILES OF TRAILS: No marked or maintained trials

HABITATS: Sonoran Desert

ADMINISTRATION: BLM, Yuma Field Office

TOPOGRAPHIC MAPS: Picacho, Picacho SW, Picacho NW, Cibola, Cibola SE, Hidden Valley

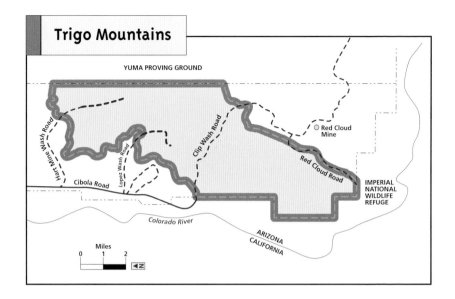

on the California side of the Colorado had a population of 2,000, making it one of the bigger towns in the area.

Gold, lead, zinc, and manganese were taken from the ground, but silver was the principal ore. Arizona's famous Silver Mining District, with more than sixty mines, was centered here. The Clip Mine, the Red Cloud, and the Silver Bonanza were among the more productive mines in the Silver District. Mining shafts, the tumble-down remains of cabins, and feral prospectors' burros roaming the Trigo Mountains Wilderness and the adjacent Imperial Refuge Wilderness are reminders of that lost era.

Creosote, bursage, ocotillo, cholla, palo verde, mesquite, smoke tree, brittle-bush, prickly pear, saguaro and other plants native to the Sonoran Desert manage to thrive in the hot, dry environment of the Trigo Mountains Wilderness. This desert region is also home to many heat- and drought-adapted animals, such as cactus wren, curve-billed thrasher, kit fox, Gila monster, sidewinder, kangaroo rat, and white-winged dove. Other animals inhabiting the wilderness include mule deer, bobcat, mountain lion, great horned owl, red-tailed hawk, desert bighorn sheep, and the seemingly ineradicable prospector's burro, which, although non-native, is among the toughest desert dwellers. Periodically, the Bureau of Land Management (BLM) captures burro herds and puts them up for adoption. Still, they manage not only to survive but to increase.

The months between November and March are favorable times to visit the Trigo Mountains Wilderness. Wildflowers often begin to appear as early as late December in the warmer deserts of Arizona. No water is available in the wilderness.

WILDERNESS ACCESS

Because no maintained hiking trails penetrate the Trigo Mountains Wilderness, all hiking and backpacking in the area is cross-country. But, as with much desert hiking, the wilderness terrain is reasonably open. My practice where no established trails exist is to follow game trails if possible. Deer, in particular, seem always to find the easiest routes in terrain where numerous arroyos have to be traversed. Another way through desert terrain is to follow dry washes, which are often broad and unobstructed by brushy growth.

The easiest access point to the Trigo Mountains Wilderness is via the Red Cloud Mine Road. From Yuma drive 25 miles north U.S. Highway 95 to the Martinez Lake turnoff and travel west to about 10 miles to the Imperial National Wildlife Refuge. Take the Red Cloud Mine Road approximately 13 miles north to the Red Cloud Mine. From the mine the Red Cloud Wash parallels the southeast boundary of the wilderness. You can reach the Red Cloud Mine in a high-clearance two-wheel-drive vehicle. To reach any other wilderness access points beyond the mine, you will need a four-wheel-drive. Consult your topo maps and the Yuma Field Office of the BLM regarding the wilderness-dividing Clip Wash Road, the Hart Mine Road, or the Lopez Wash Road.

Appendix I: Wilderness Areas

Bureau of Land Management Areas

NAME	ACREAGE	YEAR DESIGNATED
Aravaipa Canyon	19,410	1984
Arrastra Mountain	129,800	1990
Aubrey Peak	15,400	1990
Beaver Dam Mountains	19,600	1984
Big Horn Mountains	21,000	1990
Boboquivari Peak	2,065	1990
Cottonwood Point	6,860	1984
Coyote Mountains	5,080	1990
Dos Cabezas Mountains	11,998	1990
Eagletail Mountains	100,600	1990
East Cactus Plain	14,630	1990
Fishhooks	10,500	1990
Gibraltar Mountain	18,790	1990
Grand Wash Cliffs	37,300	1984
Harcuvar Mountains	25,050	1990
Harquahala Mountains	22,880	1990
Hassayampa River Canyon	11,840	1990
Hells Canyon	9,311	1990
Hummingbird Springs	31,200	1990
Kanab Creek	6,700	1984
Mount Logan	14,650	1984
Mount Nutt	27,660	1990
Mount Tipton	30,760	1990
Mount Trumbull	7,880	1984
Mount Wilson	23,900	1990
Muggins Mountains	7,640	1990
Needle's Eye	8,760	1990
New Water Mountains	24,600	1990
North Maricopa Mountains	63,200	1990
North Santa Teresa	5,800	1990
Paiute	87,900	1984
Paria-Canyon Vermilion Cliffs	112,500	1984
Peloncillo Mountains	19,440	1990

NAME	ACREAGE	YEAR DESIGNATED
Rawhide Mountains	38,470	1990
Redfield Canyon	6,600	1990
Sierra Estrella	14,400	1990
Signal Mountain	13,350	1990
South Maricopa Mountains	60,100	1990
Swansea	16,400	1990
Table Top	34,400	1990
Tres Alamos	8,300	1990
Trigo Mountains	30,300	1990
Upper Burro Creek	27,440	1990
Wabayuma Peak	40,000	1990
Warm Springs	112,400	1990
White Canyon	5,800	1990
Woolsey Peak	64,000	1990

Fish and Wildlife Service Wilderness Areas

NAME	ACREAGE	YEAR DESIGNATED
Cabeza Prieta Refuge	803,418	1990
Imperial Refuge	9,220	1990
Kofa Refuge	516,300	1990

National Park Service Wilderness Areas

NAME	ACREAGE	YEAR DESIGNATED
Grand Canyon	1,218,376	N/A
Organ Pipe	312,600	1978
Petrified Forest	50,260	1970
Saguaro East	59,930	1976
Saguaro West	13,470	1976

Forest Service Wilderness Areas

NAME	ACREAGE	YEAR DESIGNATED
Castle Creek	25,517	1984
Cedar Bench	16,005	1984
Chiricahua	87,700	1933, 84
Escudilla	5,200	1984
Fossil Springs	11,550	1984
Four Peaks	60,740	1984
Galiuro	76,317	1932, 84
Granite Mountain	9,799	1984
Hellsgate	37,440	1984

Appendix 1: continued

NAME	ACREAGE	YEAR DESIGNATED	NAME	ACREAGE	YEAR DESIGNATED
Juniper Mesa	7,554	1984	Saddle Mountain	40,610	1984
Kachina Peaks	18,960	1984	Salome	18,530	1984
Kanab Creek	68,596	1984	Salt River Canyon	32,100	1984
Kendrick Mountain	6,510	1984	Santa Teresa	26,780	1984
Mazatzal	252,500	1940, 84	Sierra Ancha	20,850	1933, 1951, 64
Miller Peak	20,190	1984			
Mount Baldy	7,000	1984	Strawberry Crater	10,141	1984
Mount Wrightson	25,260	1984	Superstition	160,200	1939, 84
Munds Mountain	18,150	1984	Sycamore Canyon	55,937	1935
Pajarita	7,420	1984	West Clear Creek	13,600	1984
Pine Mountain	20,100	1984	Wet Beaver	6,700	1984
Pusch Ridge	56,933	1978	Woodchute	5,923	1984
Red Rock-Secret Mountain	43,950	1984			
Rincon Mountain	38,590	1984	Blue Range Primitive Area	173,762	1933

Appendix 2: Addresses for Further Information

Arizona State Land Department
PHOENIX OFFICE
1616 W. Adams
Phoenix, AZ 85007
(602) 542-2119

TUCSON OFFICE
233 N. Main Street
Tucson, AZ 85701
(520) 628-5480

Bureau of Land Management Offices
ARIZONA STATE OFFICE
222 North Central Avenue
Phoenix, AZ 85004-2208
(602) 417-9200

ARIZONA STRIP OFFICE
345 Riverside Drive
St. George, UT 84790-9000
(801) 688-3200

KINGMAN FIELD OFFICE
2475 Beverly Avenue
Kingman, AZ 86401-3629
(520) 692-4400

PHOENIX FIELD OFFICE
2015 West Deer Valley Road
Phoenix, AZ 85027-2099
(602) 580-5500

SAFFORD FIELD OFFICE
711 14th Avenue
Safford, AZ 85546-3321
(520) 348-4400

TUCSON FIELD OFFICE
12661 E. Broadway
Tucson, AZ 85748-7208
(520) 722-4289

YUMA FIELD OFFICE
2555 E. Gila Ridge Road
Yuma, AZ 85365-2240
(520) 317-3200

Fish and Wildlife Offices
CABEZA PRIETA REFUGE
1611 North Second Avenue
Ajo, AZ 85321
(520) 387-6483

IMPERIAL REFUGE
Martinez Lake
P.O. Box 72217
Yuma, AZ 85365
(520) 783-3371

KOFA REFUGE
356 W. First Street
Yuma, AZ 85366-6290
(520) 783-7861

Appendix 2: continued

National Park Service Offices

**BACKCOUNTRY OFFICE
GRAND CANYON NATIONAL PARK**
P.O. Box 129
Grand Canyon, AZ 86023
638-7888 (recorded info)
(520) 638-7875
  (weekdays between 1 and 5 p.m.)
River Permits Office (520) 638-7843
Website: www.thecanyon.com/nps

**ORGAN PIPE CACTUS
NATIONAL MONUMENT**
Route 1, Box 100
Ajo, AZ 85321 (520) 387-6849
Website: www.nps.gov/orpi/

PETRIFIED FOREST NATIONAL PARK,
P.O. Box 2217
Petrified Forest National Park, AZ 86028
(520) 524-6228
Website: www.nps.gov/pefo/

SAGUARO NATIONAL PARK
3693 South Old Spanish Trail
Tucson, AZ 85730-5601
(520) 733-5153
Website: www.nps.gov/sagu/

National Forest Offices

**APACHE-SITGREAVES
NATIONAL FOREST**
309 South Mountain Avenue
P.O. Box 640
Springerville, AZ 85938
(520) 333-4301
Ranger Districts
  Alpine (520) 339-4384
  Clifton (520) 865-2432
  Chevelon (520) 289-3381
  Heber (520) 535-4481
  Lakeside (520) 368-5111
  Springerville (520) 333-4372

COCONINO NATIONAL FOREST
2323 E. Greenlaw Lane
Flagstaff, AZ 86004
(520) 527-3600

Ranger Districts
  Beaver Creek (520) 567-4501
  Blue Ridge (520) 477-2255
  Flagstaff (520) 527-7450
  Long Valley (520) 354-2480
  Mormon Lake (520) 774-1147
  Peaks (520) 526-0866
  Sedona (520) 282-4119

CORONADO NATIONAL FOREST
300 W. Congress Street
Tucson, Arizona, 85701   (520) 670-4552
Ranger Districts
  Douglas (520) 364-3468
  Nogales (520) 281-2296
  Safford (520) 428-4150
  Santa Catalina (520) 749-8700
  Sierra Vista (520) 378-0311

KAIBAB NATIONAL FOREST
800 South 6th Street
Williams, AZ 86046   (520) 635-2681
Ranger Districts
  Chalender (520) 635-2676
  North Kaibab (520) 643-7395
  Tusayan (520) 638-2443
  Williams (520) 635-2633

PRESCOTT NATIONAL FOREST
344 S. Cortez Street
Prescott, AZ 86301   (520) 445-1762
Ranger Districts
  Bradshaw (520) 445-7253
  Chino Valley (520) 636-2302
  Verde (520) 567-4121

TONTO NATIONAL FOREST
P.O. Box 5348
Phoenix, AZ 85010 (602) 225-5200
Ranger Districts
  Cave Creek (602) 488-3441
  Globe (520) 425-7189
  Mesa (520) 379-6446
  Payson (520) 474-7900
  Pleasant Valley (520) 462-3311
  Tonto Basin (520) 467-2236

National Forest Website for Arizona:
www.fs.fed.us/recreation/states/az.html

Appendix 3: Map Sources

Many wilderness area maps are available for free public perusal at public and university libraries or for sale at map and outfitter's stores throughout Arizona. Trail guides and maps, some of them free, are also available from agency offices listed in Appendix 2.

Arizona State Parks has published a four-volume *Arizona State Trails Guide,* which is updated periodically to add new trails and new information. The complete set is expensive; many libraries make the maps available on a non-circulating basis.

For information contact:
ARIZONA STATE PARKS
1300 W. Washington
Phoenix, AZ 85007
(602) 542-4174 or 1-800-285-3703
Web Site: www.pr.state.az.us

The Forest Service and USGS have cooperated to offer maps of National Forests online. The URL for the web site is:
www.fs.fed.us/links/maps.html/

As of this writing, Region 3, in which Arizona is located, was a non-participant in this service. Keep checking.

Appendix 4: Selected Bibliography

Aitchison, Stewart and Bruce Grubbs. *The Hiker's Guide to Arizona.* Helena, MT: Falcon Press Publishing Co., 1987.

Annerino, John. *Adventuring in Arizona.* San Francisco, CA: Sierra Club Books, 1991.

Barnes, Will C., *Arizona Place Names.* Tucson, AZ: University of Arizona Press, 1988.

Bowers, Janice Emily. *Shrubs and Trees of the Southwest Deserts.* Tucson, AZ: Southwest Parks and Monuments Association, 1993.

Brown, David E. ed. *The Wolf in the Southwest: The Making of an Endangered Species.* Tucson, AZ: University of Arizona Press, 1984.

Carothers, Steven W. and Bryan T. Brown. *The Colorado River Through the Grand Canyon: Natural History and Human Change.* Tucson, AZ: University of Arizona Press, 1991.

Elmore, Francis H. *Shrubs and Trees of the Southwest Uplands.* Tucson, AZ: Southwest Parks and Monuments Association, 1976.

Ganci, Dave. *Hiking the Southwest: A Sierra Club Totebook.* San Francisco, CA: Sierra Club Books, 1983.

Gehlbach, Frederick R. *Mountain Islands and Desert Seas: A Natural History of the U.S.-Mexican Borderlands.* College Station: Texas A&M University Press, TX, 1981.

Grubbs, Bruce. *Hiking Northern Arizona.* Helena, MT: Falcon Publishing Co., Inc., 1994.

Hanson, Roseann Beggy and Jonathan Hanson. *Southern Arizona Nature Almanac.* Boulder, CO: Pruett Publishing Company, 1996.

Lowe, Charles H. *Arizona's Natural Environment.* Tucson, AZ: University of Arizona Press, 1964.

Lowe, Charles H., ed. *The Vertebrates of Arizona.* Tucson, AZ: University of Arizona Press, 1964.

MacMahon, James A. and others. *Deserts.* New York, NY: Alfred A. Knopf, Inc., 1985.

Molvar, Erik. *Hiking Arizona's Cactus Country.* Helena, MT: Falcon Publishing Co., 1995.

Appendix 4: continued

Murie, Olaus J. *A Field Guide to Animal Tracks.* Boston, MA: Houghton Mifflin Company, 1974.

Nations, Dale and Edmund Stump. *Geology of Arizona.* Dubuque, AZ: Kendall/Hunt Publishing Company, 1981.

Niehaus, Theodore F. and others. *A Field Guide to Southwestern and Texas Wildflowers.* Boston, MA: Houghton Mifflin Company, 1984.

Peterson, Roger Tory. *A Field Guide to Western Birds.* Boston, MA: Houghton Mifflin Company, 1989.

Sheridan, Thomas E. *Arizona: A History.* Tucson, AZ: University of Arizona Press, 1995.

Smith, Robert L. *Venomous Animals of Arizona.* Tucson, AZ: College of Agriculture, The University of Arizona, 1981.

Stevens, Larry. *The Colorado River in Grand Canyon: A Guide.* Flagstaff, AZ: Red Lake Books, 1983.

Thybony, Scott. *Official Guide to Hiking the Grand Canyon.* Grand Canyon, AZ: Grand Canyon Natural History Association, 1996.

Walker, Henry P. and Don Bufkin. *Historical Atlas of Arizona.* Norman, OK: University of Oklahoma Press, 1989.

Warren, Scott S. *Exploring Arizona's Wild Areas: A Guide for Hikers, Backpackers, Climbers, X-C Skiers & Paddlers.* Seattle, WA: The Mountaineers, 1996.

Index

NOTE: Entries in boldface denote major areas; citations followed by the letter "p" denote photos; citations followed by the letter "m" denote maps.

A.B. Young Trail day hike   139
Abbey, Edward   20
Abineau Trail loop hike   61–62
A.D. Bar Trail day hike   99
Alder Creek Trail loop hike   184–85
Algonquin Trail day hike   107
Altitude sickness   30
Amethyst Trail loop hike   184
Apache Maid Trail day hike   164
Aravaipa Canyon Wilderness   170–72, 170p, 171m
Arizona: diversity of wilderness in 13–16; future of wilderness in, 22–23; history of wilderness in, 11, 15–16; history of wildlife in, 19–20; weather in, 25; wilderness areas by region, 8m–9m
Arizona Desert Wilderness Act (1990)   11, 16
Arizona Strip   14, 36
Arizona Trail   216p
Arizona Wilderness Act (1984)   11, 16
Ash Creek Trail destination hike   203
Aspens   31p, 68p

Barnhardt Trail day hike   126–27
Barnhardt Trail loop hike   127
Barrel cacti   262p
Basin and Range province   13, 15, 168–69, 242–43
Bathtub Campground   176
Bear Canyon loop hike   218
Bear Canyon Trail day hike   199
Bear Flat Trail day hike   119
Bear Jaw Trail loop hike   61–62

Bears   20, 95, 109
Bear Saddle loop hike   194
Bear Wallow Creek   94p
Bear Wallow Trail day hike   95–96
Bear Wallow Wilderness   94–96, 94p, 95m
Beaver Dam Mountains Wilderness   38–40, 38p, 39m
Bell Rock   17p
Bell Trail day hike   163–64
Ben Avery Trail day hike   252
Big Horn Mountains Wilderness   244–45, 244p, 245m
Black bears   20, 95
Blue Cabin Trail day hike   99
Blue Crossing Campground   103
Blue Lookout Trail day hike   99
Blue Range Primitive Area   97–105, 97p, 100m
Blue River destination hike   103
Blue River Trail shuttle hike   104–5
Bog Springs Campground   208
Bog Springs loop hike   208
Bonanza Bill Trail day hike   101
Bootlegger Campground   139
Boucher Trail destination hike   49
Boyer Trail day hike   146
Boynton Canyon Trail day hike   141–42
Bright Angel Campground   48, 50, 54
Bright Angel Trail destination hike   48
Brins Mesa Trail day hike   142
Brittle bushes   234p
Brower, David   23
Browns Canyon   253p
Browns Trail loop hike   184
Buckskin Gulch destination hike   79–80
Buckskin loop hike   80
Bull Basin Trail loop hike   70
Bull Pasture loop day hike   281–82

Cabeza Prieta Mountains   246p
Cabeza Prieta Refuge Wilderness
   246–49, 246p, 248m
Cacti: barrel   262p; cholla, 23p, 268p;
   claret cup, 241p; crested saguaro,
   276p; fish hook barrel, 274p; organ
   pipe, 279p; prickly pear, 186p;
   saguaro, 224p, 259p, 283p, 285p
California condors   14, 78
California fan palms   269
Camping. *See* Hiking and camping
Cane Spring Trail day hike   183–84
Cane Spring Trail loop hike   184–85
Canyon Lake Trailhead shuttle hike   236
Carr Peak loop hike   194
Carr Peak Trail day hike   193–94
Casner Mountain loop hike   158
Castle Creek Trail day hike   107
Castle Creek Wilderness   106–8,
   106p, 108m
Centella Point   21p, 173p
Center Mountain Trail day hike   152
Chillicut Trail day hike   184
Chiricahua Wilderness   12p, 21p,
   31p, 35p, 173–78, 173p, 174m
Cholla cacti   23p, 268p
Claret cup cacti   241p
Clear Creek Campground   54
Clear Creek Trail destination hike   54
Colorado Plateau   13–14, 36–37
Colorado River   265p
Columbines   33p, 124p
Conenose bugs   78
Coon Creek Trail day hike   153
Coon Spring Trail day hike   154
Coronado National Forest   31p
Cottonwood Campground   54
Courthouse Butte   93p
Cow Flat Trail day hike   101–2
Cow Head Saddle Trail
   destination hike   228
Crested saguaro cacti   276p

Crest Trail day hike   193
Crest Trail shuttle hike   178
Crisler, Lois   19
Cross-country hiking   25
Cunningham Camp   201

Davenport Wash Trail loop hike   128
Deadman Trail day hike   198
Dearhead Spring day hike   226
Deep Creek Trail day hike   154
Deer Creek Trail loop hike   128
Dehydration   29
Dos Cabezas Mountains Wilderness
   179–81, 179p, 181m
Douglas Spring destination hike   228
Dry Creek Trail shuttle hike   143
Dutch Henry Canyon Trail
   day hike   201
Dutchman Grave Trail loop hike   130
Dutchman's Trail shuttle hike   236, 238

Eagletail Mountains   250p
Eagletail Mountains Wilderness
   250–52, 250p, 251m
East Divide Trail destination hike   191
East Pocket Trail day hike   139
Echo Canyon loop hike   178
Equipment, hiking and camping
   25, 28, 32
Escudilla Trail day hike   110
Escudilla Wilderness   109–10,
   109p, 110m
Espero Canyon shuttle hike   221
Estes Canyon day hike   281–82
Etiquette, wilderness   25
Exposure   29, 30

Fires, while hiking and camping   26
Fish hook barrel cacti   274p
Flash floods   26, 32
Florida Trail shuttle hike   208
Foote Creek Trail shuttle hike   105

Fossil Springs Trail day hike   113
Fossil Springs Wilderness   111–13,
    111p, 112m
Four Peaks Trail day hike   183
Four Peaks Trail loop hike   184–85
Four Peaks Wilderness   182–85,
    182p, 185m
Frye Canyon Trail day hike   199

Galiuro Wilderness   186–91,
    186p, 190m
Giardiasis   28
Grand Canyon   14, 36–37, 41p, 56p
Grand Canyon National Park   41–55,
    41p, 46m–47m
Grand Gulch Bench Road day hike   57
Grandview Trail day hike   48
Grand Wash Cliffs Wilderness
    56–57, 56p, 57m
Granite Mountain Trail   114p
Granite Mountain Trail day hike   116
Granite Mountain Wilderness
    114–16, 114p, 115m
Grant Creek Trail day hike   201
Grant Creek Trail shuttle hike   105
Grant-Goudy Ridge Trail
    day hike   201–2
Grass Canyon   243p
Grinding holes, Indian   179p
Grizzly bears   20, 109

Hack Canyon day hike   64–65
Hagan Corral Trail shuttle hike   105
Half Moon Trail day hike   127
Happy Valley Campground   226
Harquahala Mountains   253p
Harquahala Mountains Wilderness
    253–55, 253p, 254m
Harquahala Mountain Trail day hike
    254–55
Hassayampa River Canyon Wilderness
    256–58, 256p, 257m

Heart of Rocks loop hike   178
Heat exhaustion   28
Heat stroke   28–30
Hells Canyon Wilderness   259–61,
    259p, 260m
Hellsgate Trail day hike   118–19
Hellsgate Wilderness   117–20,
    117p, 119m
Hell's Hole Trail day hike   146
Hermit Creek Campground   49
Hermit Trail destination hike   48–49
Hiking and camping: altitude sickness,
    30; campsites, 26; cross-country
    hiking, 25; dehydration, 29; disposing
    of wastes, 26; equipment, 25, 28, 32;
    flash floods, 26, 32; group size, 25;
    hyperthermia, 28–30; hypothermia,
    29, 30; insects, 78; lightning strikes,
    30, 32; making fires, 26; making
    noise, 28; minimum impact camping,
    25; snakes, 78; sun protection, 29, 30;
    survival equipment, 32; using pack
    animals, 25, 26, 28; water treatment,
    28; weather considerations, 25;
    wilderness etiquette, 25
Hinkle Spring Trail day hike   102
Horse Ridge Trail day hike   102
Horses, wild   272
Hot Loop Trail day hike   137
Hugh Norris Trail day hike   231
Hummingbird Springs Wilderness
    262–64, 262p, 263m
Humphreys Trail day hike   60–61
Humphreys Trail loop hike   62
Hyperthermia   28–29, 30
Hypothermia   29, 30

Imperial Refuge Wilderness   265–67,
    265p, 267m
Indian Hollow Campground   52, 53
Inner Basin Trail day hike   61
Italian Spring Trail day hike   225–26

Jacks Canyon Trail day hike   137
Jesus Goudy Ridge Trail day hike   202
JF Trail shuttle hike   238
Josephine Canyon day hike   206
Joshua trees   38p, 56p, 272p, 287p
Jug Trail day hike   146
Jumpup-Nail Trail day hike   65
Juniper Mesa Trail day hike   123
Juniper Mesa Wilderness   121–23,
   121p, 122m

Kachina Peaks Trail   58p
Kachina Peaks Wilderness   58–62,
   58p, 60m
Kachina Point day hike   82
Kachina Point destination hike   84
Kachina Trail loop hike   62
Kaibab Plateau   14, 36–37
Kanab Creek destination hike   65–66
Kanab Creek Trail destination hike   67
Kanab Creek Wilderness   63–67,
   63p, 66m
Kendrick Mountain Trail day hike   70
Kendrick Mountain Wilderness
   68–70, 68p, 69m
Ken Patrick Trail shuttle hike   55
Kent Spring loop hike   208
King Canyon Trail day hike   232
Kissing bugs   78
Kofa Refuge Wilderness   268–71,
   268p, 271m
KP Cienega Campground   99, 101, 103
KP Trail destination hike   103–4
Krutch, Joseph Wood   20

Ladybug Trail day hike   199–201
Land Policy Management Act, Federal
   (1976)   16
Lanphier Trail loop hike   104
Lemmon Trail loop hike   220
Lengthy Trail shuttle hike   105

Leopold, Aldo   18, 19, 109
Life zones   59
Lightning strikes, protection from
   30, 32
Lithodendron Wash day hike   82
Little Colorado River   132p
Log, balanced   81p
Long Canyon Trail day hike   142
Lower Tapeats Campground   52
Loy Canyon Trail day hike   141
Lucky Strike Trail day hike   151–52
Lupines   243p

Mail Trail day hike   113
Manning Camp   225, 226, 228
Manning Camp destination hike
   228–29
Manzanita Campground   143
Maps, legend for   9, 33
Margie's Cove Trail day hike   278
Mazatzal Divide Trail loop hike   127
Mazatzal Divide Trail shuttle hike   130
Mazatzal Wilderness   124–31,
   124p, 129m
McFadden Horse Trail day hike   151
McKittrick Trail day hike   101
Merriam, C. Hart   59
Mescal Ridge Trail day hike   120
Mexican gray wolves   15, 20, 98,
   175, 187
Mexican jaguars   175, 213
Miller Creek Trail day hike   226
Miller Peak day hike   193
Miller Peak Wilderness   24p, 192–95,
   192p, 195m
Mogollon Rim   13–14, 92
Mohave Desert   242–43
Monkeyflowers   33p
Monte Vista Peak day hike   176–77
Moody Point Trail day hike   154
Mountain lions   20

Mount Baldy Wilderness   132–34,
   132p, 133m
Mount Graham red squirrels   197
Mount Graham Wilderness Study Area
   196–203, 196p, 200m
Mount Tipton Wilderness   272–73,
   272p, 273m
Mount Trumbull day hike   72–73
Mount Trumbull Wilderness   71–73,
   71p, 73m
Mount Wilson Wilderness   274–75,
   274p, 275m
Mount Wrightson   204p
Mount Wrightson Wilderness   204–8,
   204p, 207m
Mud Springs destination hike   103–4
Muir, John   20
Munds Mountain Wilderness   17p,
   93p, 135–37, 135p, 136m

Nankoweap Trail day hike   88
Nankoweap Trail destination hike
   54–55
Natural Bridge day hike   176
New Hance Trail destination hike   50
North Bass Trail day hike   52–53
North Canyon Trail day hike   87
Northern Arizona region   36–37, 37p
North Kaibab Trail destination hike
   53–54
North Maricopa Mountains Wilderness
   276–78, 276p, 277m

Oak Creek Canyon   33p
Oaks and Willows Trail day hike   122
Off-trail hiking   25
Old Baldy Trail day hike   205–6
Old Baldy Trail shuttle hike   208
Organ pipe cacti   279p
Organ Pipe Cactus
   National Monument   243p
Organ Pipe Wilderness   279–82,
   279p, 280m

Pack animals   25, 26, 28
Paiute Mountains   74p
Paiute Wilderness   74–76, 74p, 75m
Pajarita Wilderness   209–11, 209p,
   211m
Palm Canyon day hike   270
Paria Canyon   2p
Paria Canyon-Vermilion Cliffs
   Wilderness   37p, 77–80, 77p, 79m
Paria Confluence destination hike
   79–80
Paria loop hike   80
Parsons Trail day hike   156
Pat Scott Peak day hike   194
Peloncillo Mountains Wilderness
   212–15, 212p, 214m
Peralta Trailhead shuttle hike   236
Peralta Trail shuttle hike   236
Petrified Forest National Park   27p
Petrified Forest Wilderness   81–84,
   81p, 83m
Pima Canyon Trail day hike   218–19
Pinaleño Mountains   196p
Ponderosa pine trees   92
Poppies   239p, 243p
Potato Patch Campground   167
Powers Garden Trail day hike   188
Powers Garden Trail loop hike   191
Price Canyon Trail shuttle hike   178
Prickly pear cacti   186p
Pulmonary edema   30
Pumpkin Trail loop hike   70
Pusch Ridge Wilderness   23p, 216–21,
   216p, 219m

Quartz Peak Trail day hike   284

Ramsey Creek   24p
Ramsey Vista Campground   194
Ranger Trail destination hike   65–66
Raspberry Ridge Trail day hike   176
Raspberry Trail shuttle hike   104–5

Reavis Trailhead shuttle hike   236, 238
Redfield Canyon   222p
Redfield Canyon Wilderness   222–23,
    222p, 223m
Red Hill Trail day hike   103
Red Rock-Secret Mountain Wilderness
    33p, 138–43, 138p, 140m
Reynolds Creek Trail day hike   152
Rim Country region   92–93, 93p
Rim Trail day hike   45, 152–53
Rincon Mountains   222p
Rincon Peak day hike   226
River Trail day hike   48
Rock Creek Trail day hike   127
Romero Trail day hike   219–20
Roosevelt Lake   147p
Round the Mountain Trail
    destination hike   203

Sabino loop hike   218
Saddle Mountain Trail day hike   88
Saddle Mountain Wilderness   85–88,
    85p, 86m
Saddle Ridge Trail day hike   127
Saguaro cacti   224p, 259p, 283p, 285p
Saguaro National Monument   230p
Saguaro Wilderness East   224–29,
    224p, 227m
Saguaro Wilderness West   230–33,
    230p, 232m
Salome Wilderness   144–46, 144p,
    145m
Salt River Canyon Wilderness
    147–49, 147p, 149m
S Canyon Trail loop hike   104
Scorpions   78
Sears Trail loop hike   128
Secret Canyon Trail day hike   143
Secret Mountain Wilderness. *See* **Red
    Rock-Secret Mountain Wilderness**
Sedona   135p

Sendero Esperanza day hike   233
Seven Falls day hike   217–18
Shake Trail day hike   202
Sheep Creek Trail loop hike   128
Sierra Ancha Wilderness   150–54,
    150p, 153m
Sierra Estrella Wilderness   283–84,
    283p, 284m
Snake Gulch destination hike   67
Snakes   78
Snowshed Trail destination hike   177–78
Snyder, Gary   20
Soldier Camp Trail loop hike   184–85
Soldier Creek Campground   201
Soldier Trail day hike   220
Sonoran Desert   242–43
Sonoran pronghorn sheep   19
South Bass Trail destination hike   49
South Canyon Trail day hike   87–88
Southeastern Arizona region   168–69, 169p
South Fork Trail day hike   177
South Fork Trail loop hike   128
South Kaibab Trail destination hike   50
South Maricopa Mountains Wilderness
    285–86, 285p, 286m
Steeple Trail destination hike   103
Stegner, Wallace   20
Sterling Pass Trail shuttle hike   143
Strawberry Crater   89p
Strawberry Crater Wilderness   89–91,
    89p, 90m
Strayhorse Campground   104
Strayhorse Canyon Trail
    shuttle hike   104–5
Strayhorse Trail shuttle hike   105
Sugarloaf Mountain Trail
    day hike   175–76
Sullivan Canyon Trail day hike   76
Sun, protection from   29, 30
Sunnyside Canyon day hike   194
Superstition Wilderness   234–38,
    234p, 237m

Super Trail day hike   206
Survival, equipment for   32
Sweetwater Trail day hike   231
Swift Trail   196p
Sycamore Canyon   209p
Sycamore Canyon day hike   210–11
Sycamore Canyon loop hike   158
Sycamore Canyon Wilderness   155–58,
   155p, 157m
Sycamore Pass   155p
Sycamore Trail day hike   156, 158
Sycamore Trail loop hike   191

Tanner Trail destination hike   50–51
Tanque Verde Ridge
   destination hike   228–29
Thoreau, Henry David   20
Thunder River Trail day hike   52
Tonto Creek   117p
Tonto National Forest   241p
Tonto Trail destination hike   51
Tortilla Trail day hike   189
Tortilla Trail loop hike   191
Tres Alamos Wilderness   287–88,
   287p, 288m
Trigo Mountains Wilderness   289–91,
   289p, 290m
Turkey Creek day hike   226
Twin Peaks Trail day hike   108

Uncle Jim Trail day hike   51
Upper Tapeats Campground   52

Ventana Canyon loop shuttle hike   221
Verde River Trail shuttle hike   131
Vermilion Cliffs   14, 77p
Vermilion Cliffs Wilderness. *See* **Paria**
   Canyon-Vermilion Cliffs Wilderness
Victoria Mine Trail day hike   282
Vultee Arch Trail shuttle hike   143

Wastes, disposing of   26
Water treatment   28
Weather, Arizona   25
Weatherford Trail loop hike   62
Webb Peak Trail day hike   198
West Clear Creek Trail day hike   161
West Clear Creek Wilderness   159–61,
   159p, 160m
West Divide Trail destination hike   189
Western Arizona region   242–43, 243p
West Fork Trail day hike   134, 140–41
Wet Beaver Creek   162p
Wet Beaver Creek hike/swim/float loop
   adventure   165
Wet Beaver Wilderness   162–65,
   162p, 164m
White Canyon Wilderness   239–41,
   239p, 240m, 241p
Widforss Trail day hike   51–52
Wilderness: attitudes toward   18–20;
   challenge of defining, 18–19;
   importance of preserving, 20, 22–23;
   importance of wildlife to, 19–20
Wilderness etiquette   25
Wilderness of Rocks loop hike   220
Wilderness Protection Act, Federal
   (1964)   15, 18–19
Wildflowers   12p, 35p
Willow Spring Trail loop hike   130
Wire Pass day hike   79
Woodbury Trailhead shuttle hike   238
Woodchute Trail day hike   167
Woodchute Wilderness   10p, 166–67,
   166p, 167m
Woods Canyon Trail day hike   137
Workman Creek Canyon   144p

Y Bar Basin Trail loop hike   127
Yuccas   169p

Tom Dollar
author

AWARD-WINNING AUTHOR
Tom Dollar has lived in Arizona
for over fifteen years and penned
two previous books on the state,
including *Tucson to Tombstone:
A Guide to Southeastern Arizona,*
which won the 1996 Publishers
Marketing Association award for
travel writing. His feature articles
have appeared in such publications
as *The New York Times, Arizona
Highways, Audubon, Wildlife
Conservation, Omni, Modern
Maturity, WorldTraveler, Discover,
The Mother Earth News,* and *East-
West Journal.* Currently he is at
work on a book on urban wildlife
in Arizona.

Lynne Dollar

Jerry Sieve
photographer

JERRY SIEVE HAS BEEN
photographing the American landscape for over twenty years. His
many trips across the United States,
Canada, and Mexico have resulted
in exceptional photography published in books, calendars, and
magazines nationwide. Many read-
ers will recognize him from his
work with *Arizona Highways* maga-
zine. Originally from Cincinnati,
Sieve has lived in Arizona since
1976 and is an avid outdoor enthusiast. He lives in the town of
Carefree with his wife, Kevina, and
their 15-year-old son, Tristan.

M. K. Milbradt